Religion helps one cope
Also negative
results c̄ a
punishing god

Religion provides
compensation
(brig 5) £

THE PSYCHOLOGY OF RELIGION

God not blamed for bad things   rewards
— only good   p 69   39

Coping
Leadership
    attendant power &
                        status
    Companionship
    leisure & recreational
                    activity
Group productivity
Health
Opportunity to
    destructive trends
        Drugs
        Sexual activities
    Altruistic Endeavor
            Stephen Covey
    Identity
    Specialness

THE
PSYCHOLOGY
OF RELIGION

Theoretical Approaches

EDITED BY
*Bernard Spilka and
Daniel N. McIntosh*
UNIVERSITY OF DENVER

WestviewPress
A Division of HarperCollins*Publishers*

Copyright © 1997 by Westview Press, A Division of HarperCollins Publishers, Inc.

Published in 1997 in the United States of America by Westview Press, 5500 Central Avenue, Boulder, Colorado 80301-2877, and in the United Kingdom by Westview Press, 12 Hid's Copse Road, Cumnor Hill, Oxford OX2 9JJ

A CIP catalog record for this book is available from the Library of Congress.
ISBN 0-8133-2946-9 (hc) — ISBN 0-8133-2947-7

The paper used in this publication meets the requirements of the American National Standard for Permanence of Paper for Printed Library Materials Z39.48-1984.

10   9   8   7   6   5   4   3   2   1

For those significant couples who keep making my life meaningful—Linda and Ed, Joan and Ira, and Marilyn and Dave.
—Bernie

For my parents, Alvin and Carolyn, and my brother, Michael, who first taught me how to think and to care.
—Danny

CONTENTS

PREFACE

Good psychology is premised on good theory and good research. This is as true for the psychology of religion as it is for a demanding laboratory study of factors affecting the maze learning of ants. Still, when religion enters the picture, some psychologists fear a kind of spiritual subversion that threatens their identity as scientists. This is a deformation of the fundamental objectivity of science, in which image replaces reality. Simply put, we study people, not religion, and that is not a denigration of religion but a statement of psychology's basic goal.

The study of people in relation to their faith is a compelling task for psychology. We live in a nation in which 95 percent of the populace claim belief in a deity, 89 percent report that they pray, and two-thirds are formally affiliated with a religious institution (Gallup 1987; Paloma & Gallup 1991). The significance of religion throughout the world needs no further explication. Similar data speak to issues and expressions of deep personal concern with one's faith; hence, there is a need for psychologists to understand this realm of human activity.

This interest can be fruitfully employed to teach not only the psychology of religion or its parent field, social psychology, but much about psychology in general. There is a general fascination with religion that suggests how psychologists should think—critically, constructively, and with an eye toward increasing our understanding of the human condition. There are leads here into virtually every aspect of psychology, including its applied aspects as they are evidenced in child and clinical work. Here are avenues to perception, cognition, motivation, personality, development, abnormality, and social life.

One of the greatest of twentieth-century psychologists, Kurt Lewin, is reported to have said that "there is nothing more practical than a good theory." In this volume, we have tried to illustrate this principle by showing how theory opens doors to research. Theories provide such direction. They allow us to see problems and issues from different perspectives. They prepare us for those discoveries and insights that are likely to occur to the mind that is prepared to accept them. They make us think.

We often hear that a primary weakness of the contemporary psychology of religion is a lack of theory. We believe that the chapters in this book, combined with the many good works we were forced to exclude, convincingly argue against this assertion. Past and present provide us with ample theory. What is needed is considered and careful empirical research aimed at refining and applying these ideas. To advance and fulfill the field's promise, psychologists of religion must intentionally get out of the proverbial armchair and enter more into the discomforts, difficulties, and glaring light of life and the laboratory. Our purpose in these pages is therefore to offer psychologists opportunities to read solid theoretical contributions in the psychology of religion. These can teach how one may move from the conceptual level to that of research, a central need of psychology.

In order to attain our goals, all of the articles presented here have been edited. The intent was to focus on the theoretical and "tighten" the contributions so that their research potential would be increasingly evident. We wish we could have included other fine contributions; however, in efforts such as this, there is both an element of subjectivity and an ever-present need to set limits. We do believe, even if we harbor many regrets and not a little anxiety and doubt, that there is much of lasting value in these very significant contributions. This work should be an avenue to creative and critical thinking and should stimulate professionals, teachers, and students to understand how theories are constructed and how they may be realized and assessed in research.

This work is a compilation of both previously published and original materials. We want to express our deepest appreciation to the editors of *The Journal for the Scientific Study of Religion*, the *Review of Religious Research, The International Journal for the Psychology of Religion*, the *Journal of Psychology and Christianity*, and the *Journal of Empirical Theology* for permitting us to reprint their articles. Our thanks go out to the authors included here, who sometimes felt and probably still feel that our tightening-shortening zeal eliminated many phrases, special emphases, and ideas with deep personal attachments.

For their diligent labors and positive attitudes, we also thank Nancy Pleiman, Sidney Hastings, Tara Chotiner, and Doré LaForett. Last, we recognize and appreciate our wives, who must have felt totally frustrated by competing for time with computers. Unfortunately, the future doesn't speak to alleviation from such competition.

Bernard Spilka
Daniel N. McIntosh

PART 1

Where We Are and Where We Should Go

1

AN AGENDA ITEM FOR PSYCHOLOGY OF RELIGION: GETTING RESPECT

C. DANIEL BATSON

There are at least three distinct disciplines that lie on the interface between psychology and religion, and each is at times called psychology of religion. First, there is the practice of therapeutic psychology by religious professionals—often labeled pastoral theology or pastoral psychology. One might call this discipline *psychology by religion*. Second, there is the work of psychological theorists, especially those adopting a psychoanalytic perspective, who make statements about what is or ought to be the essence of human nature. This discipline might be called *religion (or theology) by psychology*. Third, there is the scientific study of individuals' religious beliefs and behavior, including the relationship of individual religion to other aspects of psycho-social makeup. This is the discipline I have in mind when I use the term *psychology of religion*.

When I reflect on the current state of the scientific psychology of religion, I have mixed feelings. I am pleased with the vitality of the discipline; lots of people are doing research in psychology of religion. But I am also troubled by what I see. At the risk of appearing overly negative, I shall restrict my comments here to what troubles me.

I think I can best explain my concerns by referring to conversations I have recently had with other psychologists interested in the scientific

Reprinted and edited with permission of author and publisher from *Journal of Psychology and Christianity*, 5 (1986), 6–11.

study of religion. These bring the rather odd image to mind of a personi-
fication of the discipline of psychology of religion looking out of a television screen with sad and sloping eyebrows, saying in the words of
Rodney Dangerfield, "I don't get no respect."

For over a decade, we have heard this refrain from psychologists of religion. Essays have appeared on the lack of attention given to religion in
psychological texts and in major psychological journals. Informally, one
hears rueful comments about lack of collegial and institutional encouragement for psychologists interested in doing research on religion. I have
no reason to doubt these essays and comments. There is probably truth in
psychology of religion's complaint that it gets no—or little—respect.

But there is more. The Dangerfieldian character is tragically amusing
because not only does he not get respect, he does not deserve any. I fear
the same is true for the psychology of religion; our discipline does not get
respect, at least in part, because it does not deserve it.

Having suggested this less than flattering possibility, let me hasten to
add that I identify myself as a psychologist of religion. And many of the
shortcomings that limit the respect the discipline receives are as true of
my work as that of others. Moreover, let me make a sharp distinction
between the subject matter of the psychology of religion and the discipline itself. I think that the subject matter—the role of religion in individuals' lives—clearly deserves respect. It is not the subject matter but the
way we are pursuing its scientific study that is questionable. If our discipline is to get the respect we desire, then I think we need to make significant improvements in at least three general areas—theoretical analysis,
research methods, and scientific values.

WE NEED BETTER THEORIES

Since 1969, when James Dittes published his chapter on psychology of
religion in *The Handbook of Social Psychology*, and perhaps even before,
there has been frequent talk about the lack of solid theory in psychology
of religion. At the time Dittes wrote, and for most of the 1970s, the concern was that we were amassing large mounds of empirical observations
without theoretical frameworks to render them useful. It seemed as if we
had set out to build a great mansion, but rather than consulting an architect and developing a plan, we had simply called the lumberyard and
stone quarry and had truckloads of materials delivered to the site. As the
piles of lumber and stone became higher and higher, it became obvious
that the mansion was not getting built. A plan was needed to show how
the empirical pieces fit together. We heard more and more talk about the
need for theory.

In the last five years, several explicit attempts have been made to apply one or another contemporary psychological theory to religion. These attempts are all to the good, but I do not believe our troubles are over. Instead, these attempts underscore the fact that it is not enough to talk about theory; it is not even enough to have theories. We need *good* theories.

I do not presume to know what makes a theory good. But there are some very general attributes common to good scientific theories: (1) The theory should provide a conceptual structure that renders the phenomenon in question more understandable than before. Simply to describe the phenomenon is not enough; a good theory helps explain it; (2) The theory should be testable—capable of being shown wrong if it is wrong. If a theory is to be scientifically useful, it should be stated with sufficient precision that one can specify empirical observations that would contradict it; (3) The theory should help answer one or more important questions about the phenomenon. It should get us close to the heart of the matter, not just explain superficial aspects. To return to the construction metaphor, a good theory is "load bearing," not just a plan for some aspect of the facade.

When one applies even these very basic attributes of good scientific theories to recent attempts to introduce theory into psychology of religion, most of our attempts fall woefully short of the mark. Too often, our attempts do not appear to be guided by a desire to develop empirically testable explanatory theories to answer important questions about religion. Instead, our attempts seem to be guided by the conviction that we should have theory. Desperate for a plan, we grab the top one on the architect's desk—some currently popular theory from some other area of psychology—and begin to order our boards and stone as it specifies. This way, we can indeed begin to make something of our empirical observations. But such a structure is unlikely to have the third attribute mentioned above: It is not likely to address really important questions about individual religion.

My intent is not to criticize the practice of borrowing theories from other areas of psychology per se. It seems both natural and appropriate that we psychologists of religion would look to existing theories when attempting to introduce more sophistication into our discipline. But we must be sure that whatever theoretical analysis we employ illumines some important aspect of religious thought and behavior. There is no virtue in theory for theory's sake.

Moreover, I hope that we will not only borrow theories from other areas of psychology but that we will also make serious attempts to develop indigenous theories. In some cases it may be possible to find an already existing plan suited to our particular building site and needs, but in other cases it may be useful—even necessary—to develop a new plan. Whatever the source, I hope our theories will become more powerful, testable, and useful. If our discipline is to deserve respect, then we need to have more to say that is worth listening to.

WE NEED BETTER RESEARCH METHODS

Closely linked to the development of better theories is the development of better empirical methods for testing these theories. In research methods, psychology of religion is about thirty years behind other areas of psychology. This is not to say that there isn't considerable empirical sophistication in psychology of religion; nor is it to say that there have not been important advances. But the sophistication and advances have been primarily in the area of measurement. Our research designs are often simplistic to the point of being simple-minded. By far the most popular research design in the psychology of religion is still the single-session correlational design. We measure religion—or some aspects of religion—and we measure some other psychological or social variables; then we correlate the measures. I have commented elsewhere (Batson 1977; Batson & Ventis 1982) on the weakness of correlational designs of this kind when trying to test explanatory theories. Experimental and quasi-experimental designs, which are usually far superior to correlational designs in explanatory power, remain all too rare in psychology of religion.

There is, however, a specific problem with the way correlational designs are used in psychology of religion that requires further comment. The most frequently used technique for measurement in correlational studies in psychology of religion is the self-report questionnaire. Using a Likert-type scale, or some similar format, research participants are asked to indicate their agreement or disagreement with a series of statements. These may be statements about beliefs, values, or attitudes, or about behavior.

The problem with this type of instrument is that it fails to make a distinction between (1) what the respondent says he or she believes, values, and does; (2) what the respondent honestly believes that he or she believes, values, and does; and (3) what the respondent actually believes, values, and does. In some cases, the difference between these three levels of response is minor. For example, in the absence of any strong situational pressure to the contrary, we may assume that questionnaire responses about interest in religion or belief in an afterlife are reasonably accurate reflections of what the respondents actually feel or believe at the time.

But in other cases, there may be a tremendous difference. If, for example, one is interested in trying to assess the antisocial and prosocial behavior associated with various ways of being religious, then it is not enough to ask people to indicate their agreement or disagreement with questionnaire items such as "I find racial prejudice and discrimination abhorrent" or "It is extremely important to me to help others less fortunate than myself." There may be wide discrepancies between what people say is true of themselves on such items, what they actually believe is true, and how they behave. All major religions make rather clear prescriptions about the right answers to such questions. Thus, there is reason to expect a positive correlation between devotion to religious teachings and more positive responses to these questions. But what does this relation mean? Possibly nothing more than that people know what their religion teaches about these activities and can respond accordingly, regardless of whether these teachings have had any effect on their private attitudes or, more important, on their behavior.

For this reason I strongly believe the psychology of religion needs to reexamine its use of self-report questionnaires when measuring value-laden psychological and social correlates of religion. We need to use methods that allow us clearly to distinguish between the way people present themselves, the way they honestly believe themselves to be, and the way they actually are. Specifically, if we want to know how individuals who are more or less religious in some way really behave in value-laden areas, then I think we must use behavioral measures. We must look and see how these individuals do behave.

It is, I suspect, far from accidental that the research to date using behavioral measures to assess antisocial and prosocial behavior presents a picture of the relation between these activities and various ways of being religious that is dramatically different from the picture obtained using self-report questionnaires. I do not wish to suggest that self-report questionnaires are of no value, but they certainly cannot be taken at face value.

Nor do I believe it is enough to try to deal with this problem by introducing another questionnaire in order to measure respondents' tendency to present themselves in a socially desirable light. An increasingly popular practice is to administer the Marlowe-Crowne or some similar social desirability scale (Crowne & Marlowe 1964). If this scale does not correlate significantly with our other measures, we conclude that self-presentation concerns are not operating. Although such a technique may have some value, I believe that it has been greatly overused and overvalued. There are too many different facets of self-presentation and social desirability to assume that a single scale measures them all.

Admittedly, a shift from our almost exclusive reliance on self-report questionnaire measures to a more balanced use of behavioral measures presents practical problems. It is usually much harder to take behavioral measures. Little is needed to administer a battery of questionnaires—

copies of the questionnaires, a pencil, and a quiet place. But to take behavioral measures one must either find a situation in which the behavior in question occurs naturally with sufficient frequency, or one must create such a situation. Creating situations, whether in the field or in the laboratory, often requires experience and ingenuity. If in the laboratory, it also requires lab space and access to research participants. Although such resources are available in many psychology departments, much research in psychology of religion is not done in these places. Where it is done, such resources are often not available.

Because of the difficulty of doing so, behavioral measures are rarely taken in psychology of religion. The result has been a tendency to ignore the beam of measurement validity to deal instead with the mote of measurement purity. We devote much attention to improving our questionnaire measures—making them more reliable and internally consistent. This can be perfectly worthwhile, but not if we fail to confront the more fundamental problem of whether we are measuring what we want to measure. If the psychology of religion hopes to get respect, then I think it must address the fundamental problem of measurement validity—and soon.

We Need Better Scientific Values

This third need is, I believe, actually the most pressing. It is also the most difficult to discuss. A look at some recent developments in the scientific psychology of religion leads me to wonder whether the label "science" is really appropriate. The methods used are scientific in that they are empirical, and the writing in the discipline is cast in a scientific mode. But I get the uncomfortable feeling that the goal for a substantial number of contributors to the discipline is to demonstrate the positive value of religion in human life rather than to make an honest inquiry in an attempt to understand the way religion operates in human life.

Religion may well have positive value; if it does, then an open inquiry should reveal that value. But such an inquiry will occur only if we seriously entertain the possibility that religion does not have the positive value we might think it does. As Karl Popper (1959) pointed out long ago, the key to testing a scientific hypothesis is making empirical observations in situations in which the hypothesis can show itself to be wrong. William McGuire (1973) summarized Popper's principle of falsification nicely:

> The scientific psychologist can offer something beside and beyond the armchair thinkers in that we not only generate delusional systems, but we go further and test our delusional systems against objective data as well as for their

subjective plausibility. . . . Even when our theory seems plausible and so ingenious that it deserves to be true, we are conditioned to follow the Cromwellian dictum (better than did the Lord Protector himself) to consider in the bowels of Christ that we may be wrong. (pp. 452–453)

We, like Brother Juniper in Thornton Wilder's *The Bridge of San Luis Rey* (1927), need to entertain the possibility that "the discrepancy between faith and the facts is greater than is generally assumed" (p. 164).

In too much current work in psychology of religion the researchers do not seem interested in finding out if their understanding of the role of religion in human life is wrong. Instead, they seem interested in proving their understanding right. Empirical observations are made only in situations that provide clear promise of producing evidence that supports their hypothesis.

Rather than psychology of religion, such work would seem to be more appropriately labeled psychology *for* religion. It involves a psychological apology for one or another particular view of religion. This work should, I believe, be sharply distinguished from a scientific psychology of religion.

It is important to be clear about where the difference lies between this psychology for religion and a true psychology of religion. The difference is not in whether one has preconceptions or expectations about the way religion operates in human life. Anyone interested in the topic is likely to have those. Instead, the difference lies in whether one allows preconceptions and expectations to be subjected to the possibility of falsification.

The scientific process of seeking falsification can be distorted in two major ways. First, we can distort the search. Intentionally or unintentionally, we can fail to ask the relevant hard questions, the answers to which might embarrass our present understanding. Failure of this kind is, I believe, illustrated in questionnaire-based work concerning the relation between different ways of being religious and antisocial or prosocial behavior. So long as we restrict assessment of such behaviors to self-report questionnaire responses, we can be reasonably confident of finding positive relationships between measures of devout, sincere religious commitment, on the one hand, and reduced bigotry and increased brotherly love, on the other.

There is a second way the scientific process can be distorted. We can distort the result of the search. Even if we ask potentially embarrassing questions, we can fail to hear the answer given by empirical research. At the most obvious level, we can selectively perceive and report results, only taking seriously those results that support our preconceptions. One hopes this is rarely done; yet it is done—most obviously, in articles reviewing research on a given topic. There is another, more subtle way that we can fail to hear the answer being given. We can fail to show enough bias when evaluating research findings. No doubt it sounds heretical to suggest that we need more bias, so let me explain.

If we define bias as preference, then I think we need more bias in favor of quality research. Not all research is created equal. Yet there is a tendency in psychology of religion for reviewers of research simply to count the number of findings that support or contradict a particular hypothesis and to decide truth by majority vote. This one-study, one-vote approach can be quite misleading. If studies differ in quality, then this difference needs to be reflected in our assessment of what the research is saying. Again using research relating ways of being religious to antisocial and prosocial behavior, I believe that one or two studies using behavioral measures may be more informative—and so should be weighted more heavily—than several dozen studies using self-report questionnaire measures of such activities. Obviously, when quality judgments of this kind are made, there will be disagreements among different interpreters of the research. Yet, I think that such quality judgments must be made if our discipline is to deserve respect. Science is not value-free; rather, it involves adherence to a specific set of values—those directed toward enabling us to find our errors.

Having made these rather critical comments about the current state of psychology of religion, let me emphasize that these are personal views. They are not views that I would expect, or even want, everyone in the discipline to share. Moreover, I would caution against excessive "kvetching" about the right way to do psychology of religion or the right direction for the discipline to go. If it is true that one of the major agenda items for the discipline is to get more respect—both from the rest of the psychological community and from outside psychology—then we need to recognize that respect is a tricky goal to pursue. Most often, one gets respect not by seeking it but by getting on with the job and doing the job better. If and when the psychology of religion can provide important, useful, and empirically tested insights into the role of religion in human life, then we will get respect. Because then we will have done something that very much deserves it.

2

TOWARD MOTIVATIONAL THEORIES OF INTRINSIC RELIGIOUS COMMITMENT

RICHARD L. GORSUCH

Allport (1960, 1963, 1966) introduced the concept of intrinsic religious commitment, along with what he felt to be its opposite, namely, extrinsic religious commitment (jointly referred to as "I/E"). An "intrinsic" religious behavior is one that is internalized (Batson 1976) and that exists for its own sake; "extrinsic" religiousness is adopted to achieve some other goal.

After years of research, doubts regarding intrinsic religious commitment exist (Hunt and King 1971; Kahoe 1974; Donahue 1985a, 1985b; and Kirkpatrick & Hood 1990). Although I/E concepts are widely used in the psychology of religion, such concerns suggest that the construct contains problems that warrant further study.

Part of the problem seems to stem from Allport's reasons for introducing I/E. Intrinsic commitment was introduced into his theory of prejudice as an independent variable to resolve what he felt was an obvious anomaly, that church members were more prejudiced in the 1950s and 1960s than nonmembers (Allport 1966). Allport hypothesized that church members who were intrinsically committed to their faith would be less prejudiced than those who were extrinsically committed to their faith. There

Reprinted and edited with permission of the author and publisher from the *Journal for the Scientific Study of Religion*, 33 (1994), 315–325.

is some support for this position in U.S. Protestant denominations (Donahue 1985a, 1985b; Gorsuch & Aleshire 1974).

Although Allport's conceptualization of intrinsicness as an independent variable was helpful, he did not offer any theory of intrinsicness as a dependent variable. He did, however, suggest that the "mature" individual had intrinsic, functionally autonomous commitments. How such developed was left unclear and further research has not clarified it. A theoretical base for intrinsicness itself has been ignored by critics except for Meadow and Kahoe (1984). Instead, research in the Allport tradition continued using I/E as independent variables to dependent variables such as prejudice and prosocial behavior (Donahue 1985a, 1985b).

Other critiques of I/E stem from the Allport and Ross (1967) scales, which suffer from a lack of clarity and combine belief, behavior, and motivation (Gorsuch 1984). Such a mixture gives uncertain interpretations. Without a clear definition of intrinsicness that uses psychologically appropriate categories, it is difficult to develop any theory of how it relates to behavior or develops.

INTRINSICNESS AS RELIGIOUS MOTIVATION

Allport referred to religious intrinsicness as an "orientation." The scales in Allport and Ross (1967) reflect that concern, including items that illustrate not only affect and values in the religious domain but also behavior, such as church attendance.

Several scholars have also noted this problem and suggested that I/E be considered motivation: Hunt and King (1971) implied this, and Kahoe (1976) pointed to parallels in research on work motivation. Meadow and Kahoe (1984, chap. 20) suggested that I/E be considered motivations, while demonstrating that Allport saw it as an interiorized faith that includes belief statements—particularly loving one's neighbor—that are obviously a part of Protestant Christianity. In response, Gorsuch and Venable (1983) made a shift in the Allport and Ross (1967) construct by dropping the church attendance item and doing minor rewrites on several other items to increase the motivational nature of I/E. The next change in the I/E operational definitions (Gorsuch & McPherson 1989) followed Kirkpatrick (1989), who identified one intrinsic motivation and several extrinsic motivations.

The I/E-R scale (Gorsuch & McPherson 1989) has redefined intrinsic commitment as motivation for one's religious beliefs, whatever they may be. Being committed to one's own religion on intrinsic grounds would be considerably different for a follower of the Hindu goddess Kali than would commitment to the Christian God of Martin Luther King, Jr. Note that separating beliefs and motivations is *not* Allport, who believed that an intrinsic person "takes seriously the commandment of brotherhood," thus mixing motivation and theological position (Allport 1966:455).

Research using intrinsicness as motivation, as distinct from the beliefs and norms to which one becomes committed in their religion, has been accumulating (e.g., Herek 1987; McFarland 1989a, 1989b). For example, Snook and Gorsuch (1985) related motivation to attitudes toward apartheid in South Africa among those whose religion included separatism as a clear norm (Afrikaan-speaking) and those whose religion included the siblinghood of all people as a clear norm (English-speaking). The results were as predicted from a motivational theory of intrinsic religiousness and were directly counter to Allport's position: Those whose commitment to their faith was internalized and whose religious group had a norm of prejudice were indeed prejudiced; those whose religious norms included tolerance were tolerant. Hence, Allport's theory of intrinsic religiousness is disconfirmed in favor of a motivational theory of intrinsic religiousness.

Gorsuch et al. (1991) theorized that if intrinsic religious commitment were truly motivation without regard to content, then one should be able to find the same factor of intrinsic commitment in non-Christian and non-Western religions as is found in Protestant Christians in the United States. They indeed did replicate such when they compared English-speaking Christians with Asian non-Christians. The intrinsic motivational construct held up despite differences in beliefs and cultures.

Defining intrinsic religious commitment as motivation means that neither beliefs nor norms are part of that theoretical construct. Beliefs and norms need to be measured separately from motivation when relating religion to other variables. Including in the sample anyone from any religious group and using intrinsic scales without measuring the varying beliefs and norms of those people serves only to reduce our observed correlations and to confuse readers. The lack of inclusion of the beliefs or norms in most of the intrinsic research is one probable cause of the low correlations noted by Kirkpatrick and Hood (1990).

I explicitly revise Allport's definition of intrinsicness by limiting it to motivation:

Definition: Intrinsic religious commitment is the motivation for experiencing and living one's religious faith for the sake of the faith itself. The person's religion is an end unto itself, a goal pursued in the absence of external reinforcement.

Redefining intrinsic religious commitment solely as motivation clarifies the construct, but intrinsic commitment is still a broad term that may usefully be broken down into several components. Cattell and Child (1975) subdivided motivation into components. Their components match with the distinction between affect and moral value (Gorsuch 1986). *Affect is defined as a person's liking or disliking, whereas value is defined as a person's self-perceived moral obligation* (Gorsuch 1988; Scott 1965). A moral value is desirable for its own sake and generalizes to everyone and to every relevant situation.

Intrinsic commitment by either affect or value means that the relevant belief or behavior is believed or carried out for its own sake and not as a means to other ends. Affect is often intrinsic. For example, singing a joyful song because of the joy directly associated with that singing would be intrinsic. A moral value or obligation by definition exists for its own sake and is thus intrinsic.

THEORIES OF INTRINSIC COMMITMENT

Allport wrote of intrinsic religious commitment from the implicit perspective of what he called "functional autonomy" (Allport 1937). A functionally autonomous motivation would be one that had become independent of its roots and thus had become a motivation for its own sake. However, that development would not be important in the current functioning of the motivation. It might be possible to develop change programs that would increase intrinsic motivation but once a change program was completed, the motivation would no longer be tied to its development. The primary point of functional autonomy is that there would be no current reason for the behavior, even though an extrinsic reason might have existed originally.

Here, intrinsic commitment must be intrinsic only in the definitional sense that there are no obvious external causes for the commitment. This applies equally to either affect or value. The implication of functional autonomy that intrinsicness is totally independent of its origins is explicitly rejected.

Concerning how intrinsic motivation develops, a number of theories are helpful. These belong to two major categories. The first includes theories by which intrinsic commitment is seen as "indirectly extrinsic." The second set of theories includes those whereby the intrinsic motivation is "directly intrinsic."

Indirectly Extrinsic Theories for Intrinsic Religious Motivation

These include the cause of the original religious motivation but must also provide a reason for the religious motivation to be currently intrinsic— that is, an explanation for why it seems to occur without an immediate, direct link to an extrinsic cause.

Unconscious Habit.   Assume the religious beliefs and practices were originally explicitly extrinsically motivated. With sufficient recurrences, the extrinsic motivation develops a religious habit. The motivation for the habit could have been one of the classical extrinsic motivations—personal or social. Other possibilities also exist for religious habit. One such need might be the desire to have the respect of one's parents when that respect can be earned from religious beliefs and participation. Or another could be the fear of parental punishment if religious beliefs and practices are not as the parent desires.

In this theory of intrinsic religiousness, the person was originally following the religious beliefs and practices for an extrinsic reason. How then does it become intrinsic? By habit and forgetting.

When a religious belief/behavior is performed often enough, it becomes a habit, that is, automatic. Automatic processes require no conscious involvement. As time passes, the original extrinsic reason for the belief/behavior is forgotten. At that point, since the belief/behavior continues and the extrinsic motivation can no longer be consciously recalled, it fits the definition of intrinsic when measured by self-report.

To be successful, the theory requires that habits themselves be motivational—that breaking of a habit would engender fear of not being reinforced, but since the extrinsic motivation is no longer known, that fear would be a generalized anxiety, a feeling of uneasiness. Following the habit would reduce that generalized anxiety and therefore give a sense of relief. Hence, this view, being powered by avoidance of a negative emotion, explains intrinsic affect.

Under this theory an intrinsically motivated religious person would continue religious habits until there was a major interruption from an extrinsic source that prevented the habit from operating for a considerable length of time. Initially, there would be some anxiety about not fulfilling the now unknown extrinsic motivation. But the individual would find out over time that the anxiety was unfounded, and desensitization would take place. Hence, a unique prediction of this theory is that if there were an extrinsic reason for not engaging in religious habits for an extended period of time, the person would lose those habits and would no longer be intrinsically motivated.

Misattribution of Source.   A behavior may be extrinsically based, but the person may not know it. Unlike the above theory, this position assumes that the extrinsic reinforcement still occurs but the person does not realize it. Self-report would indicate intrinsic religiousness.

Debates over attributions of causation are widely known in psychology. In social psychology, attributing a cause to a personal source rather than to environmental forces is referred to as the fundamental attribution error. The same behavior may be explained in several different ways by the person and by a psychologist. Hence, what we label as extrinsic motivation may be considered by the person to be intrinsic motivation and would be reported as such. This misattribution could apply to both affect and value.

Multiple Complex Sources.   Cattell and Child (1975) have explained religious motivation by using a variant of general drive theory. A complex behavior such as religiousness relates to several basic drives that reinforce that religious commitment. Three of the drives that Cattell and Child believe underlie religion are the need for appeal, need for self-submission, and need for self-assertion. When any or all of these needs are high and religion satisfies them, then there is motivation for religion.

    How then does the religious motivation become intrinsic? From a generalized drive theory perspective, religious motivation is intrinsic to the degree that it satisfies such a wide range of needs that one of the needs underlying religion will always be there to motivate it, or else each need may be just below the threshold of consciousness—or the threshold of observation by another person—but the sum of several needs would be a noticeable force seemingly without a base.

Social Norms.   The social norm theory for intrinsic religious commitment states that people have been taught to report such commitment and they value the people who establish their norms too much to violate that social rule. Thus, they would answer affect or value questions on the basis of the norms rather than according to "what is really true." Batson (e.g., Batson & Ventis 1982) appeared to be functioning from this type of theory. The observed belief or behavior is never for truly religious goals or truly non-self-oriented goals but only appears that way due to social desirability effects.

    If the social norm includes both (1) beliefs, motivations, and behaviors and (2) consistency among beliefs, motivations, and behaviors, it may be difficult to distinguish from other sources. For example, even when the person is not being observed by someone from the social norm group, that person may still behave as if he or she were being observed in an attempt to uphold the norm of consistency among behavior, motivation, and beliefs.

    The danger in this theory is that it can be tautological. Anyone who does indeed behave as the norms call for is seen automatically as behaving solely due to the norms. In that case, of course, there is by definition no place for any other motivational base—and then the theory becomes meaningless. Spilka's (Allen & Spilka 1967) distinction of consensual (versus committed) may be useful to separate out those with a social norm approach versus other types of religious commitment in a manner that allows both to possibly exist.

Characteristics of Indirectly Extrinsic Theories

"Indirectly extrinsic" theories are more easily related to affect than to value. First, at the heart of each is an initial external reinforcement producing an affect that becomes associated with religion. Second, such theories could be generated from a position that assumes that "all behaviors are extrinsic, even the highest; there are just those who know it and those who don't." But if the theory fits everyone, it is theoretically meaningless for distinguishing the religiously committed from other people. Third, these theories often fall back on the rationale that there is an extrinsic source of the intrinsic commitment—it is just not yet observed. Then, "we just need to identify another drive or to claim that our measurement is insufficient."

Directly Intrinsic Religious Motivation

The following positions explain intrinsic religious commitment from solely intrinsic rationales. They assume that one does not take a tautological reinforcement or enlightened hedonist position, since in that case "self-satisfaction" or some other such tautology would be used for the extrinsic rationale. Self-satisfaction when a value is fulfilled is not seen in the following theories as the reinforcement for the value but rather as an indicator of what the value is.

Familiarity.   Zajonc (1968, 1980) has conducted a series of studies showing that exposure is sufficient to develop a positive attitude toward that to which one is exposed. Hence, by hearing a strange new music sufficiently often, one develops familiarity with that music, and it no longer seems unpleasant but actually becomes pleasant. The theory assumes that there are no major positive or negative external reinforcements in the situation. This is grouped with the directly intrinsic theories because there is no postulated underlying drive that causes a person to be exposed to the same stimuli over a period of time.

This theory could apply easily to the affect part of intrinsic religious motivation. It seems insufficient, however, to account for values unless another theory, such as cognitive consistency, were also involved with it.

Cognitive Theories.   Cognitive theories are only indirectly motivational, but they do seek to explain some of the same phenomena. The basic drive appears to be one of preferring a schema that incorporates several narrow structures within a greater whole and that can, by the more complex and yet more unified structure, relate to a broader range of experiences. These theories appear most appropriate for values.

Piaget (1974), with some other cognitive theorists, assumed an innate need to relate to the environment through unified schemata. Hence, there is a need for developing such schemata, using principles such as differentiation (making schemata more complex so that they relate to a broader range of phenomena), assimilation (bringing new elements into current schemata), accommodation (change schemata to change new elements), and reciprocal assimilation (combining schemata).

These thinkers may well provide elements applicable to the development of religious belief systems. Although the motivation for schemata development might lead to behavioral consistency, we may need a motivation for cognitive consistency per se in order to provide the underlying power to such approaches. Rokeach (1973, chap. 8) has suggested that the development and change of values is based upon the need to relate to such elements in a logically consistent manner. When we then perceive inconsistency between our view of God and our behavior, that produces an intrinsic motivation to remove that inconsistency. This appears to be a special case of the broader cognitive models.

Cognitive stage theories are also relevant here. Venable (1982) noted that one test for an intuitively compelling higher stage is that a person understands up to the stage at which that individual is but does not truly understand the higher stages: If one really understood the higher stage, then one would immediately move to that stage. The corollary is that a person at Stage 1 can only repeat Stage 2 reasoning by rewriting it down into Stage 1 thinking or giving an incomprehensible explanation. However, a Stage 2–level person can repeat the rationale for Stage 2 and also repeat the rationale for Stage 1.

In almost the only developmental study of intrinsicness and extrinsicness, Venable (1982) found the expected result with intrinsic and extrinsic understanding. Intrinsics were able to reproduce extrinsic thinking better than extrinsics reproduced intrinsic thinking. But more research would need to be done on the other criteria for stage theories.

The only motivation here is to have a more unified and complex structure that relates to more of reality. When religion itself provides that structure, then the person becomes intrinsically motivated to maintain that. All stage theories have a tautological answer concerning why people must then live out their current stage. Does "intuitively compelling" then become comparable to "functional autonomy" in that it is only a descriptive label with no explanatory power? Certainly one would need to add a careful explanation of how and when different stages were used in answering particular problems and whether there were some other need being satisfied each time the stage was engaged.

Religion as Its Own Need.   The position that "people have a need to serve God" states that the reinforcement is a given of the human psyche. The theologically oriented would say that God made us to serve religiously and we are only complete when doing so. The nontheologically oriented might hold that such a need was an accident of nature or that the underlying end could be met better by other commitments.

One might suggest that a need for religion is biologically based but that we just have not found the part of physiology in which that base is located. Differences in physiological sensitivities to "the religious need" may reflect what is theologically conceptualized as predestination. Theoretically, it would also explain why only some people are intrinsically religious. Of course, just speculating is insufficient; the physiological source would need to be identified.

If there is a built-in need to be religious, then cultural learning would affect how that need is satisfied. An analogy can be made with food. Different cultures have access to different types of foods and prepare them in different ways, but they all satisfy a person's hunger needs. Hence, under this theory most of the religions found among humanity would be able to satisfy the basic religious needs.

An evaluation of different religions could, under this need theory, be examined in the same manner. But a major problem is that each religion itself usually defines the criteria by which all religions are to be judged and, of course, the religion that defines the criteria is most likely to meet the criteria.

Both affect and value can be intrinsic if religion is a true need unto itself. Positive affect would result when that need is met in, for example, worship. If the need is seen as universally essential to a worthwhile life, it would also be an intrinsic value.

Deci and Ryan's Intrinsic Motivation.   Deci and Ryan (1985) have theoretically and empirically examined intrinsic motivation, researching it in laboratory experiments, education, sports, and work environments (religion is not mentioned). Kahoe (1974) and Meadow and Kahoe (1984) noted that the earlier work along this line showed promise as a motivational base for intrinsicness.

Intrinsic commitment is, for Deci and Ryan, characterized by an interest in that belief/practice for its own sake. They add that the person has a sense of joy and flow when participating in it. From the earlier discussion regarding the nature of intrinsic motivation as affect and value, it is apparent that joy refers to the affect, whereas interest and flow could be affect or value. The affect is seen not as reinforcement but as a result of meeting the intrinsic motivation.

The need for intrinsic motivation is based in a need for efficacy in relationship to the environment. For Deci and Ryan, this resembles the cognitive assimilation and consistency models. In addition, a sense of self-determination is included.

The Deci and Ryan approach is useful from several perspectives. For example, they have shown empirically that extrinsic reinforcement applied to a behavior that was originally intrinsically motivated will, unless under special conditions, shift the behavior to being extrinsically motivated. Also, information regarding success increases intrinsic motivation. Education is then found to be more intrinsic when grades are seen not as motivation but as information and the student feels there is a choice in learning.

Deci and Ryan's view could be our initial theory for intrinsic religious commitment, except for a major area of religious commitment that is not accounted for with this theory. Their approach has difficulty with the reports of religious experience of "twice-born" people. Many Christians feel that God gave them the intrinsic motivation to be religious. And they then have joy, a sense of flow, and a feeling of efficacy and self-determination in their lives. However, the religion was not something they chose; rather, God chose them. Such experiences seem to meet the Deci and Ryan criteria for intrinsic motivation after God has touched a person's life. Still, the theory is unclear about why an externally based event such as these mystical experiences should produce intrinsic motivation.

Which Theory Is Best?

There are pros and cons regarding a number of these theories—such as the fact that drive theories have fallen into disfavor because higher-order needs do not seem to be radically different than drives and the power of secondary reinforcement is too weak to produce higher-order drives. We need more data before we can determine which of these theories might or might not apply to intrinsic religious commitment.

Another reason for presenting the several theories is that more than one may apply and these may differ from one individual to another. This is not found by our ordinary statistical analyses because they assume that the same need or pattern of needs operates for everyone. From a multivariate belief-motivation perspective (Schaefer & Gorsuch 1991), there may well be many motivational influences in operation, but operating for different people. Some people may become intrinsic because religion is a habit and they have forgotten the original extrinsic source of the motivation. Others may become intrinsic because of the need for cognitive consistency and unity that encompasses all their experiences, including religious ones. Still others may be involved because of social norms. Logic suggests that there may well be four or five different causes for different people within the same research sample. Therefore, when we correlate any one cause with religious commitment, the correlation is low, at best.

It is important to consider several theories of motivation so that we can develop guidelines for checking for each type of motivation when using intrinsic religious commitment as a dependent variable. First, we need to sort people according to the type of religious development that they have had, and, second, we should examine how this relates to their religious beliefs, motivation, and behaviors.

The affect/value distinction is useful for hypothesizing which motivational theory relates to what part of religious commitment. Affect is more likely to develop from unconscious habit, multiple complex sources, familiarity, and religion as its own need. Value is more likely to develop from cognitive consistency and Deci's intrinsic motivation as the need for efficacy. A distinction between affect and value is needed to test such theories appropriately.

Despite the lack of research, one or two theories seem especially relevant to the different ways a person becomes religiously committed. James (1902) differentiated between "once-born" and "twice-born" Christians. The former were generally raised in a Christian environment and gradually came to accept their faith as they grew up. They do not remember a time when they were not Christian.

What theories might apply to the intrinsic commitment of a once-born person? Familiarity is one that immediately comes to mind. Those raised in Christian families will have been around churches from their earliest days and thus be very familiar with them. Assuming no major negative experiences in that situation, familiarity theory seems to be reasonably explanatory.

Once-born religious commitment may also be found in the multiple complex sources theory. The Christian faith has a complex subculture in which a number of rewards are possible. These include extrinsic rewards that are not religious per se, such as the prominence that comes from being respected within a religious community and the joy that comes from confidently carrying out ministerial assignments.

For the once-born, cognitive consistency may also play a role, including stage developments for theological beliefs. Cognitive consistency could work internally among the beliefs and behaviors. For example, it would resolve the potential problem over why the people one respects are religious. Since they are valued, it is difficult to reject their beliefs and still maintain that respect for them. Accepting their beliefs makes the system consistent. Thus, cognitive consistency would suggest that the person should become religious.

The twice-born person's religious commitment may lie theoretically in other areas than that of the once-born. Some positions applicable to the once-born, such as familiarity, might not be applicable to the twice-born. But cognitive consistency may help to explain that which Deci's intrinsic motivational theory cannot: the person who has a mystical experience that makes one religious. Saul, from his experience on the road to Damascus, had conflicting beliefs, needing to incorporate the notion that Jesus was indeed divine (after all, he appeared in a vision to him) with his own behavior of persecuting people for calling Jesus the Son of God. Since Saul was intrinsically committed to a Jewish deity and since he saw Jesus as an extension of that deity to which he was already committed, he could reduce cognitive dissonance by then becoming intrinsically religiously committed to the Christian movement. Then cognitive consistency would be restored.

These are just samples of situations to which the different theories might apply. We need to be careful in our research not to assume that everyone in a research study has the same causative patterns of intrinsic religious commitment, but rather to examine which models work best for each person.

COMMENTARY: WHERE WE ARE AND WHERE WE SHOULD GO

In Chapter 1, Batson sounds a clarion call for a scientifically rigorous psychology of religion, particularly one that embraces an experimental approach. No one can object to that. Still, treating religion as an independent variable seems far easier than making it a dependent factor. The main barrier is that we have not thought of either conceptualizing or manipulating faith in this manner. Certainly, one can set up experimental and control groups and construct conditions that theoretically should affect religious commitments, especially influencing various religious expressions such as intrinsic or extrinsic orientations. Naturalistic observation, for example, tells us that faith commitments may be influenced by crisis, and since they appear to be so affected (dependent), their effects should be seen in other aspects of a person's life (also dependent). The situation is complex, but it would be beneficial to exercise our thinking along the lines Batson recommends. Lastly, getting respect may result in the long run from the way we *study* religion *in relation to people* and from making this last point clear to colleagues who stop thinking when the word religion is uttered. Still, there is much more to be overcome in a profession historically nurtured by psychoanalysis and behaviorism. The road may well be long in our attempts to overcome the form of scholarly irrationality that masks an antireligious stance.

In Chapter 2, Gorsuch takes the classic intrinsic-extrinsic issue in the psychology of religion and theoretically charts a path through this morass by stressing I/E as motivational constructs. With his students, he has attempted to construct measures that stress this aspect of a person's religious orientation. It is now necessary to create conditions that enhance or lessen I or E tendencies, or both, and demonstrate that they really do function as motivations. For example, we know that raising drive level speeds up simple problem-solving but impedes its complex alternatives. Such notions open the door to further study of motivational effects on cognition.

Gorsuch specifies a number of theoretical generic directions for the assessment of I/E as motivational constructs. He even spells out some implications of these. Research scrutiny of these possibilities in the realm of the psychology of religion is called for. On one level, testing of dissonance-consistency versus reinforcement approaches is possible. We need to create materials containing either dissonant or consistent content relative to I and E "motivations" in a fourfold scheme and to look for effects (e.g., in response to vignettes dealing with coping situations). Theory suggests various response tendencies. We might also benefit from comparisons of the Gorsuch-McPherson motivational I/E scales with predecessor instruments—Allport-Ross, Hoge, and so on—to determine the meaning of differences (e.g., cognitive). This leads to the possibility of taking Allport's notion of I/E as orientations, and this concept suggests I/E may be translated into measures whose primary focus is cognitive. In other words, I/E can probably have utility as motivation and as cognition. In different situations, religious salience may sometimes be more cognitively or more motivationally focused. Consider (in Chapter 13 of this volume) McIntosh's use of religion as schema, which may be more cognitively oriented than Hill's attitudinal emphasis (in Chapter 14). What about the "availability hypothesis" from attribution theory? Where does motivation or cognition fit in activating availability?

Gorsuch further cites needs that religious commitment meets, noting Cattell's reference to appeal, self-submission, and self-assertion. Relative to the work presented later on attribution theory, one might look toward needs for meaning, control, and esteem. Research along these lines may explicate additional possibilities for I/E as motivation. Lastly, such consideration has pertinence in terms of Maslow's perspectives on deficiency and growth needs.

It is not difficult to envision a combination of Batson's call for experimental research and Gorsuch's I/E viewpoint. Gorsuch offers extensive entrée to realizing Batson's aspirations.

PART 2

Why Religion? Functions of Religious Beliefs and Behavior

3

TOWARD A THEORY OF RELIGION: RELIGIOUS COMMITMENT

RODNEY STARK AND WILLIAM SIMS BAINBRIDGE

We are launched on the task of constructing a general theory of religion. We propose to deduce from a set of axioms about what humans are like and how they behave, as well as from a larger number of definitions, a series of propositions explaining why religions exist, how they originate, how religious movements are transformed—indeed, answers to the whole list of classic questions.

This task is necessary because although the past several decades have produced an amazing array of new and well-tested facts about religion, we lack theories to organize these facts and tell us which are relevant to what. The task seems possible because although little theorizing has gone on in the social-scientific study of religion (and indeed in much of sociology), important progress has been made in microeconomics, social psychology, and anthropology.

This chapter is the pivotal work in a series of articles that present a new exchange paradigm for analyzing and explaining religious phenomena and that subject it to a variety of empirical tests. Our object here is to present the basic set of axioms, key definitions, and the first of literally hundreds of propositions we have derived about religion and its social context. We only carry the deductive process to the point where some nontrivial, testable, and perhaps counterintuitive propositions about *religious commitment* have been obtained.

Reprinted and edited with permission of authors and publisher from *Journal for the Scientific Study of Religion*, 19 (1980), 114–128.

The form of deductive theories requires selecting some small number of rules (axioms) governing the phenomena to be explained. If these are the correct axioms, the logical permutations will give rise to a number of propositions (derived statements) that will predict or prohibit certain relations within the domain addressed by the theory. Thus, if the axioms are correct and complete, the propositions must hold. The correspondence of such theories to the real world is determined empirically. In the case of a theory, such as our own, that is still evolving and is as yet incompletely formalized, empirical research can also uncover faulty logic in the derivation of propositions and establish appropriate means for operationalizing concepts.

Our primary reason for having some confidence in the theory thus far is that it has successfully confronted data at several points. Moreover, the deductive process has yielded a number of well-known middle-range propositions. Since our purpose is to advance this field, it is extremely encouraging to find that such classics as Malinowski's theory of magic or Durkheim's argument about why religion produces stable organizations but magic cannot derive from the deductive chain.

The theory rests on six axioms (we include a temporary seventh axiom to facilitate the presentation, since the deductive chain by which it can be deduced from the other six is quite long). *Axioms* are designated by the letter "A". The theory also contains a number of *definitions*. These link the axioms to the empirical world, and are designated by the abbreviation "Def." Finally, statements logically deduced from the axioms and definitions are propositions designated by the letter "P."

We begin with an axiom that is so basic that standard social scientific theories seldom mention it. Yet it is essential before we can understand anything else. The first axiom places human existence in *time*.

A1   Human perception and action take place through time, from the past into the future.

Def. 1   The *past* consists of the universe of conditions that can be known but not influenced.

Def. 2   The *future* consists of the universe of conditions that can be influenced but not known.

The second axiom is a restatement of the first proposition in exchange theory, operant learning theory, and microeconomics (Homans 1974).

A2   Humans seek what they perceive to be rewards and avoid what they perceive to be costs.

Def. 3   *Rewards* are anything humans will incur costs to obtain.
Def. 4   *Costs* are whatever humans attempt to avoid.

Our first proposition derives directly from A2, Def. 3, and Def. 4.

P1   Rewards and costs are complementary: a lost or forgone reward equals a cost, and an avoided cost equals a reward.

Proposition 1 extends Axiom 2 by expressing in another way the relationship between its terms. *Seeking* and *avoiding* are opposites. To obtain a reward, a person accepts costs. When a person attempts to avoid a cost, he *seeks* the *avoidance* of that cost, and this avoidance is by Definition 3 a reward. If rewards and costs were not complementary, there could be no human action. But human action is still not possible without a further principle:

A3   Rewards vary in kind, value, and generality.

Def. 5   Reward A is more *valuable* than reward B if a person will usually exchange B for A.
Def. 6   Rewards are *general* to the extent that they include other (less general) rewards.

All our experience supports the truth of this axiom. We know we desire some things more than others. This implies that there are rewards that the person does not possess at any given moment, whereas other rewards may already be possessed.

The second proposition is derived from the previous statements and gives the condition under which human action is possible:

P2   Sometimes rewards can be obtained at costs less than the costs equivalent to forgoing the reward.

Proposition 2 says that human action can be profitable. Over time, one may gain some desired rewards through the expenditure (as costs) of less desired rewards. If rewards did not differ in *kind*, then there would only be one reward and it is difficult to see that a profit might result from trading in it. If rewards did not differ in *value*, there would be no sense in giving up one to acquire another. The fact that rewards differ in *generality* is implied by the mathematical possibility of addition. When a person seeks a collection of rewards, by Definition 3 this collection is a reward in itself, and yet it includes other lesser rewards. Thus, any set of rewards is more general than any single reward in the collection. If reward A is more valuable than reward B, then they must differ in kind or generality, or both.

These axioms and propositions give us the context in which human action is possible, but they do not sufficiently specify the necessary characteristics of the human actor. Axiom 4 expresses the human capacity to perceive and act effectively in a complex environment:

A4   Human action is directed by a complex but finite information-processing system that identifies problems and attempts solutions to them.

Def. 7   The *mind* is the set of human functions that directs the action of a person.

Def. 8   Human *problems* are recurrent situations that require investments (costs) of specific kinds to obtain rewards.

Def. 9   To *solve* a problem means to imagine possible means of achieving the desired reward, to select the one with the greatest likelihood of success in the light of available information, and to direct action along the chosen line until the reward has been achieved.

Definition 9 states how the human mind must operate if it is to achieve its task in complex circumstances. This reminds us of what our minds actually do, while intentionally being quite nonspecific. To say that the mind is finite means that it is limited in the amount of information it can store and process.

Because rewards differ, problems differ; and solutions must differ as well if complex human action is to be possible. Solutions must often be somewhat novel, since humans constantly encounter circumstances they have not previously experienced. Yet solutions are not the result of random experimentation. Efficiency requires that organisms deal with novel circumstances as variations on circumstances with which they are already familiar. Thus, humans attack new situations as mixtures of the familiar and the unfamiliar and attempt to analyze novelty into combinations of familiar elements. Conceptual simplifications of reality—models of reality designed to guide action—may be called *explanations*.

P3   In solving problems, the human mind must seek explanations.

Def. 10   *Explanations* are statements about how and why rewards may be obtained and costs are incurred.

Because humans *seek* explanations and by Def. 3 whatever humans seek is a reward, it follows that

P4   Explanations are rewards of some level of generality.

Explanations differ along the dimensions that other rewards do. For example, they differ in generality. An explanation can guide action on more than one occasion and can potentially provide several lesser rewards. Explanations tell us what costs to expend under what circumstances and in what time sequence in order to obtain the desired reward. Given an effective explanation Xl, we can imagine another explanation X2 identical to Xl but with the addition of some costly action C that does not alter the value of the reward obtained. Thus, we can deduce that

P5   Explanations vary in the costs and time they require for the desired reward to be obtained.

Explanations should also vary according to the kind, value, and generality of the rewards to be obtained through them, but they vary even when the reward achieved is held constant. There are an infinite number of ways of *attempting* to accomplish anything, thus there are an unlimited number of competing explanations, and usually there are many routes to success, each of a distinctive length.

Often, it is fairly easy to find a successful explanation and solve the problem of obtaining a desired reward. But sometimes this is not the case. Axiom 5 introduces this fact and is the turning point on which the crucial parts of our argument hinge:

A5   Some desired rewards are limited in supply, including some that simply do not exist.

Def. 11   A *limited* supply means that individuals cannot have as much of a reward as they desire.
Def. 12   Rewards that do *not exist* cannot be obtained by any person or group.

People always want more rewards than they can have. Put another way, aggregate demand tends to exceed supply. Although this may not be true of a given reward at a given time, it is true of the sum of rewards. Natural resources and human productive capacities limit the supply of many rewards.

How do humans get those rewards that do exist? Much of what we desire can come only from someone else, whether the reward be affection or apples. When we seek a reward from someone else, that person usually must pay a cost for providing us with the reward. Thus, in order to induce another to supply us with a reward, we must offer an inducement—some other reward—in return. Proposition 2 tells us that a deal is possible. Sometimes we can offer the other person a reward that he or she evaluates more highly than what is given in return, while we likewise value what we get over what we give. Thus, through seeking rewards, people are forced into exchange relationships (Homans 1974).

P6   In pursuit of desired rewards, humans will exchange rewards with other humans.

People will not engage in these exchanges in an aimless way. Our discussion explains that they tend to act rationally to maximize rewards and minimize costs. It follows that

P7   Humans will seek high exchange ratios.

Def. 13   *Exchange ratio* is a person's net rewards over costs in an exchange.

So far, we have been dealing with abstract "individuals" who are equally constrained by our propositions. But real people do not possess equal rewards, nor are they treated equally by each other. There are many ways of indicating that some have greater resources than others; the way we find most convenient for our deductions is stated in Axiom 6.

A6   Individuals and social attributes that determine power are unequally distributed among individuals and groups in any society.

Def. 14   *Power* is the degree of control over one's exchange ratio.

Usually power is defined as the ability to get one's way even over opposition. Getting one's way has to do with gaining rewards or avoiding costs and is lodged in exchange relationships. It proves fruitful to define power as controlling the exchange ratio with the consequence that the more powerful, the more favorable it is.

With power so defined, attention must turn to capacities or attributes that enable persons or groups *to be powerful,* to control exchange ratios with others. Some of these capacities are biological features of human organisms—height, strength, beauty, health, and intelligence, for example. But it will also be obvious that many achieved and ascribed characteristics serve as power-giving capacities. Achieved skills, training, knowledge, and experience tend to give power. Ascribed statuses such as sex, race, family background, and the like also often serve to give power.

Among the determinants of power are the outcomes of previous exchanges. Power may be used to accumulate resources that confer more power. This tendency may have limits. For example, some rewards may be difficult to concentrate in great quantities, whereas any that are unlimited in supply cannot be concentrated at all. But rewards that exist only in limited supply are particularly susceptible to the exercise of power. Scarce rewards will tend to flow into the hands of the powerful and away from the weak. In other words,

P8   Exchange ratios will vary among individuals and groups in any society.

P9   Rewards that exist in limited supply will tend to be monopolized by powerful individuals and groups, thereby becoming relatively unavailable to others.

When people seek scarce, valuable rewards, they usually do not give in easily. Humans are persistent in pursuit of strongly desired rewards. They are willing to pay great costs for great rewards. Some problems can be solved only through costly effort, and among them are the satisfactions of several strong desires. Difficulty in obtaining strongly desired rewards not only produces *frustration* but also leads to a knotty intellectual and logical quandary. How do people evaluate the explanations on which they base their action?

P10   Explanations can be evaluated correctly only by reference to their known ability to facilitate the attainment of the desired reward.

Def. 15   *Evaluation* is the determination of the value of any reward, including explanations; value is equivalent to the maximum cost a person would pay to obtain the reward.

As noted in Proposition 5, explanations vary in the costs and time required before they can give us the desired reward. As A4 pointed out, the human mind has to compare explanations to decide which is the cheapest way of getting what is wanted. If our current situation is very similar to past situations, we can simply repeat what worked for us before. That means that evaluations, in terms of Axiom 1, are used to influence the *future* but must be based on knowledge of the *past*.

In A5 we noted that some desired rewards are scarce and others do not even exist. Here, we are postulating a fact that we cannot prove. No one is reliably known to have survived death. Although some religions report evidence on outstanding cases, other religions do not accept their claims. Logically, some rewards cannot exist because their terms are contradictory. As we usually interpret the words, we cannot have our cake and eat it too. It is a fact of life that some of the most desired, most general rewards have not been shown to exist, and we suspect that they do not in fact exist. If A5 is a little unsettling as it is stated, we could interpret it to say that some desired rewards are so scarce that they do not seem to exist *in this world*.

However, unless the definition of a given desired reward contains a logical contradiction, we cannot be absolutely sure that there is no solution to the problem of obtaining it. This follows from Axiom 1, because until the end of time—until we run out of *future*—we will not have complete information about all possible explanations, that is, we cannot evaluate the success of all possible courses of action. This is true in lesser degree for scarce rewards that can be obtained only through relatively costly action, including rewards that require lengthy sequences of exchange. Suppose we compare the values of two competing explanations for obtaining a scarce reward. We cannot honestly end the test until we have expended at least twice the cost required by the explanation that is in fact the cheaper of the two. We must have succeeded with one and have invested slightly more than an equal amount in the other before it is ideally justifiable to abandon the one that has not yet led to success. Until some course of action succeeds for us, we cannot completely reject any others under the given circumstances. It is not surprising that people often stick with explanations that seem to work without ever testing others. Because explanations can only be evaluated through a process that actually invests the minimum cost required to obtain the desired reward, the following propositions hold:

P11   It is impossible to know for certain that a given reward does not exist.

P12   When a desired reward is relatively unavailable, explanations that promise to provide it are costly and difficult to evaluate correctly.

P13   The more valued or general a reward, the more difficult will be evaluation of explanations about how to obtain it.

These three propositions explain why people often persist in following an incorrect explanation or one that has not proven fruitful, especially when strong desires are concerned. Some explanations will be invalidated, because they set specific terms for themselves. If they state the exact interval of time required for the reward to appear, then they will be discredited if the time passes and nothing happens. False explanations that *can* be discredited easily will drop by the wayside, leaving explanations (whether correct or not) that are not as vulnerable. Therefore,

P14 In the absence of a desired reward, explanations often will be accepted that posit attainment of the reward in the distant future or in some other nonverifiable context.

Def. 16 *Compensators* are postulations of reward according to explanations that are not readily susceptible to unambiguous evaluation.

The concept of *compensators* is the key to the theory of religion that follows. When humans cannot obtain strongly desired rewards they persist in their efforts and may often accept explanations that provide only compensators—empirically unsubstantiated faith that the rewards *will be* obtained—not the rewards themselves. Such faith is quite distinct from actually obtaining the reward.

P15 Compensators are treated by humans as if they were rewards; compensators are intangible substitutes for a desired reward, having the character of IOUs, the value of which must be taken on faith.

P16 For any reward or cluster of rewards, one or more compensators may be invented.

P17 Compensators vary according to the generality, value, and kind of the rewards for which they substitute.

Def. 17 Compensators that substitute for single, specific rewards are called *specific* compensators.
Def. 18 Compensators that substitute for a cluster of many rewards and for rewards of great scope and value are called general compensators.

These propositions hint at a major orphan generalization in social science analysis of the functions of religion. Malinowski's (1948) celebrated theory of magic—as an attempt to provide people with a compensatory sense of control over dangerous or vital events they cannot control—is pertinent here. So are Marx's ruminations about false consciousness and opium of the people, Durkheim's analysis of primitive religions, Freud's conjectures about religion as illusion, and much of church-sect theory. As it stands, however, these propositions *do not equate* compensators with religion. Many compensators have no connection with religion.

All societies utilize compensators. Perhaps the most universal is some promise of a triumph over death. If means were provided to evade death here and now, that would be a reward. But at present, immortality is to be achieved somewhere (somewhen?) else, and the validity of the promise cannot be determined. Thus, the desire for immortality is not satisfied with a reward but with an intangible promise, a compensator. The validity of this promise cannot be determined empirically but must be accepted or rejected on faith alone. If the promise turns out true, then at that point compensators are redeemed as rewards. If not, not.

It must be seen that some rewards are so general as to require explanations that are also so general that they are at best philosophies of life, theologies, or solutions to questions of ultimate meaning. Humans have a habit of asking why—a habit captured in our axioms. When human "whys" are repeated along certain logical chains, they lead eventually to questions about the fundamental meaning and purpose of the existence of humans and of the natural world. Some of these desired explanations are not susceptible to unambiguous evaluation. That is, we cannot surely discover whether those explanations are correct. According to our definition, such untestable and extremely general explanations are compensators. This is not to suggest that they are untrue. But we cannot find out anytime soon. It is this, and *only* this, aspect of such explanations that leads us to identify them as compensators.

Insofar as the empirical world is concerned, at any given moment a more favorable exchange ratio is possible if one can obtain a reward in trade for a compensator. Unlike bonds and other financial IOUs, compensators do not pay interest to the holder. On the contrary, they are often costly to keep and maintain. Any compensator entails the risk that it cannot be redeemed for the promised reward and therefore must be judged less valuable than that reward.

P18   Humans will prefer rewards to compensators and will attempt to exchange compensators for rewards.

Intangible IOUs represent a low cost to the giver. If you demand a better deal and I can keep things as they are by issuing promises, I can continue to enjoy a more favorable exchange ratio. Drawing together many pieces of the argument to this point, we can specify when people will succeed in obtaining rewards and when they will be forced to accept compensators instead:

P19   It will be impossible to obtain rewards rather than compensators when (1) a reward does not exist, (2) a compensator is mistaken for a reward, (3) one lacks the power to obtain the desired reward.

Obviously, one can accept a compensator if the desired reward does not exist. Malinowski's Trobriand Islanders undoubtedly would have preferred ocean liners to outrigger canoes. But in their world, liners did not exist. The best they could do was use magical compensators for the risk of sailing on the open sea. By the same token, humans would prefer not to die. Lacking scientific means to achieve immortality, they can at best settle for compensators in the form of hopes for the life to come.

People will often fail to obtain a reward and will accept a compensator instead if they cannot distinguish one from the other. One capacity influencing power—control over one's exchange ratio—is the ability or knowledge to make discriminations. This also reminds us of how compensators sometimes have been used to con the unsuspecting out of their treasure.

Finally, awareness is not enough if we are unable to control our exchange ratios. Proposition 9 states that scarce rewards will tend to be monopolized by powerful persons, leaving the powerless to content themselves with compensators. Here one thinks of the transvaluational character of religions of the poor and dispossessed. For example, folks who belong to fundamentalist sects in Appalachia know perfectly that jewels, fancy clothes, and other material luxuries exist. They also know well that they have little chance to get any, so they define these things as sinful and accept the compensatory belief that by doing without now, they will triumph in heaven, where the first shall be last and the last, first. However, in keeping with Proposition 18, when the economic circumstances of such groups change, they tend quite rapidly to become worldly and materialistic—which is, of course, what church-sect theory is partly about.

We have now reached the point at which we can introduce the concept of *religion* itself. We do so in a *definition* appended to a proposition about compensators. Thus, we show that religion must emerge in human society, and we derive its existence entirely from axioms and propositions in which religion is not an original term. It follows most immediately from Proposition 13, Proposition 14, Proposition 17, and Definition 18.

P20   The most general compensators can be supported only by supernatural explanations.

Def. 19   *Supernatural* refers to forces beyond or outside nature that can suspend, alter, or ignore physical forces.

Def. 20   *Religion* refers to systems of general compensators based on supernatural assumptions.

Earlier, we mentioned very general compensators that offer explanations for questions of ultimate meaning. It is evident that many humans desire answers to such questions: Does life have purpose? Is death the end? Why do we suffer? Does justice exist? Why did *my* child die? Humans are bound to raise questions about how great rewards can be obtained and why great costs are sometimes incurred.

When we consider such questions it is self-evident that some of them *require* a supernatural answer. To seek the purpose of life is to demand that it have one. The word *purpose* is not compatible with blind chance but assumes the existence of intentions or motives. These assume a consciousness. For the universe to have a purpose, it must be directed by a conscious agent or agents—the capacity to form plans or have intentions is to be conscious.

Conscious agents on this scale are beyond the natural world. Their existence is not subject to empirical inspection. Thus, to answer certain common questions about ultimate meaning it is necessary to assume the existence of the supernatural.

Our decision to restrict the definition of religion to very general compensator systems that rest on *supernatural assumptions* is in keeping with a very long and fruitful tradition in social science (Goody 1961; Parsons 1957; Spiro 1966; Swanson 1960; Tylor 1924/1871; Wallace 1966). A few scholars have dissented in order to apply the definition of religion to systems of thought that inspire devotion even when these are explicitly opposed to supernatural assumptions (Bellah 1970b; Luckmann 1967; Yinger 1970). Berger (1967) has demonstrated the futility of this too-inclusive definition of religion. If we define all systems of very general compensators as religion, then we are forced to define in what way science, for example, is *"different* from what has been called religion by everyone else . . . which poses the definitional problem all over again" (p. 177). We prefer to honor the commonly understood meaning of the term religion, especially when we can anticipate increased theoretical utility from so doing.

Before we can discuss the contrasts between churches and other kinds of religious organizations, we must show that such organizations can exist. Through a lengthy analysis of exchanges between individuals in populous and economically developed societies, it is possible to derive the statement that we present below as provisional Axiom 7. We offer it as an axiom here only because such a derivation lies beyond the scope of our current analysis. Observation of complex societies exhibiting advanced division of labor supports the following statement:

A7 (Provisional) Social organizations tend to emerge in human society as social enterprises that specialize in providing some particular kinds of gratifications.

General compensators supported by supernatural explanations are very special merchandise. Even a fairly rudimentary division of labor leads to the establishment of independent enterprises primarily dedicated to providing this product. Competition with organizations dedicated to selling secular products will tend to limit the tendency of religious enterprises to expand very far beyond the scope of their primary business. Because the demand for general compensators is universal, we can conclude:

P21 Religious organizations will tend to emerge in society.

Def. 21 *Religious organizations* are social enterprises whose primary purpose is to create, maintain, and exchange supernaturally based general compensators.

The role of religious organizations in producing and promulgating compensators will be obvious. A major emphasis in religious proselytization is that religion will provide a cure for pain and trouble. Indeed, because religions have recourse to a supernatural realm, they have an unmatched capacity to create and sponsor compensators. But it also should be emphasized that religious organizations, like other organizations, also have the *capacity to provide rewards*.

Because compensators function *as if* they were rewards, humans are prepared to expend costs to obtain them. Religious organizations provide compensators through exchanges in which at least some measure of real rewards is collected. Proposition 18 should not be misinterpreted to mean that individuals will *never* give up a reward to obtain a compensator. Just as they will exchange a lesser reward for a more valuable one, so they will readily exchange a reward of lower value for a compensator that promises to provide a reward of great value. Upon reflection, it is obvious that although religions usually cannot match the reward-generating capacity of some other societal institutions, they do in fact provide rewards. For example, through religious organizations, one can gain leadership positions (with attendant status and power), human companionship, leisure and recreational activity, and the like. Any organization that provides a stage for human action and interaction will produce scenes in which all manner of rewards are created and exchanged.

P22 As social enterprises, religious organizations will tend to provide some rewards as well as compensators.

This proposition permits us to introduce our derivations concerning *power* into the religious realm, in the three propositions that follow.

P23   The power of an individual or group will be *positively* associated with control of religious organizations and with gaining the rewards available from religious organizations.

P24   The power of an individual or group will be *negatively* associated with accepting religious compensators, when the desired reward exists.

Power means control of one's exchange ratio. Control of religious organizations facilitates control of one's exchange ratio by increasing one's ability to exchange compensators for rewards. Furthermore, those most able to gain rewards will tend to gain a bigger share of religious rewards, too. Because the powerful are more able to gain rewards, they will find less need for compensators. But this does not mean that powerful individuals and groups will have absolutely no use for compensators. Some rewards are so scarce—or nonexistent—that even the powerful will not be able to obtain them. Therefore,

P25   Regardless of power, individuals and groups will tend to accept religious compensators when desired rewards do not exist.

Some will interpret Propositions 23 and 24 in Marxist fashion—that the powerful will profit while the poor pray. If so, then by the same token Proposition 25 is un-Marxist and reflects basic functionalist assumptions: that all members of a society can have significant common interests, that they will tend to pursue these interests in a cooperative fashion, and that there will be considerable consensus on such matters (to say nothing of the integrative functions of such common interests). Of course, in a pluralist society, competing religious organizations may exist, and there is always the competition offered by secular organizations in those areas where demonstrable rewards and less general compensators are offered.

P26   If multiple suppliers of general compensators exist, then the ability to exchange general compensators will depend upon their relative availability and perceived exchange ratios.

Religious organizations vary in terms of how well-developed and credible a set of compensators they offer. Furthermore, they vary in terms of their degree of formal organization and the extent to which they are differentiated from other social institutions. Such variations are likely to matter.

Furthermore, in some societies, other institutions and organizations offer serious competition to religion in offering both rewards and compensators. The quasi-religious character of some political movements has long been recognized. Although there are substantial differences between, for example, the location and character of socialist and Christian utopias, the two nevertheless compete. By the same token, a scientific perspective may compete with religion in offering very general explanations concerning the most important human rewards and costs. Proposition 26 is crucial for understanding the great complexity found in the real world, but in present form it is so general as to be a truism. We must plead that we can neither break it down into the needed subset of propositions nor derive all of them in a short space. This task we postpone to a later opportunity. Our final proposition is another truism, but a vital one.

P27   All patterns of human perception and action are conditioned by socialization.

Def. 22   *Socialization* is the accumulation of explanations over time through exchanges with other persons.

Clearly it matters, for example, whether an American is raised by Baptists or Unitarians. Furthermore, regardless of the content of socialization, the effectiveness of socialization varies. Variations in socialization will probably account for much variation in religious behavior across individuals—and probably across groups as well. This is an area that deserves extensive exploration.

*   *   *

Limiting ourselves for the moment to the topic of variations in religious commitment, what does this theory tell us that was not already well known? First of all, it shows that the long tradition of deprivational theories of religious commitment was very incomplete. In Proposition 24 we derive such a theory. However, Proposition 23 permits us to see that religious organizations are not merely "otherworldly" purveyors of compensators. They also serve as a source of direct rewards. This permits us to explain forms of religious commitment not prompted by deprivation, those that are, instead, a *religious expression of privilege*. Finally, Proposition 25 allows us to take into account the fact that vis-à-vis certain kinds of desired rewards, *everyone is potentially deprived*. Thus if Proposition 24 points toward a *sectlike* mode of religious commitment and Proposition 23 points toward a *churchlike* mode, Proposition 25 points towards a *universal* dimension of commitment, variation in which is not the result of power differences, but rather of socialization and competition with competing sources of compensators (science and politics, for example).

The question is, do these predicted patterns of relationships hold? Briefly, yes. If we consider socioeconomic status (SES) as a measure of power-giving attributes, then studies ought to show SES is *positively* related to those aspects of religious commitment that can serve as direct rewards: church membership, church attendance, holding office in religious organizations, and the like. Conversely, SES ought to be *negatively* related to aspects of commitment that can serve as compensators: belief, prayer, mystical experiences, and the like. However, SES ought *not be* related to accepting compensators when no reward is known to exist, such as life after death. This is the pattern found in the data (cf. Stark 1972). Moreover, when IQ replaces SES as the power-giving attribute, the same differential patterns are found empirically (Stark & Welch n.d.). Thus, the theory clarifies and explains why different aspects of religious commitment have long been known to be differentially related to power characteristics such as SES.

These explanations of differential religious commitment are but the first small step in following out the implications of the theory. From these three propositions it can be deduced that an *internal contradiction* will exist within religious organizations. That is, within religious groups there will always be subgroups having a conflict of interest over whom the religious organization is to serve. Some will wish to maximize rewards. Some will wish to maximize compensators. It can be shown that these two goals tend to be contradictory. Therefore, the seeds of schism can exist within religious organizations. From there, it requires but a few additional steps to discover a fully developed church-sect theory: the conditions under which schisms erupt as sect movements or church movements and the conditions under which religious bodies are either transformed in a churchlike direction or remain sects. Indeed, at the end of our long chain of deductions, we will examine propositions that predict that the process of secularization is self-limiting—that it generates revivals and the formation of new religious groups. Laying out these conclusions and testing them will occupy us for the next several years. Here, we have merely tried to make explicit some basic elements of the deductive system on which our work is based.

4

IN TIMES OF STRESS: THE RELIGION-COPING CONNECTION

KENNETH I. PARGAMENT AND CRYSTAL L. PARK

Each time I knew everything would be all right because I asked God to carry me through—I know that He's got his arms around me [report of kidney dialysis patient following several cardiac arrests and surgeries].

—O'Brien, 1982

Where we find trauma and tragedy, we often find religion. Anecdotal accounts, such as the one above, and empirical studies (e.g., Koenig, George, & Siegler 1988) point to this conclusion. This is not to say that there are no atheists in foxholes. As one victim of the Holocaust put it: "I didn't need the Holocaust as proof of God's nonexistence. I was never in doubt that He didn't exist" (Brenner 1980:96). Nevertheless, it remains the case that religion is commonly called upon in times of stress.

Surprisingly, social scientists have had little to say about the relation between religion and stress. Typically, religion has been viewed as a dispositional construct—a general set of beliefs and practices. Its applications to life's most critical moments have gone largely unstudied. And yet, these moments may offer a particularly clear window into the workings of religion. "As one stands face to face with the ultimate realities of life and death," Anton Boisen (1955) wrote, "religion and theology tend to come alive" (p. 3).

Coping theory provides one framework for understanding the role of religion in stressful times. Specifically, this chapter will treat the religion-

Original contribution, edited with permission of authors.

coping connection via three questions: What forms does religion take in coping? What determines the level and form of religious coping? How helpful or harmful is religion in coping? We will see that religion adds an important dimension to coping theory and research, one that should not be reduced to simple stereotypes. We will also look at some of the questions about religion and coping that remain unanswered.

DEFINITIONS

Coping

The term "coping" has a reactive connotation to many people, as if coping is simply a reflexive response to crisis. Coping is partly reactive. Life threatening illnesses, unexpected tragedy, and death are only a few of the events that have a press of their own, forcing people to respond in one way or another. But coping is not merely reactive. Coping is a goal-directed process; it moves to the future. People cope with crises to maximize whatever is of significance to them. Significance may be material, physical, psychological, social, or spiritual. And it may be socially valued (e.g., loving relationships) or condemned (e.g., drug addiction). No matter how it is defined, coping involves attempts to preserve, maintain, or transform the things that people care about most deeply. In this sense, coping has a dual character, embodying both action and reaction. It is a search for significance in stressful times (Pargament, Van Haitsma, & Ensing 1995).

Current theory considers coping to be a transactional process that involves personal, situational, and social variables (Aldwin 1994; Lazarus & Folkman 1984). Underlying the coping process are several basic assumptions: (1) individuals initiate coping when they appraise events as threatening, harmful, or challenging to objects of significance and when their personal and social resources are appraised as insufficient to the tasks of coping; (2) people draw on an orienting system of resources (e.g., financial, physical, psychological, social, spiritual) to generate specific ways of coping with negative events; and (3) the effects of stressful life events on adjustment are mediated by the individual's resources, appraisals, and coping methods. There is a large body of empirical support for these basic assumptions.

Religion

Like coping, religion is also a process. It too is a search for significance, but a search of a special kind. What gives religion its unique character is the involvement of the sacred, however it may be defined, in this search (see Pargament 1992). Religion provides a number of special coping methods by which people attempt to conserve the things they care about most deeply. When conservation is no longer possible (e.g., the loss of a loved one), religion also offers a number of coping methods to help people transform significance—to give up what has been lost and to discover or create new objects of value.

It is important to add that religion is not simply a tool. It has as much to do with the *ends* of significance in living as it does with the *means* for attaining these ends. The world's religions offer their members a vision of what they should strive for in living. According to most traditions, finding and living close to the spiritual is the ultimate goal of life. Of course, the spiritual does not have to be defined in narrow terms. Many seemingly secular ends can be spiritualized or invested with sacred status—from baseball, politics, and war to the search for meaning, personal growth, and a better world.

Both religion and coping are concerned with the search for significance. However, not all coping is religious, for not all means and ends of coping are sacred in character. Similarly, not all religion is coping, for religion is concerned with the full range of human experience, not only the times of greatest stress. There are, though, many occasions when religion and coping come together—when people strive for significance in stressful times in ways related to the sacred.

THE MANY FACES OF RELIGION IN COPING

When it has received mention in the coping literature, religion has usually been described in a negative, stereotypic fashion. From Sigmund Freud to Albert Ellis, there has been a tradition of viewing religious involvement as a defense against confronting the painful realities of existence (see Pargament & Park 1995). A closer look suggests a more complex picture. Religion can be a part of every element of the coping process (Pargament 1990). We can speak of religious events (e.g., marriages, funerals), religious appraisals (e.g., God's will, God's punishment), religious resources (e.g., generalized religious beliefs, practices, orientations), specific religious coping activities (e.g., seeking spiritual support, doing good deeds), and religious objects of significance (e.g., closeness with God). In the process of coping, religion may serve as the independent variable, shaping coping outcomes, and as the dependent variable, shaped by the coping transaction. The broad and varied roles that religion can play throughout the coping process contradict simplistic religious stereotypes.

Functions of Religion in the Coping Process

Certainly there are times when religion serves the purpose of a defense, a protective device allaying anxiety for people faced with difficult and painful realities. Religion is more than a method of anxiety reduction (Pargament & Park 1995). People look to religion not only for comfort, but for meeting other important needs, including needs for intimacy, meaning, self-actualization, and spiritual fulfillment.

Various theorists have attempted to describe the central function of religion. Durkheim (1915) believed that the primary role of religious beliefs and practices was to unite individuals into a common society. Geertz (1966) considered meaning-giving as the most essential function of religion. Religion, he argued, is designed to fulfill the human need to find something comprehensible about the deepest problems of existence, such as suffering and injustice. Fromm (1950) asserted that humanistic religion has as its aim the promotion of human strength and growth. Finally, some theorists argue that the most basic function of religion is spiritual; to transcend oneself and embrace a larger order in the universe is the essence of religious life, a function that cannot be reduced to psychological terms.

Although theorists have debated about the most important purpose of religion, from our perspective there is no need to choose. Much of the power of religion in the coping process grows out of its ability to serve many different purposes and meet many different needs. To view religion simply as a defense against anxiety is to underestimate the multipurpose nature of religious life.

Religious Appraisals. In contrast to another common stereotype of religion, religious coping does not simply entail avoidance of difficult or undesirable situations. It provides many ways to appraise and respond to situations that challenge individuals' understanding of the world; some are passive and avoidant, but many are not.

Appraisals of potentially stressful situations involve determining the extent to which a situation is a threat, a loss, and a challenge to those things one finds significant and the extent to which their resources are perceived as adequate to meet the situational demands. Although some individuals experiencing crises may refuse to believe that God would allow such a negative event to occur, such blanket denials are uncommon. In this vein, a study of cancer patients found that measures of religiousness did not relate to reports of the presence of pain (Yates et al. 1981). Interestingly, however, the religious measures were tied to reports of lower levels of pain. Findings such as these suggest that religion may be more subtly involved in appraisal processes. Rather than being denied, negative events may be appraised in a more constructive religious light (e.g., as the will of a purposeful God, as an opportunity to share in the pain of Jesus Christ, or as a challenge to grow spiritually). Not everyone, however, forms constructive religious appraisals. Religion can add negative appraisals of its own; stressful events may be viewed as punishments from an angry God or as outside the control of a loving, but limited, God.

Religious Coping Activities.   Similar to nonreligious coping methods, religious coping activities run the gamut from avoidant and passive strategies to active approach-oriented strategies. For example, Pargament and his colleagues (1988) distinguished among three religious approaches to achieving control and mastery in coping. The first type reflects the form of religion often criticized by social scientists. Deferring religious coping places the responsibility for problem solving on God. Solutions are said to emerge through the active efforts of God alone and, as a result, the individual adopts a passive coping stance. The second type reflects more traditional mental health values. Self-directing religious coping assumes that God gives the individual the skills and resources to solve problems. Thus, the responsibility for coping rests with the individual alone. Pargament et al. (1988) defined and measured a third type of religious coping that involves active roles on the part of both the individual and God. Collaborative religious coping rests on the assumption of a partnership with God in problem solving. Neither the individual nor God is seen as passive; rather, both are active participants in coping. Not surprisingly, the deferring approach was associated with lower scores on measures of general psychosocial competence. In contrast, both the self-directing and the collaborative approaches were tied to higher levels of competence. These findings underscore the importance of distinguishing between types of religious coping.

In a more inductive approach to measuring religious coping, Pargament (1992) identified a number of other methods through interviews, surveys, and factor analyses: seeking spiritual guidance and support, doing good deeds, seeking support from clergy and congregation, pleading for a direct intercession from God, expressing religious discontent, and distracting oneself from the situation through religion.

The variety of religious appraisals and coping methods seems to parallel the variety of purposes of religion. To appraise a tragic event as the will of God may allow the individual to find some sense of meaning in an otherwise incomprehensible situation. To defer responsibility in coping to God may allow an experience of secondary control in an otherwise uncontrollable situation. To engage in a religious mourning ritual may facilitate the transition of the individual from spouse to widow to single adult in a situation that might have otherwise resulted in a loss of identity. In short, religious methods of understanding and dealing with negative life events may facilitate the conservation and transformation of many types of significance (Pargament in press).

Determinants of the Level and Form of Religious Coping

Why is it that some people engage in religious coping while others do not? There are two key determinants of religious coping. First, religion must be *available* to the individual. People cope with the tools that are available to them. Those who bring an underlying framework of religious beliefs and practices to crises are more likely to understand and deal with the situation in religious terms (e.g., Johnson & Spilka 1991). Similarly, people who are more involved in religious groups and institutions are more likely to draw on those resources for help in stressful times (Gurin, Veroff, & Feld 1960). The larger the part religion plays in an individual's general orientation to life, the more often and easily it appears to be accessed in the coping process.

But religious coping is more than a matter of convenience. Such solutions must not only be available, they must be *compelling*. This term has an emotional as well as a cognitive connotation. Compelling solutions not only make sense, but they feel right to the individual. In boundary situations, those that confront people with the inexplicable and irresolvable (cf. Little & Twiss 1973), religion may become particularly compelling. Pushed beyond their own personal and social resources, people may view religious solutions as the only viable routes to significance. Studies have found that religion is increasingly called upon in coping as situations become increasingly threatening and harmful (e.g., Lindenthal et al. 1970).

As the previous discussion suggests, a variety of individual, social, and situational forces come together to determine whether religion becomes available and compelling in the process of coping. These same forces converge to shape the specific form religious coping takes in times of stress. For example, Pargament et al. (1990) found that intrinsic, extrinsic, and quest religious orientations were associated with distinctive methods of religious coping with negative life events. Secure and insecure attachments to God might also translate into different forms of religious coping in stressful situations (Kirkpatrick 1995). Ebaugh, Richman, and Chafetz (1984) reported sharp variations in response to crisis among members of Catholic, Charismatic, Christian Science, and Bahai faiths. Different types of religious coping have also been found among people faced with different types of stressful situations, including deaths of loved ones, work-related problems, interpersonal conflicts, and health-related difficulties (Reilly & Pargament 1988).

Individual, social, and situational forces affect the specific forms of religious coping employed in the resolution of stressful encounters. In several studies, situation-specific methods of religious coping have proven to be considerably stronger predictors of adjustment to negative life events than general measures of religious belief, practice, and orientation (e.g., Pargament et al. 1990). Findings such as these suggest a mediating model of religion and coping in which life events and personal and social resources trigger particular levels and types of religious coping that, in turn, contribute to adjustment to crisis. Religious coping methods, then, are pivotal constructs. They help to explain how people translate the generalities of their orientations to the world into the specific resolutions of life's most difficult moments.

The Efficacy of Religion in Coping

How effective are religious attempts to cope with stressful life events? A straightforward approach to this question involves investigations of the relations between various aspects of religious coping and outcomes of the coping process. A more sophisticated answer to this question requires an assessment of the integration or fit between given religious strategies and the demands of the situation, the resources of the individual, and the larger social context.

The Straightforward Approach. Studies assessing the effects of specific religious appraisals and coping efforts are uncommon. However, accumulating research suggests that some kinds of religious coping are usually associated with more favorable outcomes. These include benevolent religious appraisals, spiritually based support, congregational support, and collaborative religious coping. For example, studies of attributional processes have found that negative events seem to be easier to bear when people understand them within a benevolent religious framework, such as the belief that a death or illness is the will of God or an opportunity for spiritual growth (e.g., Jenkins & Pargament 1988). Perceptions of support and guidance by God in times of trouble appear to be one of the most helpful forms of religious coping; higher levels of spiritual support are associated with favorable psychological outcomes (e.g., Park & Cohen 1993) and positive health-related outcomes, including lower mortality (e.g., Oxman, Freeman, & Manheimer 1995). Support from clergy and congregation has also been related to favorable outcomes in coping with difficult life circumstances (e.g., Gibbs & Achterberg-Lawlis 1978). Finally, empirical research has found that those who report having a collaborative relationship with God in coping have better psychological adjustment to their stressors (e.g., Rutledge & Spilka 1993).

In contrast, some types of religious coping are associated with poorer adjustment. Several studies report that attributions of negative events to a punishing God are related to negative mood (e.g., Pargament et al. 1990). Expressions of discontent toward one's congregation or God tie to less favorable adjustment (e.g., Pargament et al. 1993). It is important to note, however, that these studies are cross-sectional in design. Although the correlations between these constructs may indicate that distress is elicited by coping, it is also possible that distress is mobilizing coping. Cross-sectional studies shed no light on whether religious coping has short-term or long-lasting effects. The relationship between feelings of punishment by God or anger toward God and distress may be short-lived and such responses could be indicators of a religious struggle with beneficial implications in the long run: Consider the story of Job.

The Interactional Approach.   A more complex and interactional view of the efficacy of religious coping focuses less on the value of particular coping methods in themselves and more on the degree to which these methods are appropriate to the demands of the situation, well-integrated with the resources of the individual, and consistent with the characteristics of the larger social system (cf. Folkman 1992).

Demands of the Situation.   Problems vary in their controllability. Research has suggested that active, problem-focused coping may be more effective when problems are controllable and, conversely, that passive, emotion-focused coping may work best when problems are not controllable (Vitaliano et al. 1990). Similarly, interactional effects might be expected in various types of religious coping. In this vein, Bickel (1994) examined whether self-directing and collaborative forms of religious coping were a help or a hindrance to Presbyterian church members dealing with situations they perceived to be controllable or uncontrollable. With uncontrollable events, self-directing coping style was associated with more depression. In contrast, a collaborative coping style was associated with significant reductions in levels of depression among those dealing with uncontrollable events. Other studies have also shown religion to be especially helpful to those in greatest distress (Zuckerman, Kasl, & Ostfeld 1984).

Individual Resources.   Various types of religious coping may be more helpful to some individuals, with their own unique backgrounds and constellations of resources, than to others. For example, Park, Cohen, and Herb (1990) found that the efficacy of religious coping varied by denomination; for Protestant students, unlike Roman Catholic students, intrinsic religiousness buffered the effects of uncontrollable life events on subsequent levels of depression. For Roman Catholics, religious coping buffered the negative effects of controllable, but not uncontrollable, life events. The authors speculate that these results could reflect the relative emphasis on faith versus works in Protestant and Roman Catholic denominations. Other studies indicate that religious coping is particularly helpful to groups that tend to be more religious, such as the poor, elderly, female, less educated, African-American, and churchgoers (Veroff, Kulka, & Douvan 1981). By virtue of their ability to draw on a more fully developed religious orienting system, these groups may find it easier to generate compelling religious solutions to difficult problems (see McIntosh, Silver, & Wortman 1993).

The Larger Social Context.   Coping takes place within social forces that have pushes and pulls of their own. When people fall out of harmony with their social systems or when social systems fail to create viable niches for their members, coping becomes more difficult. Rosenberg (1962), for example, found that Protestant, Roman Catholic, and Jewish high school students reared in religiously dissonant neighborhoods (25 percent or less coreligionists) were more likely to have lower self-esteem, greater depression, and more psychosomatic symptoms than their counterparts who were raised in religiously consonant environments.

WHAT'S SO SPECIAL ABOUT RELIGION?

Although religious methods of coping have been repeatedly linked to adjustment to major life crises, it could be argued that religious coping is simply a subset of nonreligious coping. Spiritual and congregational support, for instance, may be functionally redundant with more generic social support. Religious discontent could reflect a more general emotionally cathartic approach to coping. If this were the case then there would be no need to give religious coping methods any special attention. Measures of nonreligious coping would be sufficient. Several studies, however, have found that religious coping activities predict the outcomes of negative life events above and beyond the effects of more established nonreligious measures of coping (e.g., Maton 1989; Pargament et al. 1990).

What is the special dimension religion adds to the coping process? Religion offers a response to the problem of human insufficiency. As hard as we try to achieve significance through our own insights and actions, we remain human, finite, and limited. At any time, we may be pushed beyond our own immediate resources and left with our basic vulnerabilities exposed. Religion holds solutions for those times when mastery, agency, and control—the usual guiding principles of coping—fall short. Faced with the insurmountable, the language of the sacred—forbearance, mystery, suffering, hope, finitude, surrender, divine purpose, and redemption—becomes more relevant. Spiritual support is available when other forms of social support are lacking; religious explanations become more plausible when other explanations seem unconvincing; ultimate control is still possible through the sacred when life seems to be out of control; and religion helps in the search for new objects of significance when old ones are lost or are no longer viable. In any case, religious coping complements nonreligious coping by offering responses to the limits of personal powers. Perhaps that is why the sacred becomes most compelling for many people when human powers are put to their greatest test.

CONCLUSIONS

From a distance any object, even the largest in the sky, looks faint and undifferentiated. Only when we get closer does it take on more dimension. Scientists as a group have been removed from religious phenomena, and their views of it have often been undifferentiated. But when we move closer to religion, we see that it too is multidimensional. The study of religion in times of stress offers a clear window into the concrete, intricate workings of this elusive realm. In this chapter, we have tried to show that religion serves many purposes and expresses itself in many ways through coping, in ways that do not conform to stereotyped views. We have noted how a complex of individual, social, and situational factors come together to determine the forms of religious coping that are available and compelling to people in stressful circumstances. We have identified methods of religious coping that are associated with better and poorer adjustment to crises, but we have also suggested that the efficacy of religious coping may have more to do with the degree to which the methods are appropriate and well integrated in the coping process. Finally, we have noted that religion seems to add another dimension to the coping process; it offers unique solutions to the problem of human limitations. These religious solutions deserve further research attention. They may shed light not only on religion but on the nature of coping itself. To push the point even further, we might suggest that studies of coping that ignore the religious realm remain incomplete.

Theory and research on religion and coping is only beginning. We have made a good start, but further work is needed. Microanalytic studies of specific forms of religious coping (e.g., confession, mourning rituals, or religious reframing) with specific life crises represent one promising direction for research. Macroanalytic studies of religious coping measured simply and efficiently are also needed to model religion's role in the coping process. This research should go beyond its current focus on Western religion to consider the coping practices of other traditional and alternative religious groups. Longitudinal research is also needed to distinguish effects produced by the mobilization of religious coping under conditions of stress from the immediate and long-term effects of religious coping on adjustment. The study of religion and coping offers promise for the development of a more unified bio-psycho-socio-spiritual understanding of the search for significance in times of greatest stress.

5

PROPOSED AGENDA FOR A SPIRITUAL STRATEGY IN PERSONALITY AND PSYCHOTHERAPY

ALLEN E. BERGIN AND I. REED PAYNE

Implementing spiritual values in psychotherapy is a worthy goal, but such an enterprise exists in a context, and a broad spectrum of effort must be pursued if value-oriented therapeutic practices are to attain optimal meaning and efficacy. We propose that those motivated to develop such an approach address an agenda of tasks to establish a spiritual strategy. We use the term "strategy" as defined by Liebert and Spiegler (1990), who refer to the major approaches to personality and psychotherapy in this manner.

This implies that existing major approaches are not technically theories as such but are strategies or approaches to the main issues of personality and therapeutic change. Modern versions of these strategies are actually collections of "microtheories" concerning related topics rather than "macrotheories" that explain all behavior in a single overarching conceptualization. Strategies include concepts regarding the origins, development, and dynamics of personality, the organization or structure of personality, the assessment or measurement of personality, and personality change. Liebert and Spiegler outline the details of the traditional theories within this structure, such as the psychoanalytic, dispositional, phenomenological, and behavioral strategies.

Specific approaches to therapy based upon Christian and other religious traditions are actually embedded in a broad array of assumptions

Reprinted and edited with the permission of the authors and publisher from *Journal of Psychology and Christianity*, 10 (1991), 197–210.

and professional procedures that are part of the beginnings of a new "spiritual strategy" in the psychosocial and mental health fields. The assumptions on which these works rest need to be specified as part of a plan for a comprehensive approach.

A spiritual approach contributes distinctive factors to a strategy of personality and therapeutic change, but such an approach necessarily partakes of characteristics of other approaches. A spiritual approach contributes uniquely to (1) a conception of human nature, (2) a moral frame of reference, and (3) specific techniques of change. In addition, if it is to be a viable option in the professional domain it needs to be (4) empirical, (5) eclectic, and (6) ecumenical. Finally, specialized aspects of a spiritual strategy can be (7) denominationally specific and contribute meaningfully to the religious diversity and plurality that exists among clientele.

A Conception of Human Nature

A spiritual approach to psychology has profound implications for personality theory. The assumptions that this approach brings to theory are rooted in theology (Bergin 1988a, 1988b; Collins 1977, 1980). One essential point is recognizing the existence of a spiritual reality as a fundamental assumption. The exact nature of a person's spirit may be disputed in its details across denominations, but there is a clear agreement that the essential identity of a person is eternal, has a spiritual or invisible aspect, and can respond to the spirit of God through prayer and other means of inspiration that have direct effects upon thought, feelings, and conduct. There are many other fundamentals that derive from a spiritual perception of the world and of man's place in it that could and should shape a new perspective on personality. Some of these concern "identity," "agency," "integrity," "power," "intimacy," "family," and "value systems." It is essential that the hard work required to develop and integrate such concepts be undertaken. Although hermeneutic, existential, humanistic, cognitive, and social constructionist thought all open the way to a spiritual approach to theory, none of these has bridged the secular-to-sacred gap. Although no truly systematic spiritual strategy has yet appeared, there are worthy beginnings in efforts to tie theology to concepts of personality and psychotherapy.

One example of this is Jones's (1989) attempt to show the relationship between a Christian perspective and rational-emotive theory and therapy. Jones points out a number of apparent similarities between the two perspectives that have been noted by other Christian writers; but his analysis points to incompatibilities at a fundamental level. He notes that the rational-emotive conception of self is basically atomistic and that it "undermines persons seeing themselves as agents, as substantive selves; as responsible moral agents with continuous identities through life" (p. 117). Another key point of potential conflict is in the definition of "rational." Theology suggests beliefs, such as dependence upon God, that may be viewed as irrational by secular theorists. We are thus challenged to show what healthy dependency is and how it is an integral aspect of human nature. Still, his outlines provide a meaningful attempt toward a Christian strategy of personality.

Spilka and Bridges (1989) compare and contrast theological assumptions with psychological theories. They evaluate contemporary "process," "liberation," and "feminist" theologies and show certain parallels between them and social cognitive theory. "The importance of the role of the self and needs for meaning, control and self-esteem are stressed, indicating that theology can serve as psychological theory and that both psychology and theology might benefit from increased interaction between the disciplines" (p. 343). Their article is not denominational in orientation but deals with modern struggles to interpret God in relation to groups that have suffered social oppression and seem alienated from traditional religious identifications. The authors note that one approach to process theology emphasizes the themes of God as "presence," "wisdom," and "power" (p. 347). This does not deny biblical conceptions of God but attempts to show that "a sense of God's presence may be tied to feelings of self-worth." God as wisdom may be associated with meaningfulness through the faith that "no matter what threats and contingencies we may experience, God is faithful and is leading us to creative modes of dealing with problems" (p. 347). Finally, God as power "may reflect personal capability in being able to influence the world" (p. 347).

The notion is that if people can perceive God's influence along these dimensions then therapeutic change in one's life may be more likely. "Meaninglessness, powerlessness, and low self-esteem are correlates of cultural realities that deprive people of opportunities to realize their potential" (p. 347). This thinking has implications for a theory of personality and shows how such a theory can be enhanced by theological thought. A further task for a spiritual strategy would be to link traditional concepts of sin, forgiveness, and salvation in a significant way to meaning, a sense of personal capacity and self-esteem.

A Moral Frame of Reference

A spiritual perspective anchors values in universal terms. Since psychotherapy is a value-laden process, this makes the spiritual strategy immediately relevant to the therapeutic situation. Although therapists are often unaware of their particular moral frames of reference and how they impact upon clients, this situation is rapidly changing. It is becoming abundantly clear that values must be dealt with more systematically and effectively if therapeutic change is to be lasting. To be optimal, values must also affect one's lifestyle and one's impact upon others (Bergin 1991).

In contrast to earlier assertions that values are "relative" and that psychotherapy should be "value-free," it seems more likely that there are certain values that mental health workers see as "better" or as underlying healthy adjustment. Many values "imply a frame of reference for guiding behavior and regulating lifestyle so as to prevent or ameliorate psychopathologies" (Bergin 1985:106). Making these implicit values explicit in therapy, particularly spiritual ones, may in actuality promote freedom in the therapeutic environment by promoting open deliberation about values (Bergin 1988a, 1988b).

In a national survey of mental health care workers, Jensen and Bergin (1988) found much consensus on values pertinent to both mental health and psychotherapy. These included (1) being a free agent; (2) having identity and feelings of worth; (3) having skill in interpersonal communication, sensitivity, and nurturance; (4) being genuine and honest; (5) having self-control and personal responsibility; (6) being committed in marriage, family, and other relationships; (7) having orienting values and meaningful purposes; (8) having deepened self-awareness and motivation for growth; (9) knowing adaptive coping strategies for managing stress and crises; (10) finding fulfillment in work; and (11) practicing good habits of physical health. These, in essence, are traditional values, which are correspondingly many of the same values that underlie practices and beliefs espoused in religious environments.

Sprinthall and McVay (1987) show progress toward a conception of universalistic values that may bridge the gap between such "clinical" values and spiritual values. They note an increasing consensus between religious and secular value theories in a common ground of universal and humane principles. Whereas religion as an organized system concerns itself with universals, spirituality *is* a universal. Dombeck and Karl (1987) state, "Every person can be understood to have a spiritual life, although some persons do not subscribe to any established religion" (p. 184).

When value-related problems are encountered in therapy, both the client's and the therapist's values may need to be examined to provide an ethical and open atmosphere. Although a therapist and client's values may differ at points, this need not discourage value exploration and problem solving. Some divergence may be preferred to total value agreement (Beutler, Crago, & Arizmendi 1986; Propst et al. 1992). If values become a problem in therapy, the therapist should approach them openly, and if conflict between client and therapist persists, referral elsewhere may be required. Referrals based on value discrepancy, client need, or therapist bias need to be made from a position of value knowledge and professional integrity. Therapy techniques or strategies need to be justified and explained, especially if they are other than what traditional therapy might offer (cf. Bergin 1991).

Is it ethical to provide services to people who have diverse backgrounds if those backgrounds are not understood? This point has been made when dealing with cross-cultural counseling or therapy with minorities and might well be made with clients who have a distinct religious or value orientation. Psychologists will encounter more religious diversity than any other kind of diversity.

Both Meyer (1988) and Lovinger (1984) suggest becoming acquainted with major teachings and dilemmas typical of clients of diverse religious orientations. To deny service to a client who wants to deal with spiritually related issues seems to Meyer no more appropriate than "to deny service to a student coping with educational issues or a terminally ill patient struggling with medical concerns" (p. 488). According to Meyer, clarification of values and biases with regard to religion could be better understood through research, role playing, exploratory papers, or additional education aimed at understanding spiritual issues. In understanding religious clients, it is important for the therapist to both appreciate the value pattern of the individual's particular group and understand the individual's personal value pattern within that group (Worthington 1986).

It is paradoxical that traditional psychology and psychotherapy, which foster individualism, free expression, and tolerance of dissent, would be so reluctant to address one of the most fundamental concerns of humankind—morality and spirituality. In fact, therapeutic efforts have studiously avoided controversy, concern, and needs associated with religion. Regarding this conspiracy of silence, one could accusingly reflect: We speak of wholeness but insist on parts; we value openness but stay partly closed; we like to be accepting but only of some things; it is good to be tolerant but not of things we don't understand. In the larger matrix of sociocultural variables, religion cannot be avoided as subject or object, cause or effect, noumena or phenomena.

The danger of a moral philosophy or moral frame of reference not anchored to spirituality or religion is that of relativeness, expediency, and an ever-changing hierarchy of values. With no standard of measure or no reference point, it is easy to manipulate moral issues to meet merely expedient needs. Ignorance of spiritual constructs and experience predispose a therapist to misjudge, misinterpret, misunderstand, mismanage, or neglect important segments of a client's life that may impact significantly on adjustment or growth. Therapy may clumsily tread on sensitive areas.

If the therapist is blind to the spiritual or moral realities of the client, resistance and transference will remain only partially appreciated.

Spiritual, religious, and moral diversity are givens that we must acknowledge. A moral frame of reference might be advantageously anchored to the spiritual and religious. The therapeutic process encounters value dilemmas on every side. As therapists, we must prepare to understand and address these complex issues more effectively. This will require an interaction and combining of traditional techniques adapted to value issues and techniques emanating from moral and spiritual strategies.

SPECIFIC TECHNIQUES OF CHANGE

A spiritual strategy implies hypotheses and techniques of change. Although these have applicability to normal and mildly disturbed persons, which is the special province of spiritual approaches, they are also frequently applicable to more severe disorders.

Essentially two categories of counseling techniques are used in dealing with religious or spiritual issues: (1) those grounded in traditional psychological theories or emanating from professional secular sources, which are then adapted to religious content; and, (2) those originating specifically from within spiritual or religious frameworks, which are used therapeutically in coping with both standard symptoms and religious issues.

Illustrative of applying traditional techniques with religious content, Propst (1980) found that cognitive behavioral therapy with religious imagery and a religious placebo (group discussion of religious issues) showed more treatment effect in mild depression for religious subjects than did a nonreligious imagery treatment. In a subsequent study, subjects in the religious content treatment and pastoral counseling treatment reported significantly lower rates of posttreatment depression and better adjustment scores than controls or those in nonreligious cognitive therapy. Nonreligious therapists, using the religious approach, had the highest level of treatment effect.

In an article addressing religious values and therapy, Aust (1990) reviews techniques mentioned by several authors (Frank 1973; Propst 1980; and Worthington 1978). Wilson (1974) notes client improvement with "Christian therapeutic maneuvers" consisting of (1) commitment or rededication, (2) confession or uncovering, (3) forgiveness of self and others, and (4) fellowship or community. Moral Reconation Therapy (Little & Robinson 1988) is a step-by-step treatment program applied to treatments for antisocial or drug abuse clients. The approach appears to promote moral growth and behavior improvement. They also indicate that it fosters commitments to goals and development of identity.

One of the unique aspects of Moral Reconation Therapy is the requirement for clients to render a payback to society in the form of public service. Briefly, the treatments appear to involve the following behaviors: The clients are responsible for their own treatment as well as the treatment of others, confrontation is an important aspect, and a formal written assessment of the self is required. Activities that raise the person's awareness of relationships with others are implemented. A connection between freedom and responsibility is taught. The client must provide service to others where there is no overt gain for the client. The strategies include an effort to decrease clients' decisions based on pleasure and pain. Also, they are taught to tolerate delays in gratification. They are exposed to problems and moral dilemmas at the various stages of moral development. Trust and honesty in relationships are points of focus. Ongoing self-assessment, in conjunction with receiving assessment from other clients and staff, is required. Preliminary research suggests an encouraging level of success.

The concept of forgiveness, with its roots in religion, has been espoused as a spiritual therapy technique (Bergin 1980; Brandsma 1985; Hope 1987). "Forgiveness is a core value of Christianity and other major religions . . . understanding the dynamics of forgiveness can serve as a powerful therapeutic tool" (Hope 1987:240).

Forgiveness, Hope (1987) indicates, is a voluntary act, a decision about how a person deals with past injustice, disappointment, and humiliation. One needs to learn how to reinterpret or accept the past in a way that frees one for future growth. Lasting change requires transcending one's sense of victimization. By choosing to forgive, we increase our options and freedom to grow. It is suggested that "forgiveness can be seen as a meta-action, as a reframing of how one views the world" (p. 242). The opposite is a desire to seek vindication, which delivers a person into a crippling state of ambivalence toward people. Forgiveness of others, then, may be a necessary requisite for forgiving oneself. Hope also explains, "For those who also view life from a spiritual dimension, forgiveness becomes an act of faith, a way of actualizing religious beliefs" (p. 242). He quotes Fillipaldi (1982:75) who states that "forgiveness is a focus on the present that frees from the past and opens up the future."

Confession and contrition are seen as preparatory acts to healing (Harrison 1988). Involved in these processes is the radical lowering of one's defenses, often a reordering of values and the freeing of energies that are bound up in the process of trying to hide. Contrition is equated with desire to change and is the opposite of defensiveness. It implies pliancy. In practicing each virtue, the complementary vice is rendered ineffective or nonexistent. "The individual is made a new creature bit by bit and each aspect of moral goodness is acquired by deliberate choice" (p. 315).

Specific therapy techniques mentioned by Lovinger (1984) include using (1) religious imagery, for example, comparing Christian charity with being a Christian doormat; (2) alternative Bible translations considering context, special use of words, and other interpretations of scriptures; (3) contradictory imperatives, wherein the meaning is modified by other scriptural statements; (4) corrective experiences; (5) literary resources; (6) denominational resources; (7) forgiveness; and, (8) service. It is mentioned that the hallmark of effective therapy is increased capacity to work and to love.

Some Cautions

Because religious techniques are espoused for a variety of reasons, it need not be assumed that those who promote spirituality-based methods are always competent, honest, or ethical in their approach. There may be hidden agendas and manipulations for implicit reasons, which reflect something less than integrity.

Potentially, the directness, evangelism, and conversion agenda of a pastoral counselor or a religiously oriented therapist may not be compatible with the traditional therapeutic value of autonomy and independent choice. However, there is no inherent reason for a spiritual approach or moral frame of reference to be any more directive than other approaches to psychotherapy.

Many therapists may not know how to deal with values and spiritual concerns in a constructive, helpful manner because they have not been taught to do so. They have avoided the process of helping others cope with spiritual issues and controversial values in a religious context. Although working with a client's spiritual values may promote growth and change in a positive direction, the therapist should remain "within" the client's own value system in this endeavor. To impose the therapist's own religious values onto a nonreligious client may not only be counterproductive, it may also violate professional ethics.

The usefulness of religious therapeutic techniques is predicated on several criteria such as religiosity of the client, desire by the client to employ such procedures, comfort level of the therapist, skill of the therapist in the use of religious techniques, and ultimately, empirical proof of efficacy.

Dual or unwarranted roles should be avoided as well. Both the client and the therapist should understand that though the therapist may be sensitive to and discuss the client's religious issues, the therapist does not possess the same role assigned to members of the client's particular ecclesiastical leadership. A proper referral in cases where the client may need to speak with an appropriate member of the faith may be necessary to comply with the expectations of a client's religious affiliation.

Despite such cautions, there is a vast untapped potential for spiritual approaches to therapeutic change. The way is open for creative counselors within faith traditions and for others to develop and assemble a repertoire of useful techniques that add to what is already known and can be done. At the same time, we need to remember our obligation to be empirical, eclectic, and ecumenical.

The Empirical Dimension

It is essential that a spiritual strategy have an empirical dimension if it is to have credibility in the profession at large and if we are serious about using all of the sources of truth given to us. Certainly, the scientific method in its various forms (experimental, correlational, qualitative, descriptive) is a rich source of truth that we cannot afford to ignore, even though we may be emphasizing processes that are not easy to observe in traditional scientific ways. Nevertheless, we can observe many of the effects or consequences of spiritual processes such as spiritual experience. It has been noted, for instance, that there seem to be material consequences to spiritual conviction. For example, the physical health of people who have a sense of coherence in their lives or a certain way of believing in God is better than others (Antonovsky 1979; McIntosh & Spilka 1990). We also note that there are correlations between the quality of one's lifestyle, the nature of one's belief system, and mental health indices (Bergin in press).

Although the psychology of religion is pertinent to the empirical dimension of a spiritual strategy, much of it is essentially secular social psychology. We need to carefully identify those subsections of research that are particularly pertinent to an approach that openly acknowledges the reality of the spiritual dimension in life. Much research simply ignores the possibility of a spiritual reality. However, Hood's work on mystical and religious experiences gives us an observational handle on a very private domain of phenomena (Spilka, Hood, & Gorsuch 1985). Hood's mysticism scale exemplifies the encounter of empiricism with spiritual phenomenology that is not intimidated by objectivistic strictures that might inhibit good research in this area.

We would not want to ignore objective research that is pertinent to the spiritual agenda. For instance, there is an abundant literature in the area of prevention of mental disorders and social pathology that shows a positive effect of religion (Payne et al. 1991). Other research areas, for example the study of intrinsic and extrinsic religious orientations, illustrate the value of standard psychology of religion research (Donahue 1985b; Kirkpatrick 1989).

In entering the empirical domain, we do not want to be limited entirely to traditional designs, however. Qualitative, descriptive research may be important in analyzing the relation between a religious lifestyle and personality traits and mental health indices. In addition, we need to consider a spiritual method itself as a form of empiricism. That is, a researcher may use a spiritual perception of the characteristics of a person being studied that is not accessible by ordinary observational techniques. In this sense, spirituality overlaps with intuition, inspiration, illumination, and creativity. Such phenomena have been noted by some therapists who have touched on the transpersonal realm and have referred to the possibility that therapists may be able to perceive characteristics of a client and to commune with the spirit of that client in a way that goes beyond ordinary empathic perception (Rogers 1980).

Spiritually enhanced perception can occur in research as well as in therapy and might become the focus of new studies in which spiritual tests become part of the realm of empirical testing. By spiritual tests we mean that the researcher tests the communications from or impressions received from a subject against a sensed perception of the truth as witnessed by the spirit to the observer. Such perception still needs to be checked against the perceptions of equally qualified observers and against consensually established scriptural criteria of truth. A balance is required between idiographic and nomothetic perceptions in order to avoid self-deception. Although this method may seem radical, it will be essential to consider it in the repertoire of assessment devices available within a spiritual strategy. This procedure takes research beyond the ordinary qualitative and descriptive methods of the empirical approach. Reports of its use are rare, but as a prototype it could become an essential ingredient of a spiritual strategy.

Eclecticism

There are resources within the behavioral sciences that can be tapped for the purpose of our effort. Therefore, as we seek to integrate psychological theory and technique, eclecticism will be a valuable guiding principle as we select what is useful.

Consider some examples of efforts toward such an integration. Jones (1989) integrated some aspects of the theory and practice of the rational-emotive approach into a religious framework, while also discarding major aspects of the theory. Smith and Handelman (1990) made similar efforts with regard to religion and psychoanalytic thought. Their goal was to bridge the gap that has existed between psychoanalysts and religious thinkers, especially in identifying healthy ego processes in religious experience and expression. Another exemplary effort is a book edited by Miller and Martin, *Behavior Therapy and Religion* (1988), which attempts to integrate spiritual and behavioral approaches to change. Of particular note is Martin and Carlson's (1988) chapter on health psychology in which they "emphasize . . . combining modern, well-tested medical and behavioral health interventions with appropriate spiritual ones" (p. 103).

Propst et al. (1992) have demonstrated the value of integrating religious content into cognitive therapy of depression. When her Religious Cognitive Therapy was conducted according to a prescribed technique manual, Christian religious clients benefited more from the religiously integrated therapy than from standard cognitive techniques. We would do well to follow the lead of these pioneers in broadening the interface between religion and secular psychology.

In addition to learning from secular approaches, a spiritual strategy has much to offer. It may be that those who currently ignore relevant spiritual and religious content would be less likely to do so if it were translated into the terms of their espoused strategy. By first understanding other strategies and then asking ourselves how religious and spiritual issues fit into their system, we will be better prepared to extend contributions from the spiritual strategy to other strategies. Miller and Martin (1988) offer the following possibilities for spiritual contributions to psychology: (1) enlarging the scope of inquiry, (2) stretching the science, (3) unlocking training, (4) raising clinical issues, (5) improving effectiveness and accessibility of therapy, and (6) broadening perspectives.

In sum, a spiritual strategy can be eclectic in two ways, first, by integrating useful technique and theory from a variety of sources within psychology, and second, by seeking to introduce a spiritual perspective to traditionally secular techniques and theories.

Ecumenical and Denominational Considerations

One avenue we must pursue to increase the utility of our work is that of breaking down barriers that can prevent productive communication of thought between denominations. In order to be of maximum benefit, our work must be ecumenical in the following ways: (1) Areas of agreement should be sought and specified, rather than focusing upon disagreement, and (2) even in areas where disagreement on specific doctrinal issues or beliefs exist, we can seek ways to apply things learned within the context of one denomination to other denominations.

The interface between psychology and religion is part of a larger ecumenical movement noted by Sprinthall and McVay (1987). They suggest that those interested in the interface between religion and psychotherapy may learn from each other and learn together in spite of divergence in belief systems or denominations. In order to be truly ecumenical, this exchange must include not only traditional Christian religion but other religions as well, and in our culture, this should include particular attention to our Judaic heritage. Hutch (1983) points out that some bridges can be built between Christian and Eastern philosophies in their approaches to anxiety, human suffering, and insight into the human condition. Perhaps there are bridges that should not be built, but generally a free interchange between denominations across cultures opens the door for research and theorizing to be done in a broad manner.

Beit-Hallahmi (1975) provides an example of how issues in therapy—even those that are denominationally specific in content—can be reported in an ecumenical manner. For example, he presents a therapy case of an individual from an Orthodox Jewish background. He discusses the importance of understanding that Israeli society is divided into a religious subculture and a secular subculture. Understanding this division and the coinciding differences in terms of beliefs, appearance (dress), and behavior allowed the therapist to work more effectively with the client in his struggles within the context of that society. This illustrates the universal problem of understanding the client's specific religious group and the client's way of defining himself or herself within it.

In addition, Beit-Hallahmi treats the issue of the gap in religiosity between the client and the therapist. He describes how the tension that resulted from the client-therapist religious difference was discussed openly and how this openness set the stage for future work on religious aspects of the client's life.

Although discussion of the client's specific religion and its influence in therapy offers clarity, the author's specification of the universal issues that the case studies illustrate insures that the article's scope of application will be ecumenical.

At the same time, the role of concepts and techniques specific to denominations must be recognized. Evangelical Christian, Latter-day Saint, and Orthodox Jewish clients present different needs embedded in languages and lifestyles that demand technical content adapted to their needs (Lovinger 1984, 1990; Spero 1985). A psychologist whose background and perspective derive strongly from a denominational context must learn to function both in the broader ecumenical world and in the fine texture of his or her own tradition. A viable spiritual strategy must be responsive to both ends of this continuum and persist in the conceptual struggle to embrace them both. An example of this was recently noted in a newsletter article on pain management ("Using Faith" 1990). Coping skills are taught for handling suffering using two types of spiritual content ("Christian" and "God and faith") and a nonspiritual format. Watson,

Hood, Morris, and Hall (1985) nicely show ways of integrating denominational Christian concepts of sin and salvation with the psychology of personal growth and self-esteem. Lovinger's (1984, 1990) work touches upon common themes across religions within an ego-analytic perspective, whereas Jensen and Bergin (1988) attempt to identify mental health values that can be endorsed by people of diverse denominational origins.

CONCLUSION

It is encouraging that a literature is evolving that could form the basis for a new approach comparable in substance to the existing major strategies. This work is still relatively primitive compared with the main secular traditions. In all areas of theory, practice, and research, major work remains to be done.

COMMENTARY: WHY RELIGION? FUNCTIONS OF RELIGIOUS BELIEF AND BEHAVIOR

The persistence of religion in human culture suggests that it has a significant and relatively unique role in human psychology. Clearly, some functions of religion can be equally well served via secular means (e.g., meeting affiliative needs). However, its near universality begets the question of what functions religion serves uniquely or, at least, singularly well. The chapters in this section underscore the need for a psychology of religion that is not merely derivative of broader theories of behavior and belief. To understand it, we must consider what makes up the distinct role religion serves. Chapter 3 addresses broadly what people get from religion, considering its contribution from a reward-theory perspective. Chapter 4 examines a specific context (coping) in which religion is often heavily involved in a variety of manners. Here, it is shown that religion is used by all and that a correct understanding of the functions of religion requires moving past that notion to a more sophisticated analysis of *how* people use their religion. Chapter 5 combines the notion that religious beliefs play important roles in life and the insight that these must be accounted for in therapeutic situations.

By framing the function of religion in a reward-theory paradigm in Chapter 3, Stark and Bainbridge identify some of the types of satisfactions that people get from religion. Religious involvement can provide typical rewards (e.g., power, affiliation) that are available in other institutions. Significantly, it alone can provide "compensators" (intangible substitutes for desired rewards) for existential questions (e.g., "Why are we here?"). This motivational language ties in well with Allport's intrinsic and extrinsic dimensions of personal faith. An extrinsic orientation relates to getting "typical" rewards (those available elsewhere, such as social contacts). An intrinsic orientation is tied to obtaining supernatural explanations—unique compensators—provided by religious faith. This is why those who report high levels of an intrinsic approach value religion "for it's own sake"; they may genuinely be motivated by that which can only be provided by religion—compensators for unattainable rewards. Batson's description of a quest orientation also fits into this motivational framework. Higher levels of quest-type religion may exist in people who have not found the compensators provided by traditional religion satisfactory and are still seeking this goal.

Following Stark and Bainbridge, we may hypothesize that a religious system helps people make sense out of their problems and maintain or enhance both their sense of mastery and self-esteem. These may be treated as rewards. The subjective costs of attaining such, however, still remain undefined. One approach would be to ask people directly about the costs they experience. One possibility is that commitment to one set of meanings may cause detrimental rigidity when people are faced with a situation in which those meanings do not fit. Stark and Bainbridge speak of exchange ratios, meaning "net rewards over costs in an exchange." Adherence to religious systems, involvement in ceremonies, the holding of various beliefs, the influence of religious experiences, and so on could be studied in terms of such rewards and costs.

How might one test the proposition that some religiously active people are motivated more by these compensators and others more by typical rewards offered through religious involvement? Looking at the types of changes people undergo over time might be informative. For example, one might track the shifts in members of a congregation connected with clergy replacements. Typically there is a "shuffling" of member's involvements in churches when there are changes in clergy. One might predict, based on Stark and Bainbridge's analysis, that when the clergy switch alters the compensators offered in a congregation (through a shift in the theology presented in services, for example), those people who were involved with the previous compensators will leave and seek another church that offers the original compensators. Alternatively, members who receive other typical rewards should stay involved, unless a shift in organization (e.g., lay leadership changes or a decreased focus on social activities) reduces their ability to acquire the desired rewards of power or affiliation. They should then seek out a way to obtain these commodities elsewhere.

A key issue is the question of determining people's motivations. Asking them is one good approach, but it is limited by self-presentational concerns of the respondents and by the possibility that they themselves are unaware of what is motivating their behavior. By examining situations in which particular rewards or costs change, it may be possible to better determine the motivations related to religion.

In Chapter 4, Pargament and Park stress how important the role of religion is in the coping process. This topic has received so little empirical attention that framing the most useful questions is a necessary chore. In presenting the key issues to consider, Pargament and Park point to the need for descriptive and qualitative work from which testable and pertinent questions can be formed. Despite the fact that we attend to coping when crisis occurs, it is a lifelong, daily exercise that is often taken for granted. As an independent variable, one's faith orientation may play an everyday coping role. This leads to the question of forms and content of personal religion and their place in the armamentarium of the individual. Although one may initially think of the intrinsic-extrinsic dichotomy, other dimensions exist, some tied to institutional participation, others independent of church and synagogue.

Precrisis religious schemata thus need to be identified so that postcrisis coping may be better understood. This will entail longitudinal work, following people from pre-event to post-event. Although such designs are difficult to create, they are essential if we are to know what functions religion serves. Possible populations used in other coping research include pre-med students before they take medical school entrance exams, older couples with a likelihood of one becoming bereaved within the course of the study, and students making a transition to graduate school. Pargament and Park emphasize coping in terms of what is significant to the struggling person. Personal values come into play, yet we still do not know the range or nature of such factors relevant to personal faith. There is a "complex" here of background influences, a hierarchy of individual "things that matter," and differences in where religion fits in this scheme, what aspects of religion are selected and employed as resources, and finally, how such are used.

When appraisals are made, we are seeking, in part, to discover what is threatening and to what degree such threats enter one's choice of faith as a resource. In addition to asking questions about meaning, we can also ask whether degree of threat can be assessed so that points may be clarified at which shifts may occur from naturalistic to religious referents and actions. To what extent are these points also a function of personal resources other than religion? A rather broad picture of the person is necessary to more fully comprehend the use of both religious and nonreligious coping mechanisms.

On the religious side, the individual may resort to prayer, but there are many forms: Which are employed? Further, what are the God images held by the supplicant, and how do these relate to a person's sense of control in trying situations? The authors point to humanistic and spiritual religious forms. There are also opportunistic utilitarian possibilities. Who is using what under various circumstances? Do these change over time, and how? The presence of others may mitigate stress. What works better, others with similar problems, with similar religious perspectives, or a combination of the two? Is one aided by additional information or by reinforcement of certain religious ideas? When primary control is in short supply, does faith support the utilization of secondary control forms—vicarious, interpretive, predictive? This may be an avenue to the authors' call for understanding the religious appraisals of the threat that probably occur.

People are loath to interpret the negative things that occur to them as God-caused, yet they rapidly invoke the deity to explain good outcomes. What motivates such judgments, and how do individuals who refer to or blame God for negative circumstance differ from those employing positive reasoning?

The authors point to the use of deferring, collaborative, and self-directive modes of God-relations in coping, but we still know very little about the characteristics of individuals who select these different patterns. Not only is this true for personality, but it is also true as regards the nature of personal faith. Such information might be therapeutically valuable.

Pargament and Park portray well the rich variety of religious appraisals and coping devices. Such variation opens the door to understanding religious attributions that might tie to specific appraisals and behavior. Then there is always the likelihood that some forms are more effective than others in offering personal comfort and stimulating corrective activities on the part of the person with difficulties. These authors also suggest that the study of attachment patterns might be productive here.

Research on religion and psychotherapy is difficult to conduct and hence is relatively rare. In Chapter 5, Bergin and Payne, however, point to the necessity of bringing "spiritual stategies" and considerations both into personality theory and therapy. One can argue that this is done in pastoral counseling, but the issue still remains that we know little about what constitutes the spiritual, how it is used, and what its effects are. In addition, distinctions between general clinical practice and pastoral approaches clearly need to be explicated.

Initially, we need a rigorous overview of the conceptual and applied literature to determine what is meant by "spiritual." We do know that theoretical and operational approaches to spirituality vary widely. A first step would be an exacting formulation of these ideas and methods. Second, when these are employed, what are the characteristics of both the therapists who utilize these techniques and the clients who receive them? Third, do different therapists classify different procedures under the rubric "spiritual"? Fourth, if so, can the effects of such variation be assessed? Finally, comparisons of the various spiritual strategies with their nonspiritual alternatives need to be conducted, preferably both within and across therapists.

In essence, Bergin and Payne discuss the importance of considering individuals' beliefs and practices in a way that respects the differing values and perspectives. Those who want to examine this area should look at the work done on cross-cultural or interethnic therapy for ideas regarding specific hypotheses and methods. Questions that arise here include advantages and disadvantages of a therapist who shares the client's "culture." Is mere training in dealing with clients with other beliefs enough, or must there be a match between the two? What factors influencing which of these options is preferable? Ethical considerations make experimental designs difficult; however, measures of the therapeutic alliance, continuation of therapy, and outcome would be helpful. This also begs the question of how to operationalize "successful therapy."

The meaning to therapists and clients of the spiritual approach versus the nonspiritual needs to be explored, especially in terms of what is actually done. Bergin and Payne emphasize "universalistic values" and offer some denotational direction for these; however, empirically, we ought to assess therapist and client identity with these ideals. Social desirability response sets would undoubtedly need to be controlled in such an endeavor. Still, the theoretical assumption is that successful therapy means a growing identification with these values, more specifically spiritual values that speak to an integrated unity and wholeness in personality and effectiveness in coping. Operational definition of these goals also constitutes a task to be resolved, a task that probably relates to one's specific religious group and its place within a social order. Here we have a mix of psychological and sociological questions and research roles. Bergin and Payne discuss many of these issues and have been explicit in noting a variety of research possibilities. Although some beginnings have been cited, if ever there was a "wide-open" field of study, this is it.

PART 3

Social Concerns

6

AN INTEGRATED ROLE THEORY FOR THE PSYCHOLOGY OF RELIGION: CONCEPTS AND PERSPECTIVES

NILS G. HOLM

Role theory aims to understand individual behavior from an analysis of social factors. This kind of analysis originally consisted of locating within a given community the human behavioral structures necessary for survival and propagation. Subsequently, emphasis was placed on the interactional perspective: By communication, a community develops roles that then become permanent through continuous social exchange. In Scandinavia there has been development toward perceptual role theory. This emphasizes intrapsychic processes and understands roles primarily as "patterns" recurring in forms of tradition: myths, legends, and narratives. The concept of role is extremely flexible and may be used in different ways. In this chapter, I wish to integrate the sociopsychological perspective with the psychodynamic approach.

Historically, the term "role" is borrowed from the theater. At the beginning of the century, the term was introduced into social science to describe the function acquired by an individual in a specific social context. Role theory always assumes that roles form part of a dual interaction; role activity thus always presupposes one or more counterparts.

Many classics in the psychology and sociology of religion use the term "role" or other concepts very close to it. For example, William James

---

Original contribution, edited with permission of author.

(1890) approached the concept when he advanced the notion of "self" in psychology. Similar developments may be found in Durkheim (1893) and Mead (1934). Most social psychologists to date have been inspired by Mead. Linton (1936, 1945) stressed the functions of role in social anthropology, and Erikson (1968a), inspired by depth psychology, also touched on role theory when he spoke of the "ritualization of everyday life." The following brief account of developments in the use of the role concept sets the stage for the integrated model I propose here.

THE STRUCTURAL-ANALYTICAL MODEL

The structural-analytical approach is concerned with analyzing the different roles of a social unit. Attention is not directed at the role performances of different individuals, but rather at a description of roles as social quantities. It is argued that every social group consists of a collection of roles, which must be present to enable the group to exist and develop. It then becomes important to study different leader roles, functional roles, pedagogical roles, sex roles, status roles, and so on. It is simply a question of the division of labor that must exist within a given group for everything to function. Representatives of this position include Linton (1945), Parsons (1951), and Dahrendorf (1959).

THE INTERACTIONIST MODEL

The interactionist stance examines the interaction between two or more individuals, studying how they fulfill socially given roles. This model isolates the different roles played by the person in various daily situations and sees how they are performed. Interest is directed at the person's efforts within the frame of a social context. This school includes Mead (1934), Turner (1962), Habermas (1973), Sarbin (1954), Newcomb (1952), and Berger and Luckmann (1966).

Mead's research emphasized interaction between individuals via symbolic behaviors (e.g., verbal and nonverbal language) that function as stimuli. The symbols acquire content when the transmitter of a symbol—linguistic or nonlinguistic—obtains a response from the receiver. Through a repeated exchange of symbols, they achieve meaning. The process may be understood as the transmitter placing himself or herself in the position of the receiver. In this way, the transmitter tries to understand the content of his or her own symbol, as the receiver might be thought to have construed it. But the receiver, too, must try to understand the intentions of the transmitter. Each must take on the other's role, trying to enter into his or her expectations, attitudes, and feelings.

It is through such role-taking that personal development occurs. The personal insight realized through such symbolic communication is referred to by Mead as the "self." This "self" can be the object of a relation to its own identity.

Mead's work proved fundamental to the development of social psychology after World War II. Sarbin (1954) asserted that social roles have an existence independent of the individual but the role is still intimately linked to a particular individual's way of performing it. Sarbin also introduced the concept of the *organismic dimension,* stressing varying degrees of proximity between the role and the self, proposing seven different levels, ranging from a situation where the self and the role are remote from each other to a level where role and self are united in deep trance. The self thus acquires significance from the way the role is understood, performed, and taken over from the other party.

Newcomb (1952) claims that another person's role can be integrated into the personality, into the "self." Through this capacity for identification, an individual can *anticipate* another person's behavior and also, over the course of time, influence it. A person thus experiences internal communication between his or her own role and the internalized one. The more internalized the role, the more intensive this communication becomes. Those with well internalized roles acquire common forms and frames of reference; good communication between individuals can be maintained.

In *The Social Construction of Reality* (1966), Berger and Luckmann present an interactionist model. This builds on a European tradition within cognitive sociology and begins with such basic concepts as externalization, objectivation, and internalization.

Every person must externalize thinking and actions. This leads to stereotyped forms and roles, which are then taken over by tradition and culture. They thus become objectified forms. Via socialization, the individual takes on these forms; in other words, they become internalized. For an individual to maintain the objectified form, a legitimation process operates. This means that the great interpretative models of that culture— its "symbolic universes"—are fixed by reinforcement and become meaningful to the individual. Such symbolic universes may be religions, which explain birth, life, and death, as well as providing the individual with an identity.

In this sense, interactionist models emphasize communication between individuals by symbols, normally linguistic ones. For this reason, these theories have been termed symbolic interactionist; they assume norms and frames of reference are established by communication and action models and roles. These roles vary in performance through a number of different factors, including quite individually based ones.

THE PERCEPTUAL MODEL

The third model may also be seen as a form of interaction, but I call it perceptual because it is mainly concerned with processes within an individual. It is an application found chiefly in Nordic countries, both in the psychology of religion and in folkloristics. Role theory in this form is used expressly to explain religious and supernatural experiences. In the psychology of religion, it has been chiefly developed by Sundén (1959).

During the 1950s, Sundén (1966) conceptualized religious experiences in a role-theoretical perspective, resulting in the book *Religionen och rollerna* (Religion and the roles). In other writings, Sundén developed his role theory of religious experiences (Sundén 1969, 1977, 1982, 1987).

The main question for Sundén is how an experience of the world in religious terms is psychologically possible. In the same way that physicists use different instruments to understand the properties of matter, so the human mind needs to be "prepared" for a religious experience to take place. The individual must, in other words, be devoted to a religious tradition and sometimes also to a ritual apparatus. Sundén thus contradicts a previous theory according to which religious experience is independent of the cultural tradition. He strongly emphasizes instead the importance of the learning process in the acquisition of religious experience.

When Sundén discusses the significance of tradition for the individual, he underlines socially given roles and emphasizes the structured experience models provided by the narratives in sacred texts. In Christianity, for example, it is important to study the Bible, which contains many descriptions of how individuals come into direct contact with God. These narratives contain roles, a role for the human party and another one for God. Sundén also transfers the concept of role to the mythical plane, to the holy models supplied by tradition. By reading the scriptures, hearing them, and seeing them function in others, individuals lay the foundation for their own spiritual experiences. Mythical narratives also become a potential frame of experience with latent roles that prepare one for religious experience.

To understand Sundén's subsequent argument, one must draw on perceptual psychology. When we undergo a visual experience, we absorb light stimuli from the environment. These are then interpreted and provide a pattern that gives meaning to the light signals that have reached us. But the brain has previously coded structures of experience, which means that a new stimulus can activate interpretation models and become a meaningful experience. As we mature, we construct models that enable us to experience the world as meaningful. If we have no properly functioning models, we experience chaos, panic, and despair. Mythical roles, in other words, become interpretation models within the human nervous system.

There should be one further condition: the motivation for an alternative form of experience. We normally feel safe and secure. If something out of the ordinary occurs, motivation is heightened so that alternative models can structure new perceptions. If there are stimuli from the external world, then, in addition to the motivation for an alternative experience, a *pattern-seeking* process within the brain can lead to *pattern discovery*. These models may be mythical roles in coded form in the nervous system. What then occurs is mainly an unconscious and automatic process: The individual *takes over* the role of the human party in a particular role performance and also *adopts* the role of God, which structures the field of perception so that what happens is actually experienced as an act of God. The individual can thus feel quite concretely that God has a hand in what is happening. A *phase shift* takes place in the human mind. The individual's field of perception is structured by a mythical role that is part of a fixed religious tradition. Important qualities in intensive experiences are *intentionality* and *totality*. The individual meets a "you" with a mission to humanity and the experience becomes all-embracing. It takes possession of the individual. A reverse phase shift to more secular, everyday, models of interpretation eventually takes place.

If one studies the stories of Abraham, Joseph, or the first Christians, for example, an individual—where the motivation for this exists—can take on the role of the human party in the narrative and thus enter into the role of any of the protagonists. What then occurs simultaneously is a foregrounding and adoption of the role of the other party, that is, God. This newly assumed role structures the field of perception so that the individual experiences God's action.

I have shown how the experience of baptism in the Holy Spirit within the Pentecostal movement can be experienced in this way (Holm 1976, 1978, 1987a, 1987b, 1991a, 1991b). In a charismatic environment, there is an idealization of the spiritual experiences of the first Christians, leading to an impulse to undergo similar experiences. This includes baptism in the spirit as described in the Acts of the Apostles on the first Pentecost. If an individual with such motivating factors takes on the role of being baptized in the spirit and the speaking in tongues is then experienced, the event—within the newly adopted god-role—is interpreted as being given and inspired by God. It becomes a kind of maximal experience, in which the participants are not only the fellow worshippers of the surrounding congregation; the transcendental figures of God and the Holy Spirit also come onto the stage.

It should be emphasized that there is not normally mechanical repetition of the role model. There is often variation in role-taking, due to personality factors and external circumstances. A fusion of different mythical roles can also occur. The essential point, however, is that the person identifies the event as the action of God within a given religious tradition.

In Sweden, Sundén's achievements within the psychology of religion led to the founding of a school. A number of his pupils have used this perceptual role-theory in their research, and one theoretically oriented study is J. Unger's dissertation *On Religious Experience* (1976). Källstad (1974) has studied John Wesley, Åkerberg (1975) has written on the Swedish archbishop and scholar of religion Nathan Söderblom, Wikström (1975) has examined the experience of God's guidance among the aged, and Holm (1976) has discussed baptism in the spirit and speaking in tongues. Pettersson (1975) has used the theory in studying the dynamics of the retention of religious experiences. Reference may also be made to van der Lans (1987) in Holland, who has applied role theory to testing experiences during meditation. In the United States, Donald Capps (1982a, 1982b) has used the theory to study the experiences of John Henry Newman as well as petitionary prayer. A recent work by Ayim-Aboagye (1993) on the function of myth in healing experiences in Ghana also used this approach. Others have also employed this theory to understand experiences within the field of folkloristics (Honko 1969, 1971; Siikala 1978).

AN INTEGRATED MODEL

I would emphasize that the role concept in the perceptual model has been transferred from immediate social reality to conceived mythical images which are often found codified in Holy Scripture. These mythical images result in a concrete role experience every time an individual actively appropriates them. Sundén's way of using role theory has made important contributions to research, particularly in the context of understanding strong and sudden spiritual experiences. Motivating factors have often been regarded as external stimuli—distress, anxiety, death, illness, and so on—which the individual encounters and is forced to deal with. That alternative patterns of experience acquire significance in such more or less dramatic situations and help the individual to integrate is quite obvious.

Setting aside major radical experiences, is there any justification for considering religious life in its more everyday forms in terms of role psychology? Can one thus broaden the discussion of motivating factors, and can one see roles in religious language of a more generally symbolic character?

Inner Existence Space

I begin my analysis with the notion that man's evolution from the womb to death, burial, and recognition by posterity are a single whole. To exist entails confrontation with life conditions and surrounding individuals. This confrontation always includes both affirmation and negation, success and failure, love and hate. It is a question, therefore, of adaptation, according to which one tries as far as possible to make the life principle emerge victorious. Unfortunately, as we all know, the forces of death win in the end. Like Sigmund Freud, we may speak of a life principle and a death principle.

Once life has begun, there emerges simultaneously a struggle for living space, for a meaningful relation to the environment. The struggle is constantly "audited" by the individual in the form of memories, conscious or unconscious, repressed or in some other way lost. We acquire a history of our own, a narrative, a world of experience. In all probability, it is the experiences of the first years that stick most clearly in our memory or at least greatly affect the way in which we are prepared for life. Through early experiences, we thus acquire powerful memory models for control, interpretation, and integration of life's experiences.

The memory we carry with us contains a cognitive component as well as an emotional one. The former fastens onto images and expressions that we encounter and stores them in an order that is not completely chronological or even logical. Emotional elements can strongly affect the way in which memory images are stored. Strong emotional charges—both positive and negative—tend to attract elements of memory, telescope them, and thus also transform them. This entire memory process, which has extensions to the dream world, has been studied by depth psychology and is used in therapeutic contexts. I speak here of condensation and displacement.

An important component in this struggle for living space is the relation to other people. First, normally, comes the mother or a person to whom the child can relate. It is in the context of this relationship that the first important "memories" are developed of how the environment receives and treats us. If the early experiences are catastrophic, then the whole encounter can produce "negative" memories that are repressed. They are forgotten, without, however, ceasing to operate as dynamic forces within the mind. Object relations theory has analyzed the child's experiences of the mother's breast and the significance this has for personality (Illman 1992). At an early stage, the child develops attitudes that become decisive for subsequent behavior.

Memory is not a mechanical storage device. It contains ever-present forces that drive and displace experiences in different directions. Not least among these forces is the imagination. By means of the latter, in combination with memory, the individual creates an *inner existence space* for the self. This space may also be described as an inner reference system (Crafoord 1987, 1993); it is a kind of theater of the mind (McDougall 1985), on which almost anything can be played out and where the individual can take on the most diverse roles. This inner existence space is very similar to what Winnicott (1971) describes as a transition area.

The inner existence space is the scene of all mental functions of which the individual is capable. Here we may encounter cognitive structures, emotional charges, volitional actions, relational patterns, and so forth. At a very early stage, we acquire a function that is central to all human life: the *symbol function*. This is linked with innate tendencies, reactions to external treatment, and other impressions from outside that continuously rework memories and fantasies. Throughout this process there is a condensation of thoughts, feelings, and intentions, so that symbolic combinations are formed. The capacity to express oneself in symbols becomes an important element in the struggle for life-space and survival. By means of symbols, shifting layers of life memories can be combined and become a powerful force for both good and evil in the individual's mind. Through the symbolic function, a major psychic memory can be preserved and instantly actuated for the individual.

The way forward to a developed symbolic function proceeds via different transitional objects. Here, I believe, it is useful to draw on the arguments of object relations theory concerning the transfer of feelings of security from the mother, via specific objects, to abstract constructions occurring in culture and religion (Rizzuto 1979).

The Objectified Symbol World

At the same time as the symbolic function in the individual develops and takes shape, an interaction also occurs with the environment. This interaction comes to consist to a very large degree of linguistic communication. In addition to this, there are of course all the other possible forms of expression, such as movement, painting, music, decoration, and the like. There is, in other words, a world of "objective" experience that the environment, by means of socialization processes, offers or even "forces on" the individual (cf. Lacan 1988).

An important stage in this process is provided by children's games. In games, early learned patterns are put to the test, as it were, in the objective world. The game is characterized by a combination of experience structures in the inner space and the objectified forms of the environment. Eventually, the game is increasingly transformed into work and active influence on the external environment.

Inner existence space must necessarily be affected by the patterns and structures of experience. Individuals find correspondences between experiences in inner existence space and expressions conveyed to them by the environment through symbols. One may thus cause a partial overflow of inner existence space into external culture and begin to acquire concrete roles in social interaction. And yet one always retains some form of inner existence space to retire to, in order to rework events and acquire new strength. The objectified symbolic structure that occurs in culture has many layers. We have private symbols and collective ones, in addition to social and religious ones.

The religious symbols found in all cultures are perhaps those that have most fired man's symbol-creating capacity. Here there has often been an objectivation of enormous proportions. This objectivation stretches over a long period of time and has specific social structures. An established social institution looks after the symbols and administers them. If these symbols are indices of identity and roots, then the individual acquires a connection with religious objects. If the institution or culture has a negative influence on interpretation and availability, however, then it can be more difficult for the individual to achieve a personal connection with the objective aspect of religion. The inner images in every individual should find some connection with the objectified symbol patterns of religion.

Religion as Symbol System

The objectified symbol system that we normally call religion mainly consists of two kinds of symbols. We have the more cognitive symbols (with their emotional implications), in addition to the external, obvious symbols, which have a more commonly shared interpretation within society. The inner cognitive symbols include, for example, God, the devil, spirits, atonement, judgment, grace, and so on. They are very similar to what we call concepts in the philosophical sense or, to use Rizzuto's terminology, inner representations. The external ones are symbols that have acquired form in movement, color, music, or anything else we can absorb through the senses. In both cases, however, there is an emotional binding that can be negative or positive, strong or weak. The symbols also include a volitional dimension that can find expression in a readiness to act. By means of symbols, people can be made to want something and perform actions, either as individuals or in groups.

Religious cognitive symbols refer to very basic experiences in the individual's life struggle. These often involve contact with the first people in one's environment, plus further experiences of good and evil, creation and death, sin and grace, as well as punishment and reconciliation or hope and despair. These are transformed into stories, legends, myths, and so forth, which are then taken over by the social institution that supports the central life experiences. These are often codified and become sacred narratives in canonic scriptures. Mythology within a given religion may thus be seen as a collective reworking, on the symbolic level, of the central motifs of inner existence space.

Man's struggle with life conditions provides central motifs in every mythology. This includes such questions as How will I be accepted and make contact with the powerful one, How will my failures be regarded, or, in short, how will I be regarded as an individual and acquire value? This process often occurs together with other individuals undergoing similar experiences, giving rise to a collective, such as a church, a congregation, that will survive. It acquires a dimension beyond time and space. It becomes eternal, in a Communion of the Saints. Finding correspondences between important features in the inner experience space and an idealized, perhaps glorified, group fellowship reinforces the strength of the individual's engagement with reality.

Every religion has thus elaborated conceptual models for time in the beginning and end of the world and in its movements and cycles. On the individual level, too, the religious symbol world acquires similar significance. It gives meaning to personal "creation," to development, and—finally—to one's extinction. A transformation miracle becomes important, and in the figure of Christ, all of this has been eloquently formulated by Christianity. But time also exists here and now. The course of the year becomes a recurrent pattern, with feasts and fasts succeeding each other, giving life a kind of security through iteration. In Christianity, the story of salvation is absorbed into this annual pattern.

In the same way, the physical space surrounding an individual is divided into different spheres of intimacy and degrees of holiness. The closest analogy to inner existence space is in temples and churches, where the holiest of holies corresponds to the source, the hidden creative force. In Hindu mythology this is extremely clear since the holiest space of all, with the divine symbol, is called *garbhagriha*, or the womb. But natural sites— the sea, the forest, a mountain, and so forth—can also be experienced as the origin of the creative force. In such places, a person often experiences safety, repose, reassurance, and peace. Everything hints at a heavenly sense of perfection, existing as a "memory" or fantasy. One can undergo a kind of mystical experience (Holm 1979). Expressions of this are legion in the conceptual world of religion, as in the pictorial arts.

When memories in the inner existence space are provided with symbolic expressions from the objectified external world, a number of complications can occur. There may be strong emotional disturbances in individuals, exercising power over the symbolic world and preventing any integrated correspondence from occurring between one's own inner system and the external objectified one. We find, in other words, something that might be called *affective anthropomorphisms* encoded in these symbolic expressions. It is often a question of bottled-up painful experiences that have not been processed. The objectified symbols may be merely experienced as obsolete and uninteresting. There are then no meaningful inner experiences that correspond to the objective expressions. The course of life, however, may gradually supply inner experiences that promote understanding of a certain religious symbol world in the life of the maturing individual.

Inner Role-taking

I suggested previously that the self can take on different roles in the inner existence space. This is a game of the imagination where memories are rather like Lego bricks. Even this may be regarded as a kind of role-taking, although the role-taking is now constantly extended to the social context and the individual takes on roles there that correspond at least partially to inner experience models. The individual acquires a place in a social community that corresponds to the self-image he or she possesses. But role-taking goes beyond this. People learn collective symbols in culture and above all in religion, where the experience structures of centuries have been "frozen" into fixed narratives. This collective heritage can be learned as objective knowledge and can be studied by science. But the stories on this symbolic plane may, at appropriate moments for the individual, be absorbed into inner existence space and there find a correspondence that transforms the symbols into powerful forces in the individual's mind. A role-taking occurs, in other words, that is not merely a given quantity at the cognitive level but also something that seizes on one's deepest and perhaps earliest individual memories. Praying "Our Father . . ." may thus conflate with early memories of one's own father, whereas the communion of the congregation under its highest symbol, God, may dissolve into personal memories of the all-embracing maternal arms. A religious symbol with this inherent dual role-play can become a living reality: One experiences a meaningful relation.

Religious language is constructed of symbols from the intimate sphere. It is often a case of images referring to the father, the mother, siblings, friends, the loved one, the strong one, the omnipotent, the omniscient, and so on. But there are also, of course, symbols of the negative: the devil, the evil one, the fiend, the sinner, the weak, the damned, the impenitent, and so forth. The world of religion is truly a collection of symbolic expressions, often arranged in narratives, where living memories important to survival are encoded. The capacity of these memories to make contact repeatedly with individual memory spheres derives from the fact that they are objectified to express highly central symbolic content. When an individual finds an analogy between structures of experience and those acquired collectively, a role-taking occurs—a role experience that can lead to greater maturity, to a healing process, to the discovery of hope and confidence.

In this perspective, *prayer* acquires much importance. It may be understood as the encounter between external circumstances and symbols in the inner world. Personal meditative prayer may thus attain significance for the reworking of events in the environment according to structures in inner existence space. A fusion of personal "memories" may occur with symbols and circumstances from the outer world, leading to maturity and acquiescence. Symbols of meditation in particular assume great importance for the integration of the mind. Processes occur here that find expression in a sense of God's guidance and of prayers being answered (cf. Capps 1982a).

We must also accept, however, that religious symbol worlds can end in destructive experience contexts. One may thus find symbols for both private and collective hate objects. This occurs when individuals in the name of religion devote themselves to war and extermination campaigns. A religious symbol system can thus be powerful in both the positive and negative senses. An ethical judgment directed principally at the cognitive dimensions of the individual should not therefore be ignored.

SUMMARY

The application of the role concept has undergone considerable development but is also still used in several different ways. From having been the label for an activity model within a specific group, it has gone on to become a term designating an intrapsychic process. In Sundén's version of role theory, which I call *perceptual*, the narratives of the sacred tradition were seen as containing roles, one for the person and one for God. That this tradition, through application from one generation to the next, can be realized and come to structure experiences is an important insight. It thus creates continuity and a sense of being close to "primeval experiences" in the idealized models of the sacred tradition.

The entire religious symbol world may reflect concrete experience in almost every individual. It is thus a question of different feelings in the presence of the mother, the father, siblings, friends, enemies, and so on. These feelings are found objectified in religious symbols, in myths, legends, parables, metaphors, and the like. Such objectified forms also have great intrinsic value and are usually available to the individual through socialization, where words, images, and music play a decisive role. When these are supplied to the individual, there is already an *inner existence space* where the earliest life experiences are stored; there is often a sense of being accepted, rejected, satisfied, or loved. All of this occurs at the level of personal relations.

Individual history is formed by memories that store experiences of different kinds. Memory is nevertheless controlled by different processes, with the result that contact with reality is not always objectively real. There is instead a displacement, a fusion, or a reinforcement, creating emotionally charged motifs. If the personal symbols find an equivalent in the collectively given religious imagery, a role-taking then occurs on a deeply individual plane, allowing the individual to feel meaning and hope in life. In positive cases, a maturing or healing process may occur. One can live in a religious world in contact with symbols of security and liberation, but it is important to remember that religious symbols can also be used for destructive purposes.

One may ask whether inner dedication to symbols may be regarded as role-taking. I find it meaningful to think so, since it is generally a case of personal relations being brought to the fore. One makes contact with a "you," and in relation to this it is possible to take on different roles. Behind the mythical role experiences that Sundén has described, there may also be dynamic forces in the inner experience space, which thus reinforce motivational factors. But if we turn to more sociologically oriented hypotheses—the structural-analytical model and the interactionist one—there are still parallels. It is highly likely that behind a correctly functioning social role-taking, there lie additional motives connected with inner existence space. The concepts of role-taking advanced by these various approaches are thus closely related, although research and analysis describes them in rather different ways. Behind the various uses of the role concept, therefore, there is a common denominator: Earlier memory experiences in personal relation to others, to a "you."

7

RELIGION AND MORAL EVALUATION
DISCREPANCY THEORY

ROBERT A. EMBREE

Making moral judgments is a distinctively human act, the purpose of which is to influence behavior (Kelley 1971b). Religious systems are often used to justify such evaluations (Nowell-Smith 1967); however, those sharing traditions may not make similar moral judgments. Moral considerations apparently depend on the circumstances and context of behavior. Why do some individuals with common socialization experiences express different moral judgments depending on the situation while others do not? Moral evaluation discrepancy theory focuses on such differences in moral evaluation in response to the varied contexts for such behavior.

Moral evaluation discrepancy occurs when identical behaviors are judged as more moral in one context than in another. The debate over elective abortion may help clarify this idea. Certain individuals strongly believe that abortion is immoral. Shouts of murder are made to influence women thinking about an unwanted pregnancy. Others feel just as strongly that such a decision is an issue to be resolved primarily by the pregnant woman. Moral claims are made for the rights of a woman to determine what happens to her body. To think otherwise would be to dehumanize women into baby-making machines. Each group attempts to influence women by using moral arguments. Both sides possess justifications for their position (Luker 1984) and hence affect future behavior.

Suppose the members of each group were asked to disclose their moral judgments about abortion. Such an inquiry may create a "fuzzy logic"

Original contribution, edited with permission of author.

(Zadeh & Kacprzyk 1992) condition or state of uncertainty. What kind of abortion do you have in mind? At what stage of the pregnancy will the abortion be done? What are the circumstances facing the pregnant woman? How did she get pregnant? In spite of the lack of information, some people will respond with a resounding, "No!" Others will respond just as strongly with an unqualified, "Yes!" Yet some will reflect on the question and declare, "Well, it depends on a lot of things." When a person takes the latter stance, moral evaluation discrepancy should be observable.

One method for measuring moral evaluation discrepancy on the abortion issue is to (1) develop a set of statements about abortion that vary relative to the circumstances for having an abortion, (2) have subjects provide moral evaluations for each of the circumstances associated with the abortion decision, and (3) compute the distances for all unique combinations of the moral evaluations. Moral evaluation discrepancy is indicated by a mean average of all those differences greater than zero. From this example it is clear that moral evaluation discrepancy is more appropriate for some behaviors than it is for others and that individuals will vary in the magnitude of measured moral evaluation discrepancy.

Since psychologists tend to assume "moral homogeneity" (Packer 1992), it is not surprising that limited research has examined moral evaluation discrepancy. This theory counters the tendency to overlook moral heterogeneity.

Kelley (1971a) proposed that in social interaction the individual acts both as a causal agent and as an attributor. One seeks to cause something to happen as well as to understand why that event takes place. Moral evaluation thus involves both "reality testing" and "achievement testing." "Oughts" or "shoulds" are expressed in behavior. Such judgments function as mediators between social-moral systems and individual response (Kelley 1971b). In social interactions, many strategies are used to influence others (Baron & Byrne 1987). When moral judgment is employed, moral obligation appeals to the "oughts" and "shoulds" of social norms (Schmitt 1964).

Norms represent a social consensus about the rules of a society (Klassen, Williams, & Levitt 1989). "Normal values" describe the social rules and "normative values" that are advocated by members of society (Reese & Fremouw 1984). Socialization develops the ability to make the appropriate judgments. Individual moral character is forged from the twin elements of moral knowledge and moral action (Hogan 1973). In short, a moral person knows something, makes choices, and accepts responsibility for his or her behavior. Moral behavior in essence is compliance with the social rules. Gibbs and Schnell (1985) call this perspective "societalism."

There are a number of problems in seeking to influence the actions of another through an appeal to social norms. Some normative values may be functional and practiced, whereas others are nonfunctional and, though promoted, are often ignored (Reese & Fremouw 1984). On some issues, moral theorists, even if not agreeing on what the norms should be, construct moral knowledge either as teleologists or deontologists. Deontologists emphasize moral absolutes, that is, universal rules or principles and rational justification of those rules. Often, such principles are attributed to a supreme power or being. In contrast, teleologists allow for observable consequences of human action to aid in the discovery of rules for human conduct and for the modification of existing moral rules (Nowell-Smith 1967). Central to the teleological versus the deontological debate is the role of empirical data in resolving moral questions (Waterman 1988). Therefore, it is not surprising that individuals have different understandings of morality, the reality testing of which can be challenging when one seeks to act in a moral way.

If Forsyth (1980) is correct in his taxonomy of ethical ideologies, there are four different moral perspectives: situationalism, subjectivism, absolutism, and exceptionism, depending on one's stance on absolutism versus relativism and the degree of idealism characteristic of the individual theorist. Although such concepts as norms, normal values, and normative values imply social consensus on morality, the cultural shift to an emphasis on individual conscience renders contemporary moral reality often contradictory and consensus elusive (Packer 1992). Perhaps even more important, the social norms of a society include immoral as well as moral values. After all, in an earlier period of American society, human slavery was defended by moralists as was a democracy that excluded women from the voting booth (Sagan 1988).

Lack of consensus on various moral issues suggests childhood association with a specific religious group or faith community as one major source of variance for moral evaluation discrepancy. Each of us is born into a family with its unique understanding of normative values. Being Roman Catholic, United Methodist, Orthodox Jew, or having an association with some other faith group interface is an "assigned component" of one's identity (Baumeister 1986). Normative values are a given, just as is the color of one's hair. Such reference groups may explain why moral discrepancy may be greater for some people than for others.

Recall that moral discrepancy is a tendency to give different moral evaluations to identical behaviors depending upon the context, circumstance, or situation in which those behaviors occur. Moral discrepancy theory is not interested in group differences in moral judgments as such; rather, the interest is in group differences in moral evaluation discrepancy.

The notion that moral evaluation is derived from the internalization of social norms has been challenged by various theorists (Bornstein & Lamb

1992; Kurtines & Gewirtz 1984; Kurtines, Azmitia, & Gewirtz 1992). Packer (1992) reminds us that the concept of an autonomous individual was invented by the seventeenth-century Enlightenment philosophers. Consequently, in contemporary American society, morality is conflicted and contradictory. Thus a dynamic tension between normative values and the individual conscience is postulated as a major source of moral evaluation discrepancy. The human infant is not only born into a culture but also experiences a long period of dependency. The child's caretaker not only socializes but also gives time and energy on behalf of the child's welfare. Having received such, the child has a felt need to give back. From this dependency, an individual conscience is said to be forged. Because dependency has many common features, morality tends to be universal rather than relativistic. Valuing and cultivating the individual conscience can result in conflict between normative values and individual moral judgments, thus contributing to the transformation of society itself. Caring for others, not mindless conformity to normative values, becomes a central component of morality. It is the individual conscience that makes moral progress possible (Damon & Hart 1992; Sagan 1988).

The work of Kohlberg and others supports the development of individual conscience as an alternative to blind obedience to normative values (Gibbs & Schnell 1985). A risk is that of self-deception, which can lead to immoral rather than moral social behavior (Gibbs & Schnell 1985). The action of a lone individual conscience can shock the very foundation of a society when that act violates the cultural norms. Still, the point is that this strain between the superego and individual conscience (Sagan 1988) or between "societalism" and "individualism" (Gibbs & Schnell 1985) is postulated as a major source for moral evaluation discrepancy variance.

Moral evaluation discrepancy theory assumes that such discrepancy in contemporary American society is also a personality trait or moral type created by a tension between the superego and conscience. The superego is derived from "reality testing" of one's society. Obviously, the institutions of law, education, the family, and religion contribute substantially to the development of moral types. Beyond this, these types are affected by one's unique sense of morality, that is, an individual conscience. Further, basic psychological needs unique to an individual put pressure on the script, resulting in more modification (Simon & Gagnon 1986). In addition, both societalism and individualism are postulated as shapers of moral types. When reality testing puts the two in conflict, different claims of moral obligation may emerge. Research is, however, needed to better understand how moral evaluation discrepancies develop and what the correlates are for those who share common moral evaluation discrepancy patterns.

The gap between moral thought and behavior has received considerable attention by psychologists (Blasi 1980). Nevertheless, one of the problems with the psychological study of moral character and moral development has been the tendency to ignore contextual or situational effects on moral judgments (Pittel & Mendelsohn 1969). As already noted, moral evaluation discrepancy theory recognizes that the ordinary person may judge the same behavior differently depending on the situation in which behavior occurs. Although considerable empirical research has been done by those interested in the psychology of religion, there has been little concern about moral evaluation discrepancy (Spilka, Hood, & Gorsuch 1985). There is even less curiosity about how mind-body assumptions (Embree & Embree 1993) may influence moral character development.

The work of Tamney and Johnson (1983) supports the position that attraction to groups such as the Moral Majority is linked with the persuasive influence of religious television programming and motivation to mold American politics in the shared image of the Christian Right. Jelen's (1988) analysis of the National Opinion Research Center (NORC) General Social Surveys affirms that attitudes toward abortion are shaped differently by various religious groups, resulting in strong opposition to elective abortion for some and considerable diversity of opinion for others. Jelen argues that such religious variety offers different justifications for opposition to abortion. Indeed, Fuchs-Ebaugh and Haney (1978) found that members of "conservative churches" oppose abortion in many if not all of the conditions presented in the survey, but members of "liberal churches" approve abortion in general. They explain these different moral evaluations in terms of variation in acceptance of "social gospel" ideology in contrast to the ideology of "biblical literalism."

"Moral community" theory claims religion acts to foster social conformity. Welch, Tittle, and Petee (1991) derived three hypotheses from the theory, which were tested on a large sample of adult Catholics. Given the context of being strongly motivated to do so, the Ss (subjects) estimated the likelihood of drinking excessively, cheating on the income tax, and making use of employer's equipment without authorization. The "moral communities" hypothesis predicts a strong link between involvement in a religious community and conformity to moral standards. Although not employed in this study, the value of such research might be enhanced by attention to the moral evaluation discrepancy variable.

Herek and Glunt (in Freiberg 1990) surveyed attitudes toward public health measures designed to reduce the risks for HIV infection. They found moral attitudes tended to parallel affiliation with various religious groups. This kind of research often overlooks a tendency for individuals to accept some but not all of the norms of their "moral community" or reference group. The work of Perry (1970) and others on intellectual and moral development during college suggests higher education often encourages the development of conscience. Greater moral evaluation discrepancy variance is an expected outcome of such developmental changes in response to higher education, as societal morality accommodates a developing individual conscience.

It has been argued here that individuals differ in how moral evaluations interact with their contexts or circumstances, with some persons being more influenced by context than others. As discussed earlier, moral evaluation discrepancy theory provides a framework for exploring the effects of reference group norms and their correlates. Another possible advantage of moral discrepancy theory is that it passes no moral judgments on people, regardless of their belief systems. At the same time, the theory recognizes that moral evaluation has consequences for both society and individuals.

The importance of understanding such consequences is illustrated by the notion of "sexual addiction." It can be argued that this is a social construction designed to achieve social control over sexual behavior. Once accepted as a diagnostic category, mental health professionals are empowered to impose a particular notion of sexual morality on individuals under the deception of treating mental illness (Levine & Troiden 1988). Including "sexual addiction" as a mental illness conceals the social reality that people differ on what is acceptable human behavior. In like manner, legislation requiring the V-chip and formal ratings of television programming may overlook the social reality that responsible citizens differ on what is or is not objectionable programming for various categories of people. Electronic technology makes a V-chip possible; however, the ratings that will control its use are moral values that cannot reflect our society's moral judgments as a whole. These concepts risk using stigmatization (Goffman 1974) for a seemingly high purpose, which may gratify basic needs for control even though such control strategies overlook genuine differences in moral values on such matters.

As discussed above, moral evaluation is rooted in the twin processes of reality testing and achievement striving (Kelley 1971a, 1971b). Moral judgment and moral behavior are often in tension between the individual's understanding of social norms and his or her personality (Damon & Hart 1992), making moral evaluation discrepancy not unexpected in a pluralistic society. Such diversity, however, may be more common for "ascetic" moral issues that tend to be linked with religious tradition (Middleton & Putney 1962). Scientific data that identify moral evaluation patterns and their consequences open the door for "metatheoretical discourse" between scientific theory and moral theory (Kurtines, Alvarez, & Azmitia 1990).

Commentary: Social Concerns

In Chapters 6 and 7, with both Holm and Embree, the individual in relation to the social context is considered. Holm discusses broadly how the social institution of religion can become integrated into a person's individual psychology. Religion provides roles to play and contexts in which to act them out. This general dramaturgical framework has proven productive for social psychological understandings of people's behaviors, cognitions, and emotions in a variety of areas, and Holm indicates several topics in the psychology of religion in which role theory has been used.

Holm's chapter broadens the application of role theory to include more typical religious experiences than has been done previously. Differences in individual experience can be seen as reflective of the different roles in scripture that may be made salient by a person's faith community. Which stories are emphasized in a denomination's literature, for example? Another suggested question regards those people not well connected with some sort of role-providing structure. Are there differences between them and those who are so connected? The notion that there is significance for people in attaching to old and consensually held symbols might provide a partial explanation as to why even new religions struggle to tie their symbols and beliefs to ancient ones. This view might help us understand psychological motives that influence the development of new religious movements.

Holm's personality-centered approach to roles should be supplemented by the role approach that has prevailed in American social psychology. This looks toward role enactments, perceptions, and expectations and asks what the individual is doing, perceiving, and expecting. Stated differently, it suggests a need to identify clearly what roles people are playing, how they perceive themselves in terms of a role, and what they expect short- and long-term outcomes of the role enactment to be. Role theory also suggests that roles involve two or more beings in interaction, hence self and other possibilities are always part of the picture. We must then assess not only the various aspects of a religious person's role but usually that of the deity along with significant others, of course from the role player's point of view.

This formulation recognizes that it is no longer enough to denote religious behavior; rather, religious role behavior must become our focus. For example, if one person attends religious services twice a month and another four times a month, as role enactments, these portend different motives, perceptions, attitudes, understandings, and expectations. To date, very little research has been conducted along these lines, but a role approach as proposed by Holm takes such an orientation as a fundamental necessity. There is now an explicit requirement to determine correspondences between religious actions, reasons for their activation, and ways they are integrated. Both correlations and cause-effect associations are essentials rounding out this picture. It makes us look to gaps in our empirical knowledge and to the incompleteness of our research conceptualizations.

Moralistic considerations are always found at the heart of religion. Holm's views are thus well supplemented by those of Embree. Encompassing the social position we have just suggested, Embree notes that people act in contexts. They may endorse the same set of moral beliefs yet be differentially flexible in how they are influenced by the contexts to which they are subject. This speaks to the discrepancy between stated general convictions, on the one hand, and behavior, on the other. Such differences are legion in everyday life, and Embree's emphasis suggests that we look to factors that counter or support such discrepancies. In the realm of religion, Embree has begun work on the form of personal faith as one such influence. Gorsuch's framework in Chapter 2 of the intrinsic-extrinsic distinction as motivation suggests one avenue for exploration. Holm's role approach further leads us to wonder how moral discrepancies are viewed in terms of what activates them and what their expected outcomes are theorized to be—actually and idealistically.

We may also ask about the import of perceived "size" of moral discrepancies in different areas. When does one's faith play an intrinsic or extrinsic role in such responses? Does Batson's quest perspective parallel queries about religion with similar challenges to morality?

Context needs to be defined rather rigorously because this approach speaks not only to moral discrepancy but to contextual effects on one's understanding and expression of religion, specifically personal faith. This sets up individual religion and morality as potentially dependent on the domain or realm in which moral and faith issues may be called into play. In addition, one should ask whether people are concerned about their behavior or about that of others; then there are judgments to be considered on the importance of the behavior and, of course, on its importance to whom or what. At all levels, the question "why" is present for these factors. Moral discrepancy fits well into the general attributional approach discussed by Spilka, Shaver, and Kirkpatrick in Chapter 12 in this volume. Moral matters are events that must be regarded as much per se as in context, and in like manner, the same holds for those involved in such decisionmaking. Nothing is ever as simple as we would like it to be, and moral discrepancy makes this principle abundantly evident. It is a research area that opens windows onto the way we live and onto our "souls."

Holm's work prompts a question on individual differences within a faith community. Embree's work provides one way of considering such differences. Embree notes that people act in contexts. People may endorse the same set of moral beliefs yet be differentially flexible in how context influences the application of these beliefs. Embree offers several content areas within the psychology of religion (e.g., moral community theory) in which attention to moral discrepancies would be useful.

Together, these contributions point out that people are socially influenced but that individuals play the provided roles in different ways. Exploring this interaction of personal differences and social influences is a rich area for continued research.

PART 4

Development of
Individual Religion

8

THE ORIGINS OF RELIGION IN THE CHILD

DAVID ELKIND

Every social institution, whether it be science, art, or religion, can be regarded as an externalized adaptation that serves both the person and society. From the standpoint of the individual, institutions afford ready-made solutions to the inevitable conflicts with social and physical reality that one encounters in the march through life. Social institutions originate and evolve out of the adaptive efforts of both society and the individual. Thus, any complete account of the origins of religion must deal both with the person and social processes of adaptation.

In this chapter, I propose to treat the origins of religion solely from the perspective of the individual and not from that of society. I hope to demonstrate that religion has an individual as well as a social lineage and that this lineage can be traced to certain cognitive need capacities that emerge in the course of mental growth. To whatever extent religion derives from society's efforts to resolve the conflicts engendered by these individual need capacities, we are justified in speaking of the origins of religion in the child.

I describe here four cognitive need capacities with respect to the age they first make their appearance, the problems of adaptation that they engender, and the corresponding resolutions offered by religion. A concluding section will take up the question of the uniqueness of religious adaptations from the point of view of the individual.

Reprinted and edited with permission of the author and publisher from *Review of Religious Research*, 12 (1970), 35–42.

Emergence of Cognitive Need
Capacities in the Child

In describing the mental development of the child, this presentation will lean heavily upon the work of Piaget. He evolved a general theory of intelligence, wherein the thinking of adults derives from the gradual elaboration of mental abilities in the child. In effect, Piaget argued that each new mental capacity carries with it the need to realize itself through action and, in the course of such realization, it comes into conflict with social and physical realities. The resolution of each such conflict results in structural changes that we call growth and that in turn pave the way for new conflicts and further growth in an unending dialectic.

Although Piaget's theory would seem to have rather direct implications for religious development, except for a few early papers (Piaget 1923, 1930), he has not dealt with the problem. It seems, however, that the major elements common to most religions provide comfortable solutions to some of the conflicts that Piaget's cognitive need capacities engender in the course of their realization. This is my way of viewing the problem and is not necessarily how Piaget would deal with the issue.

Before proceeding further, it might be useful to give a few illustrations of the way cognitive need capacities result in problems of adaptation. Once the child acquires language and a rudimentary understanding of causality, for example, the notorious "why" stage appears. It is soon discovered that parents do not appreciate such questions, particularly when they are endlessly repeated. The child's attempts to realize the capacity for causal understanding can produce conflict with the adult world. In the same way, when the child of four or five years begins to realize this emerging capacity to deal with quantitative relations, again conflict with others results. The constant concern with "who has more" is not endearing to parents or to siblings. In short, every cognitive capacity is in itself a need that prompts behaviors that can create discord between the child and the social and physical milieu.

Infancy and the Search for Conservation

During the first two years of life, the infant makes truly remarkable progress. From an uncoordinated, primarily reflex organism, the child is, within the course of a short two-year period, transformed into an upright, talking, semisocialized being, more advanced intellectually than the most mature animal of any species. Of accomplishments during this period, none is perhaps of such general importance as the discovery that objects exist when they are no longer present to the senses, that is to say, the discovery that objects are *conserved*.

To the adult, for whom the world and the self are clearly demarcated, it is hard to envision the infant's situation. The closest we can come to it is a state of reverie or semiconsciousness when the boundaries of awareness waver and we are embedded in the very pictures we sense. This is the perpetual state of the infant, for whom all awareness can hardly be more than a series of blurred pictures following one another in an unpredictable sequence. Only gradually does the child begin to separate actions from things and to discriminate among the latter, such as the human face. Even when response to the face occurs, usually in the second and third months of life, there is still no awareness that the face exists when it is no longer present. An infant, for example, who is smiling delightedly at an adult peering from the side of the crib, will turn away immediately if the adult ducks out of sight. The infant does not cry but behaves as if the adult drops out of existence (Piaget 1952).

Only toward the end of the second year does the infant give evidence that objects now exist and have permanence of their own quite independent of immediate sensory experience. At this age, the child will search for objects, such as candy, which was hidden from view. This awareness of the permanence or conservation of objects comes about when the progressive coordinations of behavior give rise to internal representations or images of absent objects. It is the two-year-old's capacity to mentally represent absent objects that results in their conservation.

The construction of permanent objects is important because it is a prerequisite for all later mental activity. All our concepts start from or involve objects in one way or another, so recognition of their permanence is a starting point for intellectual growth in general. Object permanence, however, is just the first of many such permanences or conservations that the child must construct. As mental capacities expand, new situations are encountered that parallel, though at a higher level of abstraction, the disappearance of objects. Illusions are a case in point. A spoon in water looks bent, the moon appears to follow us when we walk, and the sun seems to revolve around the earth. Similar problems present themselves on the social plane. The child must learn to distinguish, for example, a true invitation to stay at a friend's home from an invitation that is, in fact, a polite dismissal. In such cases the child has to distinguish between appearance and reality, between how things look and how they really are. Infancy thus bears witness to a new mental ability, the capacity to deal with absent objects and to a corresponding need, *the search for conservation*, a lifelong quest for permanence amid a world of change.

One of the problems of conservation that all children eventually encounter, and to which they must all adapt, is the discovery that they and their loved ones must ultimately die. In contrast to the conservation of the object, which is first transient and only later permanent, the child begins by assuming that life is everlasting and is shocked upon finding out that it is transient. After the initial recognition, the child seeks means whereby life can be conserved, a quest that continues from this time on.

In many cases, conflict between the search for conservation and the inevitability of death does not attain full impact until adolescence. Religion, to which the young person has already been exposed, offers a ready solution. This lies in the concept of God or spirit, which has been religion's universal answer to the problem of life's conservation. God is the ultimate conservation, transcending the bounds of space, time, and corporeality. By accepting God, the young person participates in this immortality and hence resolves the problem of the conservation of life. In any particular case, acceptance of the religious solution is determined by a host of personal and sociocultural factors. All I wish to emphasize here is that religion offers an immediate solution to the seemingly universal human problem posed by the search for conservation of life and the reality of death.

Early Childhood and the Search for Representation

As was true for infancy, the preschool period is one of rapid mental growth and of wide-ranging intellectual accomplishments. Foremost among these is mastery of language. When this occurs, the child goes far beyond the representation of things by mental images. Language is a series of conventional signs that bear no physical resemblance to that which they represent. The child must now painstakingly learn to represent all of those objects that were so laboriously constructed during the first years of life. One is not, however, limited to representing things by language; symbols can be employed that bear some semblance to what they represent. At this stage, the child creates playthings, transforming pieces of wood into boats and odd-shaped stones into animals (Piaget 1951). It is at this stage, too, that the child dons adult clothes and plays house and school. All these behaviors—the mastery of language, and engagement in symbolic play activities—bear witness to a new cognitive capacity, the ability to use signs and symbols, and to a new need, *the search for representation*.

Like the search for conservation, the search for representation, which makes its appearance in early childhood, continues throughout life. At each point in development, the young person seeks to represent the contents of thought and those of the physical and social environment. As personal knowledge of the self and world grows more exact, more exacting forms of representation are sought. Not only does vocabulary increase at an extraordinary rate, but there is the initial acquisition of new tools of representation, such as mathematics and the graphic arts. Yet, the more exacting the child becomes in this search for representation, the more dissatisfying the results seem to be. For example, one reason children usually give up drawing by about the fifth grade is disgust with the discrepancy between what they wish to portray and what they have drawn. In the same way, the maturing child gradually realizes that language is a lumbering means at best for conveying thoughts and is hopelessly inadequate for expressing feelings.

For the young person who has accepted God, the search for representations poses special problems. If religion provided only a concept of God and nothing else, one would be at a loss to represent the transcendent. How, after all, can that be signified which is not spatial, temporal, or corporeal? Religion, however, affords more than a God concept; it also provides representations of the transcendent. In primitive religions, the representations were totems or idols, whereas in modern "revealed" religions, the transcendent finds its representation in Scripture. Here again, however, as in the case of the God concept, individual acceptance of the religious solution is multidetermined and difficult to predict in the particular case. What must be stressed is that once there is acceptance of God, the question of representation is an inevitable outcome of the search for representation in general.

Childhood and the Search for Relations

During the school-age epoch the child is, for the first time, exposed to formal instruction and must acquire a prescribed body of knowledge and special skills such as reading and writing. The acquisition of such knowledge presupposes a mental system that is in part comparable to the mental systems of adults who transmit the knowledge. Such a system does come into being around the sixth year, the traditional "age of reason". Research on children's thinking has shown that this is quite an appropriate designation of the accomplishments of this age. It is only now that the child manifests the ability to make logical deductions (i.e., to recognize that if A is greater than B and if B is greater than C, then A must be greater than C, even if A and C are not directly compared) and to nest classes (i.e., to recognize that, say, boys + girls = children, and children − boys = girls, and so forth) (Elkind 1961, 1964; Piaget 1952).

One feature of this new ability to reason logically is that the child now tries to relate phenomena in the world in a systematic manner. The youngster at this stage wants to know how things work, where they come from, and what they are made from. Concepts of time and space are broadened, and the child can now grasp historical time and conceive of such distant places as foreign countries. In a very real sense, then, the child is trying to relate things to one another with respect to time, space, causality, and origin. It seems appropriate, therefore, to speak of the new ability that surfaces at school age as *the capacity for practical reason* and of the corresponding need as *the search for relations*.

The search for relations, which makes its appearance in childhood proper, continues throughout life. As the young person matures, relationships are sought to relate the person to the social and physical milieu and to relate worldly things and events to one another. Although this search for relations is often gratifying, it is also on occasion disheartening. There are many events in life that cannot be related to one another in any simple way. Quirks of fate and accident are of this kind and defy efforts. There is often no simple logical answer to the question "Why did this happen to me?" Therefore, although the quest for relations aids understanding, it also enhances awareness of how much one cannot know.

Within the religious sphere, the young person who has accepted the concept of God and its scriptural representation is confronted with the problem of putting the self in relation to the transcendent. Here again, in the absence of a ready-made solution, the young person might flounder and resolution of the problem would be makeshift. Religion, however, affords a means whereby the individual can relate to the deity, for it offers the sacrament of worship. By participating in worship, the young person can associate with the transcendent in a direct and personal way. To be sure, the young person's acceptance of religion's answer to the problem will again be determined by a variety of factors. Indeed, some of our research (Elkind & Elkind 1962; Long, Elkind, & Spilka 1967) suggests that many young people reject formal worship but nonetheless engage in individual worship. For the adolescent who has accepted God and his scriptural representation, the question of relating to God is an inevitable one, no matter how it is resolved.

Adolescence and the Search for Comprehension

The physical and physiological transformations so prominent in adolescence frequently obscure the equally momentous changes undergone by intelligence during the same period. As a consequence of both maturation and experience, a new mental system emerges that enables the young person to accomplish feats of thought that far surpass the elementary reasonings of the child. One feat that makes its appearance is the capacity to introspect, to take one's thought and feelings as if they were external objects and to examine and reason about them. Another feat is the capacity to construct ideal or contrary-to-fact situations, to conceive of utopian societies, ideal mates, and preeminent careers. Finally, in problem-solving situations, the adolescent, in contrast to the child, can take all of the possible factors into account and test their possibilities in a systematic fashion (Inhelder & Piaget 1968).

Implicit in all these mental accomplishments is the capacity to construct and think in terms of overriding theories that enable the person not only to grasp relations but also to grasp the underlying reasons for them. To use a biological analogy, the child is concerned with "phenotypes," whereas the adolescent focuses attention upon the "genotypes," the underlying principles that associate a variety of apparently diverse phenomena. It seems reasonable, therefore, to characterize the mental ability that emerges in adolescence as the capacity for theory construction and the corresponding need as *the search for comprehension.*

As with other capacities, the search for comprehension persists throughout life, although it takes different forms at different stages in the life cycle. The search for comprehension, like the other capacities, never meets with complete success. Whether it be in the field of science, art, history, or government, each new effort uncovers new puzzles for the understanding. The same holds true on the personal plane. To illustrate, although the adolescent now has a conception of personality that enables an understanding of people in depth, human foibles and eccentricities are still encountered that defy generalizations. And, though this newfound capacity for comprehension enables self-scrutiny, even here there is frequent failure.

In the domain of religion, the problem of comprehension arises naturally to those who have accepted God's scriptural representation and the sacrament of worship. Many young people often seek such comprehension on their own, with the result that they become bewildered and disheartened. Religion again provides a solution through a body of myth, legend, and history that provides a means for comprehending God.

In modern religions, the resolution to the problem of comprehension is provided by theology. It may be, however, that the ferment within present-day theological discussions makes it more difficult than heretofore for the young person to accept religious solution to the problem of comprehension. Be that as it may, for the individual who has accepted God and worship, the problem of comprehension must be faced, regardless of how it may be resolved.

CONCLUSION

The foregoing discussion probably raises many more questions than it has answered. I have tried to present a scheme to illustrate the extraordinary fit between certain basic cognitive need capacities and the major elements of institutional religion. It is probable that this fit is not accidental and that religion has, in part, evolved to provide solutions to the problems of adaptation posed by these needed capacities. To the extent that this is true, we are justified in speaking of the origins of religion in the child.

Psychologists who have concerned themselves with religious phenomena (e.g., Allport 1960; Dunlap 1946; James 1902) are in general agreement that there are no uniquely religious psychic elements. Insofar as anyone has been able to determine, there are no drives, sentiments, emotions, or mental categories that are inherently religious. Psychic elements, it is agreed, become religious only when they become associated with one or another aspect of religion. Nothing said here contradicts this position, with which I agree.

Nonetheless, the view that there are no uniquely religious psychic elements does not preclude the possibility that there may be uniquely religious *adaptations*. Adaptations are neither innate nor acquired but are instead the products of the individual or societal interaction. Every adaptation is a construction that bears the stamp of both nature and nurture yet is reducible to neither. The same holds true for religious adaptations. The concept of God, or more generally, of the transcendent, cannot be reduced to the search for conservation any more than it can be traced to the phenomenon of death. Contrariwise, neither the search for conservation nor the phenomenon of death is in itself religious, although it may well take part in the production of religious elements. Like a gestalt, such as a painting or a melody, the transcendent is greater than the sum or product of its parts.

As suggested earlier, once the concept of God or spirit is accepted as the ultimate conservation, it necessarily entails genuinely religious problems for the other emerging need capacities. These problems can, in turn, be immediately resolved by the ready-made constructions afforded by institutional religion, such as scripture, worship, and theology. From the standpoint of the individual, therefore, the concept of the transcendent lies at the very core of personal religion. At the same time, however, whether God is a personal construction or one acquired from institutional religion, it is always superordinate, transcending particular individual or social needs as well as the phenomenal facts out of which it arose.

9

INTEGRATING DIFFERING THEORIES: THE CASE OF RELIGIOUS DEVELOPMENT

K. HELMUT REICH

To get a sense of the overall situation in psychology of religion I turn first to Spilka, Hood, and Gorsuch (1985). These authors review many possibilities to comprehend religion: One can adopt an individual's outside/inside or a social perspective, study ritual, doctrine, religious emotions, religious knowledge, ethics, the religious community, conversion, or even apostasy. One can concentrate on the reasons people are religious (e.g., instinct, need for meaning and control, wish to avoid anxiety, desire to grow, or simply habit). And one can consider all this for childhood, adolescence, adulthood, and old age; and for persons of diverse styles (such as scientific, dogmatic, and ad hoc, Berzonsky 1992), as well as of various overriding dispositions (intellectual, emotional, justice orientation, and so on). Additionally, Pruyser (1987) and Malony and Spilka (1991:191–192) suggest studying faith groups, denominations, sects, cults, various types of individuals (liberal, Orthodox, fundamentalist, evangelical, Hindu, Shiite, Sunni, capitalist, Marxist, Anabaptist, militant, pietistic, established, in free-church tradition, freethinker, God-and-country ideologist, and so forth). Although many pieces of the puzzle exist, it is not surprising that no comprehensive systematic program has been carried out to date, given the extension and diversity of the field and the

Reprinted and edited with permission of author and publisher from *Journal of Empirical Theology*, 6 (1993), 39–49.

small number of laborers. In particular, we lack longitudinal data on reli-gious development, making it difficult to assess competing theoretical claims.

Psychologists have tried to meet these challenges via different approaches. Pruyser (1987) lists the following: (1) social-psychological, (2) behavioral, (3) cognitive, (3) classical psychodynamic, (5) ego-psycholog-ical, (6) British objective-relations, (7) clinical psychological, (8) pastoral psychological, (9) parapsychological, (10) organizational behavior, (11) life-course developmental view, (12) stress and crisis, and perhaps even (13) military view. Hence, just as in the case of mainstream psychology, the psychology of religion is so *diversified and subspecialized* that we can no longer speak of *the* psychology of religion. In such a situation, one can understand that Spilka, Hood, and Gorsuch (1985:17) predict: "The likeli-hood is that no one theory will ever suffice for this complex realm." Wulff (1993) suspects that a truly comprehensive theory of religious stability and change "is most likely to be soft to an extreme and hence not useful in practical affairs." Nevertheless, I offer a direction for an integrated the-ory, at least of religious development, and advance a speculative scheme designed to cover a variety of religious life paths.

MAJOR DIFFICULTIES IN ATTAINING THEORY INTEGRATION

These concern (1) position with respect to the reality of the transcendent, and (2) research motives and aims. With regard to the first, Wulff (1991a) placed various views in the psychology of religion into a two-dimen-sional space. The upper half defines affirmation of transcendence (under-stood literally or symbolically), the lower half disaffirmation. Clearly, an affirmative stance such as Ricoeur's second naïveté (1965/1970:28), situ-ated "high" in the upper half, and the disaffirmative stance of orthodox psychoanalysis, situated "low" in the lower half, simply cannot be inte-grated.

The second problem goes even deeper. Given the difficulty of the task, it would seem reasonable that the workers in the field should join forces to attain mutually agreed-upon milestone targets. However, Pruyser (1991) lists quite different motives and aims of the extant psychologies of religion: (1) offering apology of religion by way of demonstrating its psy-chological necessity or inevitability; (2) making subjective experiences objective and public; (3) seizing upon strange, rare practices that are seen by others as abnormal or are generally disdained and making them understandable and acceptable, possibly even respectable; (4) exposing religion as a whole as an atavism or anachronism; (5) offering exposition of the psychic roots of religion in archaic imagery of childish wishes or defense mechanisms so as to maximize the continuity between ancient and modern man or between child and adult; (6) exploring the possibility that a particular psychology (clinical, experimental, social, and so on) explains the so far unexplained altogether—or at least better explains the explainable than other theories; (7) admiring religion's historical persistence, its power, its impact on individuals and groups, and its richness of forms.

As a result of this fragmentation, "many scholars pay little attention to works produced outside their own clique, and broad cross-referencing leaves much to be desired in the bibliographies of books and articles" (Pruyser 1991:195). Consequently, efforts at theory integration can hardly count on broad support.

SUGGESTIONS FOR THEORY INTEGRATION

In this section a number of suggestions for theory integration are offered regarding promising elements, basic theoretical content, and the integration procedures. As most suggestions touch on more than one point, they are given in alphabetical order of the authors.

Epstein (1991) claims that his cognitive-experiential self-theory (CEST) elucidates broader human concerns and enterprises, such as religion or spirituality. He (1991:119) posits four basic *psychic functions*, serving (1) "to assimilate the *data of reality* (which subsumes the need to maintain the conceptual system that does the assimilating), (2) to maintain a favorable *pleasure-pain balance* [pleasure principle]; (3) to maintain *relatedness to others*, (4) to maintain a favorable level of *self-esteem*" (enumeration and emphasis added).

Mental health is said to involve a sound equilibrium between the four functions. Spilka, Shaver, and Kirkpatrick (1985) take a somewhat different view (as discussed later; cf. Reich 1992a), and Epstein (1991:120) posits four associated *basic beliefs*: Everyone has an intuitive belief about (1) the degree to which the world is benign, (2) the degree to which life is meaningful (including predictable, controllable, and just), (3) the degree to which people are desirable to relate to, and (4) the degree to which the self is worthy (including capable, good, and lovable).

Fraas (1992:24–25) makes the following three recommendations: (1) Do not rely on a particular psychological school, but make *comparisons*. In particular, compare *results* of comparable research projects based on different theoretical perspectives. Concentrate on *concordances*; (2) *Analyze in the light of theology and religious studies* psychological theories of religion that appear to be candidates for an integration: Are their religious presuppositions really compatible? and (3) Analyze candidate theories with respect to the underlying *personality theory* and check compatibility in that respect (cf. Snarey, Kohlberg, & Noam 1987, as discussed later on). Together with others, these recommendations will (partly) be followed here.

Noam (1990:365) argues that a larger context is needed as a basis for a new synthesis. In particular, "earlier vulnerabilities, strengths, identifications, and life experiences" have to be taken into account when analyzing a developmental path. This "causality of fate" is biographical, an "invariance of life history that can be dissolved by the power of reflection," as McCarthy put it (cited in Noam 1990:368). Hence, Noam introduces biographical structures, calling them *themata* (p. 390). The full theory requires a combination of (Piagetian) *schemata* with these themata.

According to Perrez (1991), a difference exists concerning conjectures, hypotheses, and hypothesis testing, depending on whether a question of *everyday knowledge* or of *ideology/mythology* (religion) is concerned. In the first case perception, information processing and genuine taking into account of personal experience will be as effective as possible for the person concerned. In the second case, a certain insensitivity to everyday and even scientific experience and evaluation is said to obtain.

In a different field, Schmidtchen (1980) considers separately the levels (1) of *measurement* (questionnaire, interview, biographical study, and so forth), (2) of *conceptual* elements (here he considers God images, dogmas, rites, prayer, and the like), and (3) *psychic* elements (unconscious drives, preconscious acts, emotions, cognitions, attributions, judgments). He recommends combining them in compatible ways.

Huston Smith (1992) summarizes the common vision of the world's religions. In the present context, that vision is not recommended as a procedural recipe but as a warning against positing a too narrow, one-sided terminus ad quem of religious development.

Snarey, Kohlberg, and Noam (1987:381) argue that various approaches to *subdomains* of human development are complementary and can usefully be brought under the "umbrella" of an appropriate *theory of ego development*. They provide a tentative alignment of the stages of various developments conceptualized by Erikson, Loevinger, Kegan, Piaget, Selman, Perry, Snarey, Kohlberg, Oser, Broughton, and Fowler (1987:372–373). Their approach is taken as one of the cues for the present endeavor.

Spilka, Hood, and Gorsuch (1985:17–28) emphasize notably (1) the ever-present *social context* (negative and positive effects), (2) the "universal" basic *forms of personal faith* (intrinsic/committed and extrinsic/consensual religion), (3) *attributions* (motivations; situational influences, event character factors, event importance, positive-negative influences, event domain, situational complexity, and event significance; and dispositional influences such as background factors, cognitive-linguistic factors, personality attitudinal factors, self-esteem, locus of control, and belief in "a just world"). Again, this is (partially) one of the inputs here.

From a different focus, Spilka, Shaver, and Kirkpatrick (1985) build their general attribution theory for the psychology of religion on three needs: (1) that for a *sense of meaning*, (2) for *control over outcomes*, and (3) for *self-esteem*. In particular, they also discuss cases in which self-esteem interferes with sound judgment.

If one cannot combine different extant theories into a single coherent supertheory, Tschannen (1991) recommends working at the (lower) *paradigmatic* level and searching in particular for shared *concepts* (whatever their various labels).

In addition to the previous comments about the shortcomings of various developmental theories of religiousness (Oser & Reich 1992; Reich 1992b, 1993), I would suggest looking carefully at the empirical validity of any theoretical elements to be integrated. Wulff (1991a) is helpful in that he presents much evidence and argues the case carefully regarding any specific theory. Reading his evaluative sections on Freud, Erikson, and Jung, one wonders how some people can exclusively concentrate on, and give almost unrestricted credit to, only one of these theories.

A UNIFIED THEORY OF RELIGIOUS DEVELOPMENT

Specifications

Taking the cue from Kuhn (1988; cf. Reich 1992b:151), a unified theory would need to

1. refer to *psychical* (intellectual, emotional, volitional, preconscious, unconscious) *processes* that take place within the organism, including those aspects of such processes referred to as meaning-making;
2. characterize development as a *gradual coordination* of individual psyche and biophysical, sociocultural, and perceived spiritual reality and explicate the relationship between the *internal* and the *external forces* in the course of development;
3. address the *social contexts* in which development occurs and the ways in which those contexts relate to individual religious attitudes, behavior, and development;
4. account for the *universal features* of religious development as well as for *individual differences*;
5. specify *mechanisms* by means of which developmental change occurs and explain the workings of factors that favor or hinder religious development, including conversion and apostasy.

TABLE 9.1   Elements to Be Incorporated into a Unified Theory of Religious Development

(Mental) Age	Cognitive Domain of Religious Development	Emotional Domain	Major Age-Related Factors
Infancy	coordination of perceptions and movements; "logic" of actions; first steps toward social relations	emotions expressed via actions (smiling; moving arms; crying); emotions give rise to dreams	native biological endowment; outcome of competition between "trust and mistrust"
Early childhood	child realism (egocentric attributions); magical thinking; animism (life and will attributed to things); artificialism (an artisan's world)	dialectics of being held securely and exploring surroundings alone; child introduces emotions into symbolic play for familiarization	"spontaneous" creation of God image as transition object; outcome of "autonomy vs. shame, doubt"
Middle childhood	concrete operations (incl. conservation, classification, reversibility); mode of necessity; analogies: comparison of external features	early use of abstract conventional language to describe inner states ("I felt tense"; "I was burning"); early grasp of cause-effect relation	possibility/impossibility of exploring environment and being supported therein; "initiative vs. guilt"
Late childhood	early formal operations; mode of possibility; analogies: comparison of functions; elements of dialectical and complementarity reasoning	simple differentiations of emotions by degrees; category ("I was not mad, more helpless"); mental forms of emotional control	discovery that others may have different views from one's own; friendships; "industry vs. inferiority"
Adolescence	formal operations (hypothetical and deductive reasoning); comprehension of metaphors/analogies; universality mode; early dialectical and complementarity reasoning	technical, nonpersonal terminology ("It was a verbal anger"); description by nonvivid and nondynamic metaphors ("I felt empty"; "things were bottled up")	transition from childhood to adulthood; search for one's own views, values, and profession; "identity versus identity confusion"
Early adulthood	dialectical and complementarity (relational and contextual) reasoning; existential mode; epistemic cognition (how to gain valid knowledge)	more complex eleborations and comparisons ("Everything is like a cyclone going around"); emotional control by complex negotiation	involvement (or not) in religious community; religious/nonreligious partner; "intimacy vs. isolation"
Middle adulthood	conscious awareness and appropriate use of various forms and modes of reasoning and logic	highly differentiated, dynamic comparisons ("I felt like someone was pulling my insides out")	raising a family; solving the "midlife crisis"; "generativity vs. stagnation"
Older	equilibrium between mythos and logos; second naïveté; wisdom	psychological integration of subjective and objective awareness	facing progressive decline; "ego integrity vs. despair"

| Major Religious Orientation | Effect on Religiousness | |
Provided by	Positive	Negative
interactive rituals of relation-ships with significant others (parents, etc.)	if endowed with basic religious sensibilities and interests; if basic trust acquired; close relationship with caretaker	if character such that fully content with "no-nonsense" occupations; if mistrust acquired; no relationship with caretaker
representation of own pre-operational thoughts; aligning religious images with pro-found feelings	loving, supporting God image; enjoyable religious experiences ("Christmas, as a child, that was the best, just great"; "Singing in church, it's so beautiful")	frightening God image ("God watches all the time to see whether we behave"); or negative "religious" experiences; possibly entirely satisfactory relations
progressively by concrete logical reasoning; God rewards good deeds and punishes bad deeds	age-related, empathic religious socialization (praying together, participation in satisfying religious ceremonies; telling of / listening to religious narratives)	religious incompetency ("I just didn't understand"; "I hate it"); indifference ("In our family, we do not believe in religion") or even atheistic socialization
opinions of significant others; traditions; also by a justice point of view; restricted autonomy	relationship with religiously engaged persons (parents, teacher, etc.) who engage in open discussion of religious questions; understanding of parables	religiously negative family climate (no, or even negative, mention of no religious activities; possibly denigration of, and opposition to, religious education)
own individuality and autonomy; third person per-spective; possibly by examina-tion of inherited beliefs	religiously open family climate (for voicing criticisms, discuss-ing doubts; asking personal questions and getting satis-factory answers); member of a religious peer group; religious camps	negative experiences with pray-ing ("No answer—there is no God") and with "religious" persons; difficulties with the theodicy ("If God existed, he wouldn't permit it"); no *causa exemplaris* in sight
possibly reactivation of relationship with spiritual reality that mediates autonomy	discovery of "new" aspects of religion / religiousness; involve-ment in continued "religious education" (e.g., discussions inside a group of young couples)	religiously negative human environment (religion con-sidered as a waste of time, hindrance to self-fulfillment, bad for mental health, unhelp-ful altogether)
multilayered meaning making beyond dichotomies; social engagement	supporting one's children in their religious development; enlarging one's religious horizons; reflecting on religion	experiencing turmoil and dissatisfaction against a religiously negative background and biography
unconditional religiousness, cosmic solidarity	sharing a religious experience which can be relied upon in difficulties	embitterment about life; possibly entire satisfaction with an areligious life

Construction of an Integrated Scheme

We now come to the construction stage. The result is shown in Table 9.1; the basic idea is taken from Snarey, Kohlberg, and Noam (1987), as already indicated. In addition to the theories of Baldwin (Wallwork 1982), Fowler (1987), Oser and Gmünder (1991), and Rizzuto (1979) and the background elements and considerations already presented, I make use of the following presuppositions and material, ordered according to the columns of Table 9.1.

(Mental) Age.   A standard subdivision is used (except that adolescence might be subdivided). "Mental" age refers mainly to the columns Cognitive Domain and Emotional Domain (in which large individual differences obtain and calendar age is known to be a notoriously imprecise developmental yardstick). Otherwise, calendar age is meant. For Religious Orientation and Effect on Religiousness, an average development of cognition and emotion is assumed.

Cognitive Domain.   Use is made of research on various forms of thought, in particular that by Basseches (1989; dialectical reasoning), Chinen (1984; reasoning in terms of modal logic), Gentner (Gentner & Jeziorski, in press; reasoning by analogy/metaphor/similarity), Labouvie-Vief (1992; mythos and logos), Piaget (1983; logico-mathematical reasoning), Oser and Reich (1987; Reich 1991; relational and contextual [complementarity] reasoning). One would also like to introduce unitary and transpersonal thinking or the like (e.g., Funk 1989; Koplowitz 1990; cf. Reich 1992a), but those hypothetical forms of thought are not yet confirmed empirically.

Emotional Domain.   The main orientation is taken from the volume edited by Bearison and Zimiles (1986), adding some psychoanalytical elements stressing early competence (e.g., Domes 1993; Knapp 1988). The formulations are largely drawn from Labouvie-Vief, DeVoe, & Bulka 1989; Labouvie-Vief et al. 1989).

Age-Related Factors.   The basic skeleton is taken from Erikson (1982), the fleshing out from the elements presented above.

Religious Orientation.   The isomorphisms of the developmental theories listed earlier serve as the main content; the formulations are mostly those of Fowler.

Effect on Religiousness. The basic idea is taken from Rizzuto (1979: 206–207). The contents are based on the literature (including Kirkpatrick 1992) and on personal research.

In summing up, I reemphasize that Table 9.1 only presents a first step toward theory integration. If considered helpful for the design of empirical studies and as a first orientation when evaluating data, improvements could be considered.

10

An Attachment-Theory Approach to the Psychology of Religion

The psychology of religion has enjoyed a resurgence of interest in recent years (Gorsuch 1988). However, two serious obstacles lie in its path. First, as noted by Gorsuch, religion research has yet to be integrated within mainstream psychology. Research on religion receives little attention in psychology textbooks (Lehr & Spilka 1989) and only rarely appears in leading psychology journals. Second, little of this work is grounded in strong theory. Studies documenting empirical correlates of religious orientation continue to accumulate, for example, but have contributed little to theoretical understandings of the dynamics of religious experience, belief, and behavior (Kirkpatrick & Hood 1990). The area of greatest theoretical activity continues to be the psychoanalytic tradition, but this paradigm is itself estranged from most contemporary research in psychology.

The solution to both of these problems must involve the development of a broad theoretical framework for the psychology of religion that draws on and extends research and theory developed within other areas of psychology. I argue here that attachment theory, which has become highly influential within developmental, social, personality, and clinical psychology, is such a theory and offers exciting prospects for the psychology of religion. To support this argument, I review a sampling of research findings and show that conceptualizing (at least some forms of)

Reprinted and edited with permission of author and publisher from *International Journal for the Psychology of Religion*, 2 (1992), 3–28.

religion as an attachment process may provide a fruitful theoretical model for approaching religious belief and behavior from a psychological perspective.

A BRIEF OVERVIEW OF ATTACHMENT THEORY AND RESEARCH

Originally introduced by Bowlby (1969, 1973, 1980) as an alternative to psychoanalytic object-relations theory, attachment theory postulates a primary, biosocial behavioral system in the infant that evolved to maintain proximity of the infant to its primary caregiver, thereby protecting the infant from predation and other dangers. This postulated motivational system is distinct from other systems involved in nutrition and reproduction and is intended to replace the outdated psychic energy model of motivation with a model more consonant with modern biology and ethology.

Active functioning of the system has its roots in the mother-infant relationship: The infant emits social signals (e.g., crying, clinging) to which the mother (or other attachment figure) is more or less responsive, which in turn influences subsequent infant behavior. When the system functions optimally, the infant develops a secure attachment to the mother in which she is perceived as a reliable source of protection and security. The secure attachment relationship is characterized by confident exploration of the environment under normal circumstances and by proximity seeking and comfort seeking in the presence of threat. In the language of attachment researchers, the mother serves alternately as a secure base and a haven of safety for the infant. The attached person experiences this process in terms of the regulation of felt security (Bretherton 1987; Sroufe & Waters 1977).

Individual differences in infant-mother attachment have received considerable attention in developmental psychology. In addition to secure attachment, two insecure patterns have been widely researched: the avoidant type, in which the infant seems to regard the mother as neither a secure base for exploration nor a haven of safety, and the anxious/ambivalent type, in which clinging, proximity- and comfort-seeking behavior alternates episodically with anger and resistance. Anxious/ambivalent infants also appear more anxious generally and do not consistently evince confident exploration of the environment in the mother's presence (Ainsworth et al. 1978). Considerable evidence now exists linking individual differences in infant attachment classifications to maternal caregiving behaviors and attitudes (see Bretherton 1987, for a review).

Main, Kaplan, and Cassidy (1985) showed that classifications based on the strange situation paradigm are fairly stable between one and six years of age. Other studies have shown that the social behavior of five- and six-year-olds can be predicted reliably from early attachment relationships (e.g., Arend, Gove, & Sroufe 1979; Lieberman 1977; Waters, Wippman, & Sroufe 1979). Patterns of attachment have also been shown to perpetuate themselves across generations, from mother to child (Main et al. 1985; Ricks 1985). These long-term effects of early attachment experience are attributed to internal working models or schemata of attachment relationships that develop early and remain relatively stable across time, although they are modifiable by significant emotional experiences or changes in life situation. Sroufe and Fleeson (1986), among others, emphasize that previous relationship patterns are carried forward into later close relationships.

Attachment and Adult Relationships

Although Bowlby's development of attachment theory was based primarily on the attachment system's evolutionary function of providing protection to human (and other primate) infants, he strongly maintained that the attachment system is an important influence on behavior "from the cradle to the grave." In recent years, the application of attachment concepts to adult relationships has emerged as a field in its own right. Weiss (1973) differentiated two types of loneliness—emotional isolation and social isolation—and related the former to attachment dynamics. Shaver, Hazan, and Bradshaw (1988) provided an extensive list of striking similarities between early attachment and adult romantic love. Hazan and Shaver (1987) showed empirically that adult romantic relationships tend to fall into three major patterns that closely resemble Ainsworth's three infant-mother attachment classifications.

It should be emphasized that attachment is not a generic term but refers to a distinctive type of relationship. Several researchers have made careful attempts to distinguish attachment bonds from other kinds of close relationships. Ainsworth (1985) distinguished "affectional bonds" from role-oriented relationships and emphasized the secure-base and haven functions as distinguishing features of attachment relationships per se. Most researchers agree that the defining features of an attachment relationship include the provision of feelings of comfort and security, the role of the attachment figure as both a haven of safety (in the presence of threat) and a secure base for exploration (in the absence of threat), and the distress or protest occasioned by potential or actual separation from the attachment figure.

For a more detailed review of attachment theory, see Ainsworth et al. (1978), Bretherton (1985), or Lamb, Thompson, Gardner, and Charnov (1985). See Ainsworth (1969, 1972), Bretherton (1987), Maccoby and

Masters (1970), and Sroufe (1986) for comparisons of attachment theory with psychoanalytic and dependency theories.

Religion Conceptualized as an Attachment Process

In this essay I argue that the availability and responsiveness of an attachment figure, who serves alternately as a haven and as a secure base and from whom separation would cause considerable distress, is considered a fundamental dynamic underlying Christianity and many other theistic religions. Whether that attachment figure is God, Jesus Christ, the Virgin Mary, or one of various saints, guardian angels, or other supernatural beings, the analogy is striking. The religious person proceeds with faith that God (or another figure) will be available for protection and will comfort him or her when danger threatens; at other times, the mere knowledge of God's presence and accessibility allows a person to approach the problems and difficulties of daily life with confidence. In the remainder of this essay, I refer to the supernatural attachment figure as God, although other deities may fulfill this role.

At least one modern theologian has also been impressed by the applicability of the attachment model to people's beliefs in God. Kaufman (1981) discussed the tremendous psychological importance of secure attachments and noted that, unfortunately, humans are at best limited and fallible attachment figures. By comparison, "the idea of God is the idea of an absolutely adequate attachment figure . . . God is thought of as a protective and caring parent who is always reliable and always available to its children when they are in need" (Kaufman 1981:67).

The analogy of the attachment relationship to Christian belief has also been acknowledged by Reed (1978), who noted that "every form of attachment behaviour, and of the behaviour of the attachment-figure, identified by Bowlby, has its close counterpart in the images of the relationship between Israel (or the Worshipper) and God which we find in, for example, the psalms" (p. 14).

The idea that religion is ultimately rooted in fear and the need for security and comfort is hardly new. Freud (1961) was a leading proponent of this view, arguing that religion was a response to the perception that one is helpless in the face of a hostile and uncontrollable world. According to Freud, people yearn for the protection of the omnipotent father figure of childhood and therefore create God in this image. Schleiermacher's (1893) well-known dictum that the distinctively religious experience is marked by "feelings of absolute dependence" similarly expresses this view. Wobbermin (1933) later expanded Schleiermacher's analysis of the basic religious experience to include, in addition to the feeling of dependence, "the feeling of security and the sense of longing" (p. 157). Other related views of religion as a fear-oriented system are reviewed by Spilka, Hood, and Gorsuch (1985), who devoted a chapter section to the "defensive-protective" tradition.

One problem with such deficiency models of religion, however, is that they frequently represent religion as inherently childish, immature, and unhealthy. Freudian concepts such as regression, fixation, and dependency imply a decidedly negative evaluation of virtually all religious involvement. Attachment theory, in contrast, replaces these concepts with less evaluative terminology and constructs. Bowlby has repeatedly emphasized, in contrast to traditional psychoanalytic thinking, that seeking protection and security from an attachment figure under threatening circumstances is a normal and healthy activity at any age. Activation of the attachment system is seen as a normative response to normative fears rather than as an immature, regressive response to neurotic fears. Although my goal here is not to serve as an apologist for religion, it seems clear that unfounded antireligious biases and stereotypes have historically impeded constructive psychological theorizing about religion (Hood 1983).

Haven of Safety

Bowlby's (1973) review of the ethological literature led him to postulate that increases in the intensity of attachment behavior in infants of lower primate species occur in response to three classes of environmental stimuli: (1) any kind of alarming event, (2) the mother moving away (i.e., threat of separation from the mother), and (3) actual separation from the mother. Similar conditions activate the attachment system in human infants as well (Ainsworth et al. 1978). If religious belief and behavior are manifestations of the attachment system in humans, one would expect to find that people turn to religion (and to God in particular) under similar conditions.

The available evidence supports such a conclusion. The popular maxim that "there are no atheists in foxholes" attests to the idea that people commonly turn to God under stressful and threatening circumstances. An amusing but revealing twist on this theme was provided by Allport (1950), who quoted one war veteran's observation that "there were atheists in foxholes, but most of them were in love" (p. 56). Allport noted the fundamental insight illuminated by this quote: "The individual in distress craves affection and security. Sometimes a human bond will suffice, more often it will not" (p. 57).

Argyle and Beit-Hallahmi (1975) concluded that religion plays a particularly important role in times of crisis. They were careful to note, however, that people specifically turn to prayer, rather than to the church, in stressful circumstances. This is important from an attachment perspective because it parallels the fact that people turn to attachment figures—rather than to those with whom they have other sorts of relationships—for comfort and security. Spilka et al. (1985) similarly observed that "prayer is probably most significant for its role in crisis" (p. 304).

Several studies have pointed to the role of prayer and God as providing a haven in times of fear and distress. The "no atheists in foxholes" maxim was literally supported by Stouffer et al. (1949), who showed that soldiers in battle do in fact pray frequently and feel that such prayer is beneficial. In a study of religious attributions, Pargament and Hahn (1986) concluded that "subjects appeared to turn to God more as a source of support during stress than as a moral guide or as an antidote to an unjust world" (p. 204). Ross (1950) queried over 1,700 religious youth about why they prayed: The two reasons most frequently cited were "God listens to and answers your prayers" and "It helps you in time of stress and crisis."

In an in-depth study of patients suffering from renal failure and facing the prospect of long-term hemodialysis, O'Brien (1982) demonstrated that religious faith is an important variable in predicting successful coping and in combatting feelings of alienation. Excerpts from interviews from these patients suggested that God was seen by many as providing comfort, nurturance, and a source of personal strength for getting through this difficult time. Duke (1977) and Gibbs and Achterberg-Lawlis (1978) found that fear of death among terminally ill cancer patients was inversely correlated with religious commitment and faith. In a study of Unification Church members by Galanter (1979), converts displayed a substantial reduction in emotional and neurotic distress after joining the church.

Insofar as loss of an attachment figure is likely to activate attachment behavior, the attachment model would predict that religious behavior and belief should increase during periods of bereavement. Loveland (1968) showed that bereaved people feel more religious and engage in more prayer than they did prior to the death, yet the specific content of their basic beliefs does not appear to be affected. Loveland also showed, along with Haun (1977) and Parkes (1972), that religious belief and commitment correlated positively with adjustment and coping to loss of a spouse. For the bereaved, God can serve as a substitute attachment figure when a spouse or other attachment figure is lost. It is also worth noting that, in most theistic religions, separation from God is the most horrific threat imaginable. In many Christian belief systems, it is the very essence of hell.

Thus, it appears that people turn to religion, and to God in particular, in response to the same sorts of events known to activate the attachment system and that doing so often provides the comfort and security associated with attachment relationships.

Conversion. Research on sudden conversions also suggests that converts may be most likely to turn to religion when they are distressed and confused. Early work generally agreed that sudden conversions are often preceded by a period of distress, depression, and anxiety (Clark 1929; Starbuck 1899). According to Strickland (1924), the subsequent crisis or turning point itself "provides a relief of the nerve tensions and consequent release from fear, anxiety, grief, or other emotional states" (p. 119). In his analysis, this turning point involves the surrendering of oneself to God and the placing of personal problems and one's faith into God's hands. Galanter (1979) showed that most converts to the Unification Church reported that they had been experiencing severe emotional distress at the time of conversion.

One extensively documented fact is that adolescence is the most common period of life for religious conversion, leading early researchers such as Hall (1904), James (1902), and Starbuck (1899) to refer to religious conversion as an adolescent phenomenon. Johnson (1959) reviewed five major studies and found that the average age of conversion was 15.2 years. It is well known, too, that cult recruiters make teenagers and young adults primary targets for proselytization. Because adolescence represents such a unique developmental period, it is not surprising that a wide range of many explanations has been advanced for the prevalence of conversion at this time, including postulated links to puberty and sexual instincts (Coe 1916; Thouless 1923), to the need for meaning, purpose, and sense of identity (Starbuck 1899), and to self-realization (Spilka, Hood, & Gorsuch 1985).

All these factors contribute to the often cited "storm and stress" of adolescence, and the resulting distress and uncertainty experienced may well lead many to seek refuge with a new, omnipotent attachment figure. Moreover, adolescence represents a period of major transition between primary attachment figures. According to Weiss (1982), relinquishing one's parents as attachment figures has several important implications for the adolescent, including vulnerability to loneliness—and, for Weiss, loneliness "indicates the absence from one's internal world of an attachment figure" (p. 178). At such time, many adolescents may turn to God (or perhaps to a charismatic religious leader) as a substitute attachment figure.

A Secure Base

In addition to providing a useful model for conceptualizing religion in terms of the haven function, attachment theory speaks equally strongly to the issue of religion as a secure base. James (1902) observed that "the sense of Presence of a higher and friendly Power seems to be the fundamental feature in the spiritual life" and added that "in the Christian consciousness this sense of the enveloping friendliness becomes most personal and definite" (pp. 274–275). He illustrated the point with this quotation from Voysey (1882; cited in James 1902):

> It is the myriads of trustful souls, that this sense of God's unfailing presence with them in their going out and in their coming in, and by night and day, is a source of absolute repose and confident calmness. It drives away all fear of what may befall them. That nearness of God is a constant security against terror and anxiety. (p. 275)

Johnson (1945) similarly remarked on the function of faith in providing a generalized sense of emotional security:

> The emotional quality of faith is indicated in a basic confidence and security that gives one assurance. In this sense faith is the opposite of fear, anxiety, and uncertainty. Without emotional security there is no relaxation, but tension, distress, and instability. Assurance is the firm emotional undertone that enables one to have steady nerves and calm poise in the face of danger or confusion. (p. 191)

These quotations capture an important aspect of religious life that has received surprisingly little research attention from psychologists of religion: the pervasive sense of calm and poised confidence that derives from the mere knowledge of "God's unfailing presence." Attachment theory captures this idea in the construct of a secure base. According to Bowlby and others, the availability of a secure base is the antidote to fear and anxiety: "When an individual is confident that an attachment figure will be available to him whenever he desires it, that person will be much less prone to either intense or chronic fear than will an individual who for any reason has no such confidence" (Bowlby, 1973:202).

Unfortunately, the diverse and conflicting research literature on religion and mental health does not paint a coherent picture vis-à-vis this hypothesis. Matters are complicated by at least two problems: (1) Few if any extant measures of religious belief have been designed to assess an attachment-related dimension of religion, and (2) religion is only one of many things to which people may turn for a secure base. However, several suggestive findings are noteworthy. For example, intrinsic religious orientation (i.e., genuine religious commitment) has been shown to correlate inversely with trait anxiety (Baker & Gorsuch 1982; Entner 1977; McClain 1978) and fear of death (Kahoe & Dunn 1975) and positively with internal locus of control (Kahoe 1974; Strickland & Shaffer 1971). In their review of research on religion and mental health, Batson and Ventis (1982) found intrinsic religiousness to be positively correlated with two conceptualizations of mental health—"freedom from worry and guilt" and "personal competence and control"—but not with other aspects of mental health. In addition, mental health conceptualized in terms of freedom from worry and guilt was positively associated with religious involvement only in studies of elderly populations. This may reflect the fact that elderly people are less likely to have living parents and spouses available to provide a secure base.

Pollner (1989) analyzed data from the General Social Survey to assess the role of divine and human relationships on well-being and life satisfaction. His measure of "divine relationships," designed to "tap the psychological proximity of a divine other and the frequency and depth of interaction with that other" (p. 95), proved to be the strongest among many correlates of three of four measures of well-being in multiple-regression analyses. Similar results were found even when background variables and church attendance were statistically controlled. Galanter (1989) reported the two best predictors of emotional well-being among Unification Church members to be the survey items "My religious beliefs give me comfort" and "I feel a close connection to God."

In an empirical study of newspaper survey respondents, Kirkpatrick and Shaver (1992) found few significant correlations between a host of religion variables and measures of life satisfaction, loneliness and depression, and physical symptoms—with one important exception. An item designed to assess individual differences in the security of respondents' attachments to God was strongly associated with the mental and physical health variables. This closely parallels results for a similar variable measuring security of attachment in human love relationships. Although the research literature on religion and mental health is replete with conflicting and ambiguous results (Bergin 1983), a specific dimension of religiousness focusing on a secure attachment to God may prove to be strongly associated with positive mental health outcomes.

God as an Attachment Figure

Empirical studies concerning people's images of God have appeared intermittently in the literature since the 1950s. This research has focused primarily on two issues: the relation of the God image to conceptions of one's parents and the relation of the God image to the self-concept. In spite of various methodological difficulties (Nicholson & Edwards 1979; Spilka 1978), studies of the former type have pointed to two general conclusions. Contrary to the Freudian hypothesis that originally motivated this line of research, God is evidently perceived as more similar to one's mother than one's father (Godin & Hallez 1965; Nelson 1971; Strunk 1959) or, alternatively, to one's preferred parent (Nelson & Jones 1957). Both findings are consistent with an attachment interpretation. If the preferred parent represents the primary attachment figure, which seems a plausible assumption, it is the image of this parent that God should most resemble. Moreover, because the primary attachment figure is more likely to be the mother than the father in Western culture (Lamb 1978), it would follow that the God image would generally resemble the mother more closely than the father. God is not an exalted father figure, as suggested by Freud, but rather an exalted attachment figure.

Studies of the relation between the God image and self-concept are similarly consistent with an attachment explanation. Bowlby (1973) emphasized that models of attachment figures and models of the self tend to be complementary: Children who believe that their attachment figures love, protect, and care about them, are also likely to view themselves as lovable and worthy of being cared for and protected. Similarly, people who view God as basically loving and beneficent have higher self-esteem and more positive self-concepts (Benson & Spilka 1973; Flakoll 1974; Jolley 1983; Spilka, Addison, & Rosensohn 1975).

Factor-analytic studies of God images lend further support to the hypothesis that attachment represents a central issue in people's beliefs about God. Gorsuch's (1968) hierarchical factor analysis of one hundred God-image variables revealed two second-order factors, one of which was labeled "Benevolent Deity." Items loading positively on this factor included "comforting," "loving," and "protective"; items loading negatively included "distant," "impersonal," and "inaccessible." Two of the first-order factors contributing to this higher-order factor were labeled "Kindliness" (e.g., "loving," "comforting") and the inverse of "Deisticness" (e.g., not "distant," not "impersonal," and not "inaccessible"). Spilka, Armatas, and Nussbaum (1964) found a large general factor in a similar analysis that included the items "comforting," "supporting," "protective," "strong," and "helpful." Using a very different set of descriptors, Tamayo and Desjardins (1976) found a first factor that accounted for 81 percent of the variance in ratings of God. This factor, labeled "Availability," included items such as "who gives comfort," "a warm-hearted refuge," "always ready with open arms," "who will take loving care of me," and "who is always waiting for me." It would be difficult to write a list of characteristics that better described an ideal attachment figure.

Evidence for a strong God-attachment dimension has not been confined to studies of individual differences in God images. Broen (1957) factor-analyzed responses to 133 statements about a wide array of religious attitudes and beliefs and found a large first factor labeled by two independent judges as "Nearness to God." According to Broen (1957), "Persons with high loadings on this factor would tend to feel that God was very real and constantly near and accessible. These persons feel they commune with God—'walk and talk' with Him" (p. 177). Again, this description bears a striking similarity to the defining characteristics of a secure attachment relationship.

In a different vein, Benson and Williams (1982) used cluster analysis to examine the God images of a random sample of members of the U.S. Congress. Two of the three clusters interpreted by the authors, God the attentive parent and God the companion, are described in terms strongly reminiscent of the secure base and haven functions of the secure attachment relationship. Similarly, Heller (1986) observed several "personality themes" in children's images of God that seem to illustrate attachment phenomena (although he did not interpret them in attachment terms). His God-the-therapist image refers to "an all-nurturant, loving figure," which closely resembles a secure attachment figure; two alternative God images parallel the two insecure patterns of attachment. This inconsistent-God image seems to correspond to an anxious/ambivalent attachment; and his God-the-distant-thing-in-the-sky image seems to capture avoidant attachment. Heller also noted several themes that transcend common familial and cultural influences, including intimacy (feelings of closeness to God) and omnipresence (God is "always there"). Although he found some of these themes to be enigmatic, they are not mysterious from an attachment perspective.

Religious Behavior

Attachment behaviors refer to actions designed to increase infant-mother proximity. Infant attachment behaviors have been divided into (1) signaling behaviors, such as upraised arms, babbling, and crying, and (2) approach behaviors, including clinging, cuddling, and physically moving toward the attachment figure (Bowlby 1969). Ainsworth (1982) argued that these proximal behaviors are useful indices of the attachment relationship only until the infant is approximately six months of age, at which time they are gradually supplanted by more distal behaviors. Older children are more easily satisfied with visual or verbal contact with the attachment figure in most circumstances, although especially severe distress may be alleviated only by physical proximity. For much older children and adults, mere knowledge of the availability of a potentially responsive caregiver may often suffice (Bretherton 1987). This decreasing dependence on physical contact and proximity makes possible an extension of the attachment model to a noncorporeal, imaginary attachment figure.

As part of their attempt to demonstrate similarities between infant-mother attachment and adult romantic love, Shaver et al. (1988) noted that many infant attachment behaviors bear striking resemblance to the behaviors of romantic love partners toward each other. For example, they pointed out that prolonged eye contact, cooing or talking "baby talk," and other intimate behaviors are similar to the actions displayed by infants to elicit and maintain contact with an attachment figure. Several of these behavioral dimensions suggest intriguing analogues in religion, such as raising one's arms in worship in many Pentecostal and other Christian worship services.

Glossolalia bears some resemblance to infant babbling; Oates (1967) explicitly referred to speaking in tongues as a childlike form of language. The combination of upraised arms and glossolalia is reminiscent of an infant waiting to be picked up by its mother. Further support for a view of glossolalia as an attachment behavior comes from Kildahl (1972), who reported that "more than 85 percent of tongue-speakers had experienced a clearly defined anxiety crisis preceding their speaking in tongues" (p. 57; but cf. Hine 1969, for a contrary view). Typically, this crisis involved feelings of worthlessness and powerlessness; said one, "I felt like a child who could only say 'Goo'" (Kildahl 1972:64). Kildahl (1972) reported that increased feelings of confidence and security resulted from the tongue-speaking experience, which he attributed to the glossolalics' perception that they had proof that they were loved and protected by God.

The activity of prayer presents a particularly good example of religious attachment behavior: According to Reed (1978), "Crying and calling, [by an infant] find a close parallel in supplicatory prayer. The prominent place of prayer in most religions is perhaps the most striking point of contact with Bowlby's observations" (p. 15). According to Heiler (1932), a devout person prays believing "that he [or she] speaks with a God, immediately present and personal," and "the man who prays feels himself very close to this personal God" (p. 356). This emphasis on God as a personal and accessible being with whom one communicates directly through prayer is clearly in line with an attachment interpretation.

Whereas prayer was discussed earlier in terms of God's role as a haven of safety and comfort in times of distress, at other times prayer is more suggestive of God's provision of a secure base. Young children exploring their environment check back with their mothers visually, verbally, and physically from time to time to reassure themselves that she is still available and attentive. Campos and Stenberg (1981) labeled such behavior *social referencing*. Some forms of prayer might similarly be construed as "God referencing," which provides reassurance that God remains an available and responsive secure base.

Church attendance, although clearly a multiply determined activity, is also interpretable within an attachment framework. Although many theistic religions regard God as omnipresent, these traditions still provide specific places where worshippers can go to get closer to God. It is also common for people to visit churches at times other than formal services, especially when troubled, to speak with the deity and feel its presence. Although an abstract image of God may suffice most of the time, in times of distress a more concrete image of God in a specific location may be required to restore feelings of security and comfort—just as children shift from distal to more proximal attachment behaviors in times of distress (Ainsworth 1982).

A DYNAMIC MODEL OF RELIGIOUS DEVELOPMENT AND INDIVIDUAL DIFFERENCES

In this section, I consider a dynamic model in which individual differences in religious beliefs and development may be traced to significant relationship experiences.

A Compensation Hypothesis: Substitute Attachment Figures

Given the importance of attachment processes in the life of a developing child, attachment theory suggests that children who fail to develop secure attachments with their parents, for whatever reason, may seek such attachments elsewhere. Ainsworth (1985) discussed the possibility of "parent surrogates to whom [a child] may become attached, and who may play an important role in his life, especially for those who find in them the security that they sought but could not attain with their own parents" (p. 799). She listed several such possibilities, including older siblings, other relatives, youth leaders, athletic coaches or special teachers, mentors, priests, pastors, and therapists. Although God and other supernatural figures do not appear in Ainsworth's list, they may be plausible additions.

Some fascinating illustrations of the need for and development of substitute attachment relationships among adults appear in a collection of autobiographies of lesbian nuns (Curb & Manahan 1985). A noteworthy feature of nearly all these accounts is an emphasis on the official prohibition of "particular friendships" within the convent. Although the development of such close interpersonal relationships is actively discouraged, these suggest that a need for attachment relationships is simply too strong to be eliminated by fiat. Many of these nuns turned to God, Jesus, or the Virgin Mary as attachment figures.

In a similar vein, Bowlby (1969) discussed the possibility that certain kinds of groups may be substituted for primary or secondary attachment figures, especially in older children and adults (who have greater capacity for abstract thinking). Weiss (1982) also observed that adolescents and adults "seem sometimes to display attachment to a small, cohesive, reliable and accepting group of peers rather than to an individual" (p. 177). Religious groups, and especially small cults or sects, seem likely candidates for this role.

More direct evidence for this compensation hypothesis comes from studies by Deutsch (1975) and Ullman (1989), both of whom found that a disproportionately high percentage of religious converts report a history of extreme difficulties in relationships with parents. Kirkpatrick and Shaver (1990) found in their adult sample that the incidence of sudden religious conversions was four times greater for participants reporting retrospectively avoidant maternal attachments than for those with secure or anxious/ambivalent attachments. Several other religion variables followed a similar pattern, although only for participants whose mothers were relatively nonreligious.

An interesting variation on this theme appears in the glossolalia literature. Although ample evidence is available indicating that glossolalics do not differ from nonglossolalics on most indices of psychopathology (e.g., Hine 1969; Richardson, 1973), several studies have pointed to differences between these groups in terms of personal relationships. Wood (1965, cited in Richardson 1973:203) suggested that Pentecostal people "have an uncommon degree of uncertainty concerning interpersonal relationships" and a "strong drive to feel close fellowship with others but . . . are uncertain that these interpersonal involvements will be satisfactory." Vivier (1960:382) found that glossolalics come disproportionately from "disturbed" homes and have a "tendency to cling to objects in the environment for emotional support." Measuring individual differences with the California Psychological Inventory, Plog (1965) found that the one test dimension on which glossolalics scored significantly lower than nonglossolalics was interpersonal relationships. From an attachment perspective, these results paint a picture of the glossolalic resembling the anxious/ambivalent attachment style described by Hazan and Shaver (1987) and the clingy interpersonal style described by Shaver and Rubenstein (1980). In fact, Kirkpatrick and Shaver (1992) found, using Hazan and Shaver's love-attachment typology, that people classifying themselves as anxious/ambivalent were significantly more likely than avoidant or secure lovers to report having spoken tongues at some time.

Other interesting variations of the compensation hypothesis remain to be tested. For example, to the extent that religious beliefs serve a compensatory role vis-à-vis attachment, an agnostic or atheistic stance would be expected to result from a history of satisfactory (secure) attachment relationships. This viewpoint also raises an interesting question as to whether agnosticism and atheism are psychologically similar. Would people with secure attachment histories be more likely to display mere disinterest in the notion of God or to reject the notion of God outright? A variety of intriguing hypotheses informed by attachment theory might be developed along these and similar lines.

A Correspondence Hypothesis: The Continuity of Mental Models

In contrast to the compensation hypothesis, other hypotheses may be developed from the attachment framework. For example, Bowlby's emphasis on the relative constancy of mental models throughout the life span suggests an opposite set of predictions—namely, that people's beliefs about attachment figures (including God, in this case) should directly reflect prior experience with attachment relationships. That is, we might expect people to experience a worldview and a relationship with the deity that shares the same features as their earlier parental relationships. According to this correspondence hypothesis, the security-insecurity of a person's attachment relationships with parents should predict that person's religious inclinations directly rather than inversely. Support for this hypothesis can be found in the studies, reviewed earlier, indicating that God images correlate positively with images of preferred parents and with self-concepts. Similarly, several studies show that loss of faith is associated with poor parental relationships (Bruder 1947; Caplovitz & Sherrow 1977), suggesting that atheism or agnosticism may be a direct reflection of an avoidant attachment pattern.

Kirkpatrick and Shaver (1992) found that participants who described themselves as secure in their love relationships described God as more loving, less controlling, and less distant than did avoidant lovers. In addition, the avoidant adult-attachment group contained a significantly higher proportion of agnostics than the secure and anxious/ambivalent groups. These findings are particularly intriguing in that data on childhood attachment to parents appears to support the compensation hypothesis (Kirkpatrick & Shaver 1990). Hints regarding how these various relationships may fit together were suggested by the additional finding that security of attachment to God showed a direct correspondence to security of adult love relationships, but only for participants who had reported insecure maternal attachments during childhood. It was suggested that when people undergo radical transformations of mental models of attachment from insecure to secure, all attachment relationships—including a relationship with God—are similarly affected. These findings underscore the importance of examining an individual's entire hierarchy of attachment figures and other personal relations in order to understand religious and human-relationship experience.

A fascinating set of findings that lends further support to the correspondence hypothesis comes from cross-cultural research on parenting styles and religious beliefs. Lambert, Triandis, and Wolf (1959) and Rohner (1975) reported strong correlations across cultures between the culturally dominant parenting style (measured on an accepting-rejecting dimension) and the society's beliefs about the supernatural. In particular, cultures in which "accepting" (loving, nurturing) parenting styles are predominant tend to embrace benevolent deities, whereas cultures in which "rejecting" parenting styles are common embrace malevolent deities. Rohner (1975) further noted that in societies characterized by "rejecting" parenting styles, adults and children are less emotionally responsive, less emotionally stable, and less able to become involved in affectionate relationships and they show more aggressive and hostile behavior.

Of course, the nature of the causal relationship among these variables represents a complex chicken-and-egg question, and there are obvious difficulties involved in extrapolating from cross-cultural findings to individual differences within cultures. But at least one attachment researcher (Bretherton 1985:26) noted that Rohner's general conclusions should be taken seriously: "I am particularly impressed with the fact that correlates of acceptance or rejection among societies read uncannily like the sequelae of secure and insecure attachment reported by Sroufe (1983) for a sample of preschoolers in Minnesota." Whether parallel correlations exist between parenting styles and beliefs about the supernatural across families within a given culture remains an empirical question, but one well worth pursuing.

Parenting and Religion

The literature linking parents' and children's religiosity offers yet another perspective on the potential role of attachment in religious development. A consistent finding is that the best predictor of children's religiosity is their parents' religiosity (Argyle & Beit-Hallahmi 1975). Presumably this reflects, at least in part, religious socialization. Although little else is known about the influence of other aspects of the parent-child relationship on religious development, the quality of parent-child relations may mediate this correlation. Spilka, Hood, and Gorsuch (1985) concluded from their review that children are likely to agree with their parents on religious issues if they come from a stable home in which parents fight infrequently and tend to agree with each other on other important issues and also if parent-child relationships are characterized by good communication and sincerity. Several studies suggest that loss of faith is often associated with poor parental relations (Bruder 1947; Caplovitz & Sherrow 1977).

In the present context, this can be restated as follows: Children with secure parental attachments are more likely to be strongly influenced by their parents' religious beliefs than are children with weak or insecure attachments. Kagan (1984:63) argued that "the major consequence of an attachment is to make the child receptive to the adoption of parental standards." Similarly, Minsky (1985) argued that the principal role of attachment is to establish a context for learning and modeling values and goals. The quality of childhood attachments may therefore play an important role in moderating the correlation between parents' and children's religiousness (compare Kirkpatrick & Shaver 1990).

Attachment, Religion, and Love

Since the publication of a seminal paper by Hazan and Shaver (1987), attachment theory has begun to prove itself a powerful framework for the study of close personal relationships, particularly romantic love. It is worth noting that many writers have previously observed a direct concordance between religious experience and romantic love. William James (1902), for example, compared the process of religious conversion with that of "falling in love." Pratt (1920) noted that "the convert feels the presence of a new friend who loves him and to whom he is endlessly grateful and whom he is coming to love passionately." In many cases getting converted means "falling in love with Jesus" (p. 160). Similarly, Thouless (1923) reflected on the "tendency of religious emotion to express itself in the language of human love" (p. 132), particularly among the mystics. Heller (1986) even found a romantic God-the-lover-in-Heaven image among young children's descriptions of the deity. If love is an attachment process, then perhaps so too is religion.

Although the attachment model has proved tremendously useful in the study of adult love relationships, I would suggest that the God-worshiper relationship fits the attachment model even more convincingly than does romantic love. The application of attachment to adult relationships is complicated by some important differences between adult and infant-mother relationships (Weiss 1982). First, adult relationships are typically with peers, who may or may not be perceived as a source of strength. The worshipper-God relationship, like the infant-mother relationship, is typically asymmetrical in the sense that the roles of caregiver and care receiver are clearly defined and relatively constant across time. According to Weiss (1986), with the change in attachment figure from parent to peer, "there has taken place a change in the character of the object from the awesomely powerful, usually protective, parent of childhood to a peer whose frailties, once the relationship has passed its initial idealizations, are apt to be well recognized" (p. 102).

Skolnick (1985) criticized Bowlby's emphasis on representing the attachment figure as the "stronger and wiser other" (a phrase commonly used by Bowlby), primarily because this view of the attachment figure seems inapplicable in many romantic relationships. Unlike romantic love partners or other peers, however, God retains the character of the "awesomely powerful, usually protective" attachment figure of childhood. In a word, God is the quintessential stronger and wiser other.

Second, adult attachments often involve a partner with whom a sexual relationship exists. This confounding of attachment and sex is typically absent from people's relationships with God or other religious figures. There are fascinating exceptions to this, of course, such as certain forms of mysticism (Moller 1965) and some new religious movements in which a charismatic leader (who may serve as an attachment figure) also engages in sexual activity with cult members. But in most religious traditions, relationships with God, Jesus, and other supernatural figures do not include an explicitly sexual component. The exceptions may provide interesting insights concerning the larger question of how attachment and sex are linked in adulthood (cf. Shaver et al. 1988).

CONCLUSION

Two particular criticisms of the attachment-and-religion model have commonly arisen: The theory is accused, on the one hand, of trying to explain too much and, on the other, of not explaining enough. These objections point to two sets of important issues that warrant closer scrutiny.

With respect to the first point, it is important to recognize that there is, so to speak, more to life than attachment. Religion clearly serves many psychosocial functions. For example, Spilka, Shaver, and Kirkpatrick (1985) have emphasized that religious attributions provide adherents with a sense of meaning, control, and self-esteem. Religious beliefs offer answers to otherwise unanswerable questions, moral direction, and values around which people can meaningfully organize their lives. Security and protection represent one important set of human motives among many. Perhaps the unparalleled success of religion as a human institution is owed to the fact that religious traditions have demonstrated remarkable breadth in their ability to address so many fundamental human concerns in so many ways.

It must also be recognized, however, that there is much more to attachment theory than the immediate experience of security or anxiety. More broadly, it represents a large-scale theory of personality development that emphasizes the degree to which significant emotional experiences and relationships influence one's beliefs about the world and one's position in it. The need for a haven of safety and a secure base, and one's history of successful and failed attempts to meet these needs, have far-reaching implications for individual differences across the life span. These differences, in turn, may influence religious beliefs and experiences in a diversity of ways. In this chapter, I have barely scratched the surface of attachment theory and its potential utility as a theory for the psychology of religion.

To illustrate, Bowlby's writings and empirical research on cross-generational transmission of attachment patterns suggest an important link between attachment and the complementary process of caregiving. Research on the role of religion in fostering altruism and helping behavior—a central feature of many religious traditions—might therefore be informed by an attachment perspective. For instance, Darley and Batson's (1973) finding that intrinsically religious subjects persist in trying to help a victim who has indicated no need for assistance is reminiscent of Bowlby's (1973) discussion of compulsive caregiving. As a second example, it might be hypothesized that people's ability to adopt an open, questioning, quest-oriented approach to religion (e.g., Batson & Ventis 1982) may depend on a history of secure attachment and perceptions of the availability of a (human) secure base. In contrast, dogmatic acceptance of religious tenets may provide a sense of security and comfort in the absence of a secure attachment history.

These considerations lead to the second issue regarding the degree to which an attachment model may be applicable beyond the context of Christianity and Western culture. Even within religious traditions that eschew an anthropomorphized deity, individual differences in attachment among adherents might be expected to correlate with perceptions about the nature of supernatural forces and a person's relationship to them. The findings of Lambert et al. (1959) and Rohner (1975) suggest that cross-cultural variation in supernatural imagery, which takes different forms across societies, is predictable from variations in child-rearing practices. Modal child-rearing practices in India and Japan, for example, differ greatly from their Western analogues. The "narcissistic self-motif" identified in Zen Buddhism by Schjelderup and Schjelderup (cited in Wulff 1991a) and in Indian spirituality by Kakar (1978) might, from an attachment perspective, be recast in terms of Bowlby's construct of compulsive self-reliance. This remains an intriguing question for future research.

Several characteristics of attachment theory make it a promising candidate for integrating and guiding research in the psychology of religion.

Like psychoanalytic theories, this theory is sufficiently broad to incorporate the diverse cognitive, affective, and behavioral aspects of religious belief and experience, but it is more amenable to operationalization and fits better with other scientifically oriented domains of psychology. Attachment theory also provides both normative and individual-difference perspectives, making it suitable for addressing a range of interesting and important questions about religion and its place in people's lives.

Another appealing feature of attachment theory is that it offers a less value-laden perspective on religious belief and experience than many alternative theories. It is no secret that Freud, for example, considered much of religion to be infantile and inevitably unhealthy. An attachment perspective, in which God and other religious figures are conceptualized in the context of other close relationships and their psychological functions, can provide the basis for a more scientific and less biased view of the psychology of religion. The availability of such an approach may be crucial for eliminating the taboo that appears to exist in psychology with respect to research on religion.

In addition to outlining a promising theoretical framework for the psychology of religion, a second purpose of this chapter is to try to persuade researchers interested in personal relationships, emotion, and other mainstream areas of psychology that religion is a topic with which they should be concerned. No understanding of attachment, personal relationships, stress and coping, self-esteem, loneliness, or related topics will be complete unless religious beliefs are explicitly considered. For many individuals, any account of their social-support and interpersonal-relationship networks that fails to include God would be incomplete. Moreover, beliefs about God may reveal important insights concerning issues such as (1) hierarchies of attachment figures, (2) substitute attachment figures, (3) the process of relinquishing parents as attachment figures, and (4) the various provisions offered by different types of close relationships.

At present, the psychology of religion seems estranged from the rest of academic psychology, to the detriment of both fields. The psychology of religion cannot exist as an island, divorced from the theories and methods of other areas of psychology. I believe attachment theory offers the exciting prospect of bringing together these two fields in a dynamic and mutually enriching manner.

Commentary: Development of Individual Religion

These chapters offer exciting directions for research in the development of individual religion. A decade ago, this area appeared neglected except for a few noteworthy efforts. Suddenly, the massive pioneering researches of Tamminen (1991) appeared, along with Hyde's (1990) monumental overview of the field. Concurrently, new vistas have been opened up by Oser and Gmünder (1991) and by their colleague K. Helmut Reich, who is represented here in Chapter 9. The article by Kirkpatrick that is also included here (Chapter 10) has clearly excited many researchers.

In Chapter 8, Elkind creatively correlates the development of need capacities in the child with religious growth. His discussions of conservation, representation, relations, and comprehension are really guidelines for a much-needed, more rigorous development of these criteria in the religious domain. Because such criteria will represent both the "forms" of this "neo-Piagetian" system and its contents, we must recognize that much more work has been directed toward the former material than the latter. An entrée is thus made to identifying the substance of childhood thoughts in the domain of faith. Additional significant insight could be gained regarding the sources in the home and culture of such cognitive elements. Elkind's trailblazing effort should stimulate progressive work in the developmental psychology of religion.

Reich is a scholar with a rare integrative turn of mind. He has always offered research perspectives that offer breadth and counter narrowness. The elements he selects for incorporation into a "unified theory of religious development" represent a lifetime of work for researchers. Each of the forty-eight cells in Table 9.1 suggests a research direction. This is supplemented by the obvious vertical developmental dimension. Further, we should not forget the necessity of correlation and coordination on the table's horizontal dimension. If one wants the "big picture," Reich has provided it.

Kirkpatrick's attachment theory approach constitutes a panorama for research, a fair amount of which the author himself denotes. In particular, witness the interpretations of glossolalia, prayer, and church attendance, among other possibilities. The notion of compensation and substitute attachment is worthy of study not only from the vantage point of religious development but from the interpersonal realm of social psychology. The language of attachment in religion is well illustrated by Kirkpatrick and presages the significance of an exhaustive study of such communication patterns by age and gender, among other possibilities. By overlaying attachment theory on Reich's categories of the emotional domain, major age-related factors, the role of the major religious orientations, and final effects on religiousness provide an extensive theoretical focus with much specification for research.

One can look at attachment as a major aspect of coping with life. A la Gorsuch's article in this volume (Chapter 2), attachment might be examined in a motivational mode and expanded in an organized manner relative to cognition and the meaning of schema (McIntosh, Chapter 13), and attitude (Hill, Chapter 14). Attachment theory speaks not only to connection in many aspects of living, not the least of which are religious, but theoretically, it should unlock many research gates, stimulating inquiry and analysis of central importance to the psychology of religion.

PART 5

Believing Is Seeing: How Religion Shapes Our Worlds

11

ATTRIBUTION THEORY AND THE PSYCHOLOGY OF RELIGION

WAYNE PROUDFOOT AND PHILLIP R. SHAVER

The study of religious beliefs and experience has not been well integrated into academic psychology. Despite a promising start, with James's *Varieties of Religious Experience*, the psychology of religion has been ignored by most research psychologists. The cognitive emphasis in the social sciences might contribute a new approach to the psychology of religion. In sociology and anthropology, there is concern with the cognitive function of religious symbols, institutions, and practices—with the ways in which these allow people to make sense of their experience (Bellah 1970b; Douglas 1966; Geertz 1973). Although rooted in the work of Weber, this orientation stands in sharp contrast to the dominant approaches of theologians, philosophers, and social scientists during the first half of this century. Little and Twiss (1973) thus argue that religion functions as a cognitive system to reduce anxiety over problems of interpretability raised by "boundary situations"—anomalous experiences and events that bring people face to face with the limits of their worlds, that is, with birth, death, inexplicable suffering, or challenges to the moral code of a culture.

Thus far, however, these formulations have been vague at the psychological level of analysis. How do crises of interpretability arise? What kinds of interpretation serve to reduce anxieties associated with these crises? What is the relation between cognitive, emotional, and volitional components of religious phenomena? Some answers may be provided by

Reprinted and edited with permission of authors and publisher from *Journal for the Scientific Study of Religion*, 14 (1975), 317–330.

work in social psychology, where topics that captured James's attention—beliefs, the self, emotions, personal experience—are again moving toward center stage. These issues are now being organized around attribution theory (Kelley 1967; Shaver 1975), a theory designed to explain how people perceive and account for their own behavior.

ATTRIBUTION THEORY

There is no firm agreement on the overall form of attribution theory. It is actually a loose coalition of smaller theories, the mutual compatibility of which was not recognized until a few years ago. Members of the coalition share a concern with the way people perceive the causes of their own bodily states and behavior. To discuss the relevance of the theory to religion, we provide a brief account of recent developments, relying heavily on the work of Schachter (1971), Bem (1972), and Weiner (1972).

Schachter's Theory of Emotion

Schachter (1971) began by reconsidering William James's statement that emotion is the perception of bodily changes (James 1890:449). James gave several examples to illustrate his meaning: A person runs away from a threatening stimulus (e.g., a bear) and only then perceives that he is afraid. Visceral stirrings precede realization of personal anxiety, fear, or excitement. Later, Cannon (1927, 1929) cast doubt on James's theory by noting that the same visceral changes occur in both different emotional and nonemotional states and that the artificial induction of visceral changes typical of strong emotions does not automatically produce the emotions.

Schachter decided that the main physiological determinant of emotional experience was not specific visceral or muscular stimulation but a general and diffuse pattern of excitement or arousal in the sympathetic nervous system. This can be induced experimentally by injecting a person with adrenaline, thereby producing heart palpitations, tremor, face flushing, and other recognizable symptoms. An early study by Marañon (1924), however, raised a problem for Schachter's formulation. In that study, a majority of subjects (Ss) receiving an adrenaline injection showed these physical symptoms of autonomic arousal without experiencing emotion. Schachter thus concluded that another determinant was required for true emotion: a cognitive label, interpretation, or attribution. According to this two-factor theory, an adrenaline injection will result in emotion only if the aroused person does not know where the symptoms come from.

This idea, which may seem implausible, has received empirical support. In a classic study by Schachter and Singer (1962), Ss who had received a disguised adrenaline injection interpreted their feelings as euphoria or anger, depending on the set created by a confederate of the experimenter. Those told to expect arousal side effects (heart palpitations, tremor, and so on) were much less likely to share the actor's mood. Later experiments have shown that arousal created by drugs, physical exercise, or natural hormonal charges can be labeled anything from euphoria, humor, love, and sexual attraction to hunger, anxiety, conflict, anger, and menstrual distress.

It seems quite plausible, given these results, that some religious experiences are due to diffuse emotional states that are given a particular interpretation. Although Schachter refers only to diffuse arousal states, we would contend that any generalized physiological change elicits evaluative needs and requires labeling. For example, certain classical meditation exercises function to decrease heart rate and to dampen rather than arouse autonomic functions. Laboratory-induced sensory deprivation has resulted in reports that are often similar to descriptions of mystical experience. For our purposes, any significant physiological change from equilibrium could have the effects that Schachter ascribes to arousal and if the person is uninformed as to the origin of the change, it will give rise to the need for a label or interpretation. Throughout this essay, we use the term "arousal" in the interests of brevity, but it should be remembered that other physiological changes might be involved as well.

Self-perception Theory

Self-perception theory (Bem 1972) is concerned with the ways people monitor themselves and form self-concepts. It extends Schachter's notion of interpretation to include behavior. According to the theory, evaluative or interpretive needs are salient not only in situations of unexplained arousal states but intermittently throughout the course of all human activity. As we shall see in our consideration of Weiner's theory of motivation, particular interpretations may affect future behavior that, in turn, calls for interpretation.

The central propositions of self-perception theory are as follows:

Individuals come to "know" their own attitudes, emotions, and other internal states partially by inferring them from observations of their own overt behavior and/or the circumstances in which this behavior occurs. Thus, to the extent that internal cues are weak, ambiguous, or uninterpretable, the individual is functionally in the same position as an outside observer, an observer who must necessarily rely upon those same cues to infer the individuals' inner states. (Bem 1972:2)

This theory explains results from attitude change experiments designed to test the theory of cognitive dissonance (Brehm & Cohen 1962; Festinger 1957). It had been discovered, for example, that people who are paid a small amount to make a counterattitudinal statement will later agree more with the statement than will people paid a larger amount (Festinger & Carlsmith 1959). Bem showed that this might be due to an inference made by the participants on the basis of observing their own behavior. These inferences might be expressed as follows: (under the low incentive condition) "I must have believed the statement I made if I was willing to make it for such a small fee"; (under the high incentive condition) "I must really not have believed the statement if they had to pay me so much to make it."

Later experiments provide other examples. In one, children were induced to believe that they were moral by seeing themselves resist a forbidden toy (Lepper 1971).

Bem (1972) reviews many studies that support self-perception theory. For our purposes it is sufficient to note that individuals, when viewed in experimental circumstances, are not always the best judge of the actual causes of their own behavior. The judgments made, however, are practical and powerfully affect future behavior.

Weiner's Attributional Approach to Motivation

An important personality dimension described as "internal versus external locus of control of reinforcement" (Rotter 1966) is also potentially relevant to the study of religion. People who score at the internal end of the dimension tend to believe that they are responsible for most of what happens in their lives; they think that their decisions and effort make a difference. People who score at the external end think that others' decisions or some external force such as chance or luck are more important than their own efforts in determining their lives. Rotter and subsequent investigators have found that scores on the internal-external dimension predict a wide range of attitudes and behaviors, from level of aspiration in achievement situations to participation in civil rights demonstrations.

Weiner (1972) has incorporated this dimension into an attribution theory of achievement motivation. He indicates that high achievers attribute successes and failures to effort, an internal variable under their own control. Low achievers attribute success to easiness of the task, an external variable, and attribute failure to low ability, an internal variable that is not under their own control. The result of these differing attributions of success or failure is that following a failure, high achievers typically try to succeed through increased effort, whereas low achievers usually give up.

Weiner and Sierad (1974) attempted to see if these characteristic attributions could be altered experimentally. Ss were either given a placebo pill or not, depending on the experimental condition to which they had been randomly assigned. One-half in each condition were high in achievement motivation, one-half were low. The experimenter led the "pill" Ss to believe that the drug they had ingested might interfere with "psychomotor coordination." Actually, it had no real effect. Following this manipulation, Ss took parts of a test requiring eye-hand coordination and were made to believe that they performed poorly. The main purpose of the experiment was to determine what effects the pill, perceived as an external block on success, would have on performance.

The results were striking. High achievers in the "no-pill" control groups increased their effort after failure and consequently performed better; low achievers, in contrast, started to give up. This agreed with earlier studies. In the "pill" condition, however, high achievers, apparently believing that effort would no longer assure success, started to give up, whereas low achievers, perhaps relieved that they did not have to blame themselves for failure, continued to make an effort. Characteristic behavior patterns were reversed by making different interpretations appropriate. This work provides direct evidence for the claim that differential attributions have important consequences for behavior.

One of the functions of religious doctrines and symbols is the attribution of power and responsibility to the actor or to natural or supernatural forces that are, in different degrees, beyond one's control. If we can understand the conditions under which such attributions are made, we can increase our knowledge of how these symbols and doctrines function.

ATTRIBUTION PROCESSES AND RELIGIOUS EXPERIENCE

A Classic Case of Conversion

Attribution theory is attractive to the student of religion because, unlike other theoretical approaches in psychology, it deals directly with a person's interpretation of experience. Moreover, some of the phenomena already studied in the laboratory bear striking resemblance to those described by religious writers.

One example is the conversion experience of Stephen Bradley, presented at length by James in *Varieties of Religious Experience*. Bradley had just returned from a revival service in which the preacher had been unusually forceful. Bradley was impressed but claimed to be unmoved.

I will now relate my experience of the power of the Holy Spirit which took place on the same night. Had any person told me previous to this that I could have experienced the power of the Holy Spirit in the manner which I did, I could not have believed it, . . . I went directly home after the meeting, and when I got home I wondered what made me feel so stupid. I retired to rest soon after I got home, and felt indifferent to things or religion until I began to be exercised by the Holy Spirit, which began in about five minutes after, in the following manner:

At first, I began to feel my heart beat very quick all of the sudden, which made me at first think that perhaps something is going to ail me, though I was not alarmed, for I felt no pain. My heart increased in its beating, which soon convinced me that it was the Holy Spirit from the effect it had on me. I began to feel exceedingly happy and humble, and such a sense of unworthiness as I never felt before. . . . My heart seemed as if it would burst, but it did not stop until I felt as if I was unutterably full of the love and grace of God. In the meantime, while thus exercised, a thought arose in my mind, what can it mean? and all at once, as if to answer it, my memory became exceedingly clear, and it appeared to me just as if the New Testament was placed open before me, eighth chapter of Romans, and as light as if some candle was held for me to read the 26th and 27th verses of that chapter, and I read these words: "The spirit that helpeth out infirmities with groanings that cannot be uttered." And all the time that my heart was a beating, it made me groan like a person in distress, which was not very easy to stop, though I was in no pain at all, and my brother being in a bed in another room, came and opened the door, and asked me if I had got the toothache. I told him no, and that he might get to sleep. . . .

I now feel as if I had discharged my duty by telling the truth, and hope by the blessing of God, it may do some good to all who shall read it. He has fulfilled his promise in sending The Holy Spirit down into our hearts, or mine at least, and I now defy all the Deists and Atheists in the world to shake my faith in Christ. (James 1902:190–193)

Bradley's testimony reads like a textbook example designed to illustrate Schachter's theory. Bradley notices his heart rate suddenly increase. He looks for its cause and, having just returned from a revival, attributes it to the Holy Spirit. The palpitations are thus assigned to an external force, not to "pain" or an "ailment" and thus present no need for alarm. But he still must make sense of this force. A thought arises: What can it mean? He sees a passage in Romans that confirms the attribution of his stirrings to the Holy Spirit. Eventually this leads him to "defy all the Deists and Atheists in the world to shake (his) faith in Christ." What began as a mysterious emotional experience ends with attributional certainty.

Bradley, like so many prospective devotees before and since, could not understand his feelings in naturalistic terms. Religious symbols offered him an explanation that was compatible with both his experience and his former beliefs. He did not consider explanations involving Krishna, Zeus, or the Koran. The content of the scripture and the experience of being moved or physiologically aroused were confidently linked together. These are the two components of emotion described by Schachter. It seems likely that religious symbols and doctrines often serve as labels for experiences of arousal that initially appear to be anomalous. As in Schachter's experiments, individuals seek plausible explanations for their feelings among whatever explanations are available in the environment.

The experience of Pentecost among the disciples of Jesus may be amenable to a similar interpretation. The disciples gathered together for the first time since Jesus' death. The setting was a religious one. Suddenly a sound came from heaven, and the disciples experienced voices speaking through them. Luke reports, "All were amazed and perplexed, saying to one another, 'what does this mean?'" (RSV Acts 2:12–13). Some observers provided a naturalistic explanation, accusing the disciples of drunkenness. But Peter, noting the early hour, rejects this interpretation and quotes from the prophet Joel: "And in the last days it shall be, God declares, that I will pour out my spirit upon all flesh, and your sons and your daughters shall prophesy, and your young men shall see visions, and your old men shall dream dreams" (RSV Acts 2:17). This interpretation carries the authority of the Hebrew prophets. It accounts for an arousing experience that was unexplained. It relates the disciples' shared experience to Yahweh's promise and their conviction of its fulfillment in Jesus, a tradition and a conviction that had recently been threatened by Jesus' death and apparent defeat.

We have cited two examples that can be illuminated by attribution theory. A recent controversial experiment in the psychology of religion can also be similarly interpreted. Pahnke (1966) attempted to induce experimentally some form of mystical experience with the aid of psilocybin. In the setting of a Good Friday service, Ss received either psilocybin or a mild control drug, nicotinic acid. The Ss receiving the hallucinogen labeled their experiences in religious terms to a significantly greater extent than those who had received the nicotinic acid, and they reported significantly greater coincidence of their experience with nine characteristics previously gleaned from reports of classical mystics. Many have cited Pahnke's experiment, along with the research of Wasson (1971), LaBarre (1972), and others, to suggest that the chance discovery of natural hallucinogens might have provided the basic experience that underlies all notions of the sacred, the holy, or the goals of religious striving.

Bowker (1973) has recently appealed to Schachter's work in order to *criticize* attempts to account for religion by appeal to some physiological mechanism, such as the effects of hallucinogens. Bowker employs Schachter's theory to argue that hallucinogens might account for some cases of physiological arousal but that a cognitive interpretation is necessary to provide a religious experience. The notion that the setting is influential in forming the experience is one that Pahnke and other experimenters have always affirmed. But most have not claimed that the activity of psychedelic agents is limited to diffuse physiological change. Pahnke's experimental design parallels that of Schachter, with the focus on a different dependent variable. Schachter attempted to hold the arousal agent constant and to manipulate the cognitive setting. Pahnke sought a constant cognitive context (the Good Friday service) and manipulated the arousal agent, which thus led him to attribute different experimental reports to that agent.

Bowker calls attention to the fact, omitted in the published accounts, that one of Pahnke's Ss seems to have been immune to the hallucinogens because of a firmly held naturalistic interpretation. This subject was skeptical from the outset and did not report any of the characteristics of religious experience. Although statistically unimportant, the case does provide some evidence for a Schachterian interpretation. The subject was unwilling to adopt the attributions suggested by the context, and thus the psychedelic experience was not labeled mystical or religious. This raises serious questions about Pahnke's inference that mystical experience is caused by some quality of hallucinogens. It may be that Pahnke's psilocybin functioned only as an agent of autonomic arousal, differing only quantitatively from the arousal provided by the nicotinic acid. The attributional component appears to be the crucial factor in an experience that is felt to be religious.

The issues raised by such experimentation are fundamental to an understanding of religious experience. Phenomenologists of religion have attempted to describe the basic characteristics of the experience of the holy or the sacred, bracketing insofar as is possible any interpretative structure of their own. Attribution theory would suggest that labeling and interpretation are fundamental to religious experience. A related point appears in Smart's (1965) critique of Zaehner's (1957) typology of mysticisms. According to Smart, Zaehner mistakenly posits substantial distinctions between different mystical experiences and ignores the role of interpretation and cultural factors in producing diverse doctrinal results from a common experience.

In the case of Stephen Bradley, our information is insufficient to account for his initial arousal. Perhaps it was the excitement of the revival meeting, though he claims to have been unaffected at the time. Relative to the disciples, it is not surprising that their first meeting following the death of their teacher, in the setting of the religious festival of Pentecost, should be a moving one. Anger, resentment, fear, despair, uncertainty, and the excitement and mutual support of being reunited may all have been involved. In the Good Friday experiment, the agent of arousal has been isolated by experimental manipulation.

What might be responsible for the initial arousal or turmoil required by the attribution approach in "natural" settings in which religious experiences are reported? Many exotic religious systems emphasizing disciplines aiming at mystical experience are attractive to adolescents and postadolescents. In this society, adolescence is characterized by release from the constraints of familial and traditional authorities, often accompanied by resentment or anger, new sexual experiences, conflicting demands and pressures, and experimentation with drugs. Any or all of these might produce diffuse tension and arousal that to the adolescent have no clear explanation. Recent evidence shows a high incidence of reports of mystical experience among middle-aged males, particularly among the relatively well educated (Greeley & McCready 1975). Concurrently, there has been a spate of articles describing the crises of middle age, the experience of meaninglessness in one's vocation, and the lack of commitment to goals that were uncritically striven for earlier. It is understandable that such crises would be more acute for the educated person, who is more likely to engage in work as vocation rather than occupation and to reflect on the meaning and value of that work. Experiences of this sort in the face of imminent death or the threat of death have been reported frequently. Common to adolescence, middle-aged crises, and the facing of death is the breakdown of ordinary cognitive systems of action and rules for the resolution of conflict. Religions are particularly attractive at such times because they are total systems, providing comprehensive interpretations of experience. These preempt, and thus render relatively insignificant, the conflicts and cares of mundane life, because they include explicit attention to the relation between belief and action.

A Contemporary Example: Nichiren Shoshu

We have recently been observing various religious groups in New York City in order to see how well attribution theory seems to fit the phenomena of religious experience. Such observations are crude, impressionistic, and subject to bias, but they may eventually lead to more rigorous tests of our ideas. We will focus briefly on one group of particular interest, Nichiren Shoshu. This is one of the fastest growing of Japan's "new religions." A Buddhist sect, it is committed to spreading the message that salvation can be attained by faith in the Lotus Sutra, especially by repeated chanting of the title of that sutra: *Nam myoho renge kyo*. A typical meeting of an American Nichiren group consists of about an hour of chanting, a

short break for sidewalk evangelism (*shakubuku*), additional chanting, testimonials, and questions and answers about the doctrine and practice of
the movement, followed by a strong appeal for commitment from the new
prospects. Testimonials provide an opportunity for different members of
the group to interpret their own experience within the supportive context
of the meeting. The central activity of both public and private worship
(chanting the *Daimoku*) is completely standardized and is almost free of
cognitive content. Even for Japanese members, the phrase is a title that
has no propositional meaning ("Adoration to the Lotus of the Wonderful
Law"). The contents of the sutra itself, of which this is the title, remain
unknown to most American adherents. The chanting is directed toward
the *Gohonzon*, a black box containing a small scroll on which is printed a
copy of a mandala by Nichiren. Thus, the devotee begins with an attributional tabula rasa, fervently chanting meaningless syllables before a
"black box."

The service opens with an hour of chanting that appears to arouse the
devotees and to create a strong sense of participation in a group effort.
Many religious communities urge prospective converts to engage in ritual action or discipline before they acquaint themselves with the beliefs of
the faith. Yogic exercises, martial arts, chanting "Hare Krishna" or "Nam
myoho renge kyo," ingesting drugs or embarking on pilgrimages to
sacred shrines are all examples. Each of these engages an individual in
actions that increase susceptibility to the appropriation of justifying and
explaining beliefs. The activity is strongly commended to the prospective
convert with only the most rudimentary reasons: "Try it. It will change
your life." Curiosity about the belief system is initially discouraged.
Emphasis is placed entirely on the efficacy of the activity. When we
inquired about the meaning of the chant, we were told that this should
concern us only after we had experienced the power of the *Gohonzon* to
produce benefits in our lives. This suggests that the beliefs eventually satisfy adherents because they make sense of an activity to which they have
already committed themselves and for which they as yet have insufficient
justification. Such a view is related to Bem's interpretation of experiments
in which Ss engaged in activities with insufficient justification and later
attributed increased significance to these activities in order to make sense
of their actions.

Once the attribution is made, confirming evidence is much easier to
find. At one session, the leader invited a new prospect to chant for just one
hundred days and see what would happen. Chanting involves, initially,
an hour or more both morning and evening. If one decides to try this
"experimentally," the rearrangement of daily life and the persistent chanting, which cannot be justified on any other grounds, presents a situation
that is quite salient. It is likely that after one hundred days the potential

convert will be attracted by a set of beliefs that give meaning to the "meaningless" activity in which the convert has been engaged and around which life has been reordered.

The testimonials are especially interesting. Two examples will be recounted here. A young man explained that he had recently suffered from test anxiety during a college math exam. He was unable to concentrate and perceived himself as failing. Rather than simply giving up or fighting himself to gain control of his attention, he began to chant "Nam myoho renge kyo" and put his trust in the rhythm of the universe. Suddenly, he became calm and the answers came to him as if from outside. Notice the similarity between this experience and the case of high test anxiety Ss in Weiner and Sierad's experiment who were given an external reason for failure. They could relax and keep trying, since the outcome would not directly reflect on them. His report was greeted with enthusiastic applause by his fellow chanters, who encouraged him to make similar interpretations and reports thereafter.

This relatively simple testimony, typical of experiences and interpretations in many religious traditions, combines both the labeling of a state of physiological arousal and the attribution of causality to an external source. The former labeling, stemming (we would say) from test anxiety, is reinterpreted as "being out of harmony with the universe." Chanting is therefore indicated, and it allows one to give up the struggle and let the burden be borne by the rhythms of the universe. The obsessive focus on the self and its possibility of failing is removed, and relaxation occurs. After the feat, success is attributed to an outside power. A changed cognitive set produces the relaxed state, but this process depends on trust in an external power. This willingness to trust may at first be born out of despair at no other alternative, but following one success, the convert will be more willing to put trust in the efficacy of the chant whenever a similar situation arises.

A second testimonial was given by a woman who had been chanting for two years when she was stricken by severe asthma. She continued to chant and was fortunate enough to find a clinic in Manhattan where her asthma was cured. She was elated and attributed the good fortune to her continued chanting. When asked by a skeptical member of the audience why she had contracted asthma after chanting for two years, she replied in all seriousness, "You don't know how much bad karma I had to work out of my previous life." This example is representative of statements made by adherents of most religions. Most, if not all, such systems have a theodicy that enables the devotee to interpret events that are potentially discouraging as further evidence for the truth of the system and for the efficacy of appropriate religious action. Anything negative that happens is attributed to bad karma or the forces of evil and can be countered only by chanting, prayer, sacrifice, or exorcism. Even among the well educated and unusually nontraditional group of forty thousand respondents studied by Wuthnow and Glock (1974), approximately 40 percent agreed that "God always answers prayer, but His answer may not be ours." Such flexible and comprehensive attributions allow people to "discover" order in seemingly chaotic and arbitrary events.

Many of the religious systems currently gaining in popularity are characterized by their encouragement of devotees to attribute responsibility to external forces. Similar external attributions can successfully overcome test anxiety (Weiner and Sierad 1974). There is also recent evidence for the relief of the symptoms of reactive depression by external attributions (Klein, Fencil-Morse, & Seligman 1974). The need to remove the mantle of responsibility may be particularly strong for individuals in our culture, as the Judeo-Christian tradition has increasingly emphasized individual responsibility. Supportive structures are fewer, experiences more diverse, and choices are demanded with fewer guidelines than in the past. It is tempting to find shelter in a faith that offers clear goals and a systematic ordering of life events. Cults celebrating Krishna-consciousness, Nichiren Shoshu, astrology, the I Ching, and the Jesus movement all share the characteristic that devotees are encouraged to give up the struggle for personal meaning, values, and fulfillment and to submit to a ready-made system. Attribution of responsibility for the flow of events is shifted from the isolated ego to the stars, the Lord, the Ching, the ritual, or the chant.

POSSIBILITY OF FURTHER RESEARCH

We have shown that attribution theory can provide plausible post hoc accounts of particular reports of religious experience. But students of religion do not suffer from a dearth of such armchair explanations. On the contrary, the problem is one of discriminating among an embarrassing wealth of hypotheses. Only careful measurement and a degree of experimental control can accomplish this.

We described earlier the ways in which some members of Nichiren Shoshu come to interpret events in their lives as evidence for the efficacy of chanting. Recently, we conducted a pilot study in which several young adults were asked to chant daily and keep diaries describing their experiences. Some of the diaries clearly show that people, even without the support offered by authentic Nichiren groups, begin to interpret the causes of feelings and events in their lives in terms of the power of chanting. Some diaries show how cynicism or commitment to naturalistic explanations blocks the attribution of special powers to chanting.

Taking cues from Schachter, it should be possible to transform such a study into a true experiment. Ss who had been randomly assigned to informed, uninformed, and misinformed conditions—ethics permitting—might receive a disguised agent of arousal (e.g., caffeine) in a controlled setting. In each condition one-third of the Ss could be exposed to a context emphasizing a particular set of religious symbols (e.g., a Christian Pentecostal worship service) and one-third to a context in which another set of symbols was salient (e.g., an Indian setting in which a guru was instructing his devotees). The remaining Ss would be placed in a more "neutral," naturalistic setting. If the arousal agent were properly disguised and the settings properly constructed, we would expect uninformed Ss in the two religious attribution conditions to feel "moved" and attribute their response to the context in which they found themselves. Ss in the naturalistic condition should interpret feelings in naturalistic terms, just as contemporary agnostic meditators interpret the relaxing effects of meditation

This is just an example—perhaps an oversimplified one. In general, experimental studies of religion could be modeled after several of the more important attribution experiments. Of course, hypotheses derived from attribution theory could also be tested in natural settings.

Attribution theory, with its emphasis on beliefs and interpretations of experience, provides a natural path into the realm of religion. In fact, if it is to account for the beliefs and explanations of real people, it cannot omit consideration of religious claims. This fact will no doubt have implications for the study of religion as well as for psychology. For example, social scientists are divided on the issue of secularization. Some contend that religion is declining, whereas others claim that only its forms are changing. We would argue that the labeling and interpretation of experience is perennial and that it may take forms that either are or are not traditionally associated with religious symbol systems. Conversions *from* such a system would follow much the same form as conversion *to* the system. Both result from anomalous experiences followed by self-perception and monitoring, ultimately leading to the adoption of a new set of attributions. One interpretation is given up only in exchange for another. The dissolution of religious faith, then, should not be seen as a gradual diminishing of concerns with ultimate meaning, purpose, and evaluation, but rather as the adoption of a new set of attributions.

As Bowker (1973) has argued, recent work in the social sciences has made cognitive claims and their evaluation more, rather than less, important in the study of religion. Such concern has not occurred to the same degree in religion itself. The relative validity of conflicting theoretical interpretations, the weighing of evidence, and the attending to questions of the truth or falsity of beliefs are being restored to their central place in the understanding of religion. Although it is neutral with respect to the ultimate validity of religious beliefs, attribution theory directs the attention of researchers to the cognitive claims of believers. Ironically, the importance of philosophical and theological interpretive schemes may be defended by social scientists at a time when many students of religion are attempting to explain religious beliefs in terms of noncognitive needs and forces.

12

A General Attribution Theory for the Psychology of Religion

BERNARD SPILKA, PHILLIP R. SHAVER,
AND LEE A. KIRKPATRICK

Around the world, in all periods of recorded history, theologies have told how the universe was created, why humans occupy a special place in the scheme of things, why seasonal changes and natural disasters occur, why some people triumph while others fail, and why everyone must occasionally suffer and eventually die. One task for the psychology of religion is to characterize the ways in which people use such religious explanations. Informal observation suggests that not everyone relies on them to the same extent and that not even the most religious people (at least in our culture) explain every occurrence in religious terms. There must be, then, factors that determine when religious explanations are appropriate. Moreover, there is a host of interpretive options within every religious framework—God's mercy, God's justice, saints, guardian angels, the devil, correctly or incorrectly executed rituals, effective or ineffective prayers, right or wrong conduct, to name a few from the Judeo-Christian tradition. What determines which, if any, of these causes will be used when a person attempts to account for a particular event?

In recent years, social psychologists have made considerable progress in understanding how people explain everyday occurrences in secular

Reprinted and edited with permission of authors and publisher from *Journal for the Scientific Study of Religion*, 24 (1985), 1–20.

terms, and these efforts have been consolidated under the general rubric of "attribution theory" (e.g., Jones et al. 1971a; Kelley 1967; Shaver 1975). This "theory"—actually a congeries of smaller theories, each designed to account for a particular attributional phenomenon—provides a rich starting point for an examination of religious explanations.

The application to religious phenomena of certain subcategories of attribution theory, namely, those dealing with emotion (Schachter 1964), self-perception (Bem 1972), and task performance (Weiner 1974), has been explored theoretically by Proudfoot and Shaver (1975) and empirically by Imhoff and Malony (1979) and Spradlin and Malony (1981), among others. Attribution theory also applies to the perception of events in the outside world such as economic fluctuations, accidents, and wars. For this reason, some have gone beyond Proudfoot and Shaver's analysis of personal experiences to view religious attributions as part of one's overall explanatory efforts (Gorsuch & Smith 1983; Pargament & Sullivan 1981; Ritzema 1979; Spilka & Schmidt 1983). To these authors, religion provides a broad-scale "meaning system" for interpreting the whole range of life events, not just a framework for labeling internal emotional states. What is needed, then, is a more general application of attribution theory to religious phenomena.

The purpose of this chapter is to integrate existing theoretical efforts, extend them by incorporating more of the attribution literature and more of the existing empirical psychology of religion, and begin organizing them into a formal attribution theory for the psychology of religion. By "formal" we mean that axioms, corollaries, and derivations will be stated explicitly. This formal approach should increase the theory's clarity and testability and make it easier to supplement and extend through future theoretical analysis and empirical research.

General Attribution Theory

All attribution theories begin with the assumption that people seek to make sense of their experiences, to understand the causes of events. Stated formally, this assumption becomes

> A1.   People seek to explain experiences and events by attributing them to causes, that is, by "making causal attributions."

In addition to this general statement, several considerations deserve mention. To begin with, both common sense and research findings indicate that more than one cause may operate with respect to a given event. In Kelley's (1967) three-factor model of the attribution process, various causal weights can be placed on "individuals," "entities," "modalities," and their interactions. We therefore propose a corollary to Axiom 1:

> C1.1.   Often, an event or experience has many possible and perhaps compatible causes, in which case the attributor's task is to choose among them or rank them in terms of relative importance or causal impact.

Other considerations arise when the causal agent is a human (or humanlike) actor rather than an impersonal object or event; such cases have been the primary focus of attribution research to date. Specifically, many researchers (e.g., Heider 1958; Jones & Nisbett 1971b) argue that people tend to attribute events to enduring dispositions and traits of actors. In fact, the tendency to underestimate environmental forces is so pervasive that it has been labeled the "fundamental attribution error" (Ross 1977). Because of its prevalence in the literature, this special case warrants a second corollary to Axiom 1:

> C1.2.   In cases where the presumed causal agent is a human or humanlike actor, attributions are frequently made to some enduring trait(s) or other characteristic(s) of the actor.

Another special consideration is that many human actions are intentional and goal directed. Buss (1978) has suggested that such actions may be explained by observers in terms of causes ("that which brings about a change") or reasons ("that for which a change is brought about"). This distinction is exemplified in a study by Bulman and Wortman (1977) in which paraplegics and quadriplegics were interviewed about their accidents. Many saw their fate as willed by God for a variety of reasons such as teaching them a lesson or setting an example for others; in contrast, others attributed their accidents to conditions (causes) that had no purpose. We recognize this distinction in a third corollary to Axiom 1:

> C1.3.   In cases where the presumed causal agent is an actor, attributions are frequently made to the actor's reason(s) or intention(s).

Having introduced some basic attribution concepts, we turn to the issues of why attributions are made and what functions they serve for those who make them.

Why Do People Make Attributions?

Most traditional approaches to attribution theory (e.g., Shaver 1975) have focused on two aspects of the attribution process, specifically, a general desire to seek meaning in the world and an attempt to control and predict events. Several writers (e.g., Greenwald 1980; Spilka 1982) suggest that, in addition to these factors, attributions are made to maintain or enhance self-esteem. Recent field studies of the attributions of cancer victims (Taylor 1983) and accident victims (Bulman & Wortman 1977) have focused on these same factors. We therefore propose the following axiom:

A2. The attribution process is motivated by (1) a need or desire to perceive events in the world as meaningful, (2) a need or desire to predict or control events, and (3) a need or desire to protect, maintain, and enhance one's self-concept and self-esteem.

The observation that people seek meaningful explanations has a long history. Aristotle opened his *Metaphysics* with the assertion that "all men by nature desire to know." Dewey (1929) spoke of a "quest for certainty," Frankl (1963) of a "search for meaning," and Maslow (1970) of the "desire to know and understand." Motivational theorists within psychology have postulated exploration and curiosity drives (Berlyne 1960; Bindra 1959), and White (1966) has speculated that "the nervous system might have an interest, so to speak, in learning about the environment for its own sake" (p. 247). As a corollary to Axiom 2, then, we propose:

C2.1. Attributional activity consists in part of an individual's attempt to understand events and interpret them in terms of some broad meaning-belief system.

Although several of the above theorists portray the search for meaning and understanding as an end in itself, others suggest that the latent goal in seeking knowledge is to maintain effective control over the environment and hence over one's experiences or outcomes (Kelley 1971a). Kelley and Thibaut (1969:6) noted that attributions represent an integral part of "successful problem-solving and coping with the demands of the environment." The idea that organisms seek knowledge of their environments in order to predict and control future outcomes, particularly when threatened, is well established (e.g., Seligman 1975). Some theorists have suggested that the "intrinsic" motive for knowing may have evolved from the more instrumental or "extrinsic" motive of control and prediction (White 1966). Much research shows that attribution processes reflect this need or desire; for example, people attribute more control and power of prediction to themselves than is warranted by objective circumstances (e.g., Langer 1975; Wortman 1975, 1976). In short,

C2.2. Attributional activity consists in part of an individual's attempt to maintain effective control over events and experiences, in order to increase the probability of positive outcomes and avoid negative outcomes.

Self-esteem and self-concept are central to nearly all human behavior and motivation (Epstein 1984; Wylie 1974). Many theorists postulate generalized drives toward self-enhancement, as, for example, in Goldstein's (1939) and Maslow's (1970) "self-actualization," Bandura's (1977) "self-efficacy," and White's (1959) "competence motivation." With respect to attributions in particular, there is considerable support for the idea that attributions are influenced by efforts to maintain and enhance self-esteem. This "attributional egotism" (Snyder, Stephan, & Rosenfield 1978) or "self-serving bias" (Miller & Ross 1975) permeates the attribution process so thoroughly that we propose the following corollary for Axiom 2:

> C2.3. Attributional activity consists in part of an individual's attempt to maintain personal security and a positive self-concept, including a general striving toward self-enhancement and the protection of both the physical self and the self-concept against threat.

Although the preceding discussion suggests that meaning, control, and self-esteem motives for attribution are conceptually distinct, they are often interrelated. Thompson (1981) noted that throughout the extensive literature linking control over aversive events and successful coping, the issue of an event's "meaning for the individual" is frequently a critical mediating factor. Also, Kelley (1971a) saw control/prediction as the "latent goal" of attaining knowledge. The impact of feelings of control on self-esteem and the ability to cope with aversive events has been emphasized by Thompson (1981) and Taylor (1983). Finally, the importance for self-esteem of perceiving events as meaningful has been discussed by these same authors, among others (Becker 1973; O'Brien 1982); in most cases, "meaningful" refers to qualities of events and experiences that support the attributor's self-view as competent, moral, worthy, and so on.

When Do People Make Attributions?

The three issues of meaning, control, and self-esteem prove important again.

1. Events that challenge one's meaning-belief system instigate attributional processes. In particular, investigators have found that novel and unexpected events trigger causal analyses (Hastie 1984; Pyszczynski & Greenberg 1981; Wong & Weiner 1981). The searches for an answer to the question "Why me?" by Taylor's (1983) cancer patients and Bulman and Wortman's (1977) accident victims are also consistent with this interpretation.

2. Events that challenge feelings of personal control and predictability of events—that is, events that have implications for the individual's future control of outcomes—also trigger attributional searches. For example, attributions about the dispositions of another person are likely when the attributor expects to be dependent on that person for future outcomes

(e.g., Berscheid et al. 1976). Restriction of control and personal freedom have also been found to instigate attribution processes (Pittman & Pittman 1980; Worchel & Andreoli 1976; Wortman 1976).

3. Events that significantly alter feelings of self-esteem instigate attribution processes. For example, failure on a task instigates causal reasoning (e.g., Diener & Dweck 1978; Wong & Weiner 1981). In addition, Taylor (1983) and Bulman and Wortman (1977) report that tragic events damage self-esteem and that the attribution process is geared toward restoring a positive self-concept. These considerations suggest the following axiom:

> A3.   Attributional processes are initiated when events occur that (1) cannot be readily assimilated into the individual's meaning-belief system, (2) have implications regarding the controllability of future outcomes, or (3) significantly alter self-esteem either positively or negatively.

If attribution processes are motivated by challenges to a person's beliefs, sense of control, or self-esteem, the particular attribution selected on a given occasion should reflect its ability to restore these variables to satisfactory levels. Thompson (1981) argues that restoration of the meaning-belief system after a tragic event involves three components: (1) assurance that future events will be endurable, (2) identifying positive outcomes concomitant with the negative consequences of the event, and (3) determination that the event was "part of a plan" and not random. Walster (1966) claims that attributions of blame for negative events are made partly to ensure personal controllability (i.e., avoidance) of similar events in the future. Finally, research on self-serving biases (Miller & Ross 1975; Greenberg, Pyszczynski, & Solomon 1982) and "ego-involvement" (Miller 1976) suggests that attributions are selected partly on the basis of their ability to maintain or enhance self-esteem. We therefore propose a fourth axiom:

> A4.   Once the attribution process has been engaged, the particular attributions chosen will be those that best (1) restore cognitive coherence to the attributor's meaning-belief system, (2) establish a sense of confidence that future outcomes will be satisfactory or controllable, and (3) minimize threats to self-esteem and maximize the capacity for self-enhancement.

Lest we seem overly negative about attribution processes by focusing on cancer, tragic accidents, and failure, we should point out that the mechanisms and motives involved in making attributions about positive events appear to be identical to those already described. For example, winning a lottery may present a challenge to one's meaning-belief system, gaining a promotion at work may influence one's sense of or mastery over the environment, and winning a difficult tennis match may produce a substantial upward shift in self-esteem. These events can be expected to instigate attribution processes in much the same way as the aversive events to which we have more frequently referred.

One general question remains to be addressed: What factors influence the degree to which a given attribution will satisfy the meaning, control, and self-esteem motives outlined above? Magnusson (1981) and Veroff (1983) have argued that attributions are a joint function of situational and personal factors; for our purposes, however, it will be useful to delineate these factors further. Specifically, we propose the following axiom:

> A5. The degree to which a potential attribution will be perceived as satisfactory (and hence likely to be chosen) will vary as a function of: (1) characteristics of the attributor, (2) the context in which the attribution is made, (3) characteristics of the event being explained, and (4) the context of the event being explained.

ATTRIBUTION THEORY AND RELIGION

All children that we know about are raised in cultures that provide religious explanations of certain events. Atheist families in predominantly religious cultures and officially atheist countries with substantial religious minorities are not yet exceptions to this rule, since almost all children reared under these conditions still find out about religious concepts. Therefore, the best explanation for the psychological availability of religious attributions is simply that cultures provide them ready-made. This leads to Axiom 6:

> A6. Systems of religious concepts offer individuals a variety of meaning-enhancing explanations of events—in terms of God, sin, salvation, and so on—as well as a range of possibilities for enhancing feelings of control and self-esteem (e.g., personal faith, prayer, rituals, and so forth).

Referring back to Axiom 2, it is clear how religious attributions might serve the fundamental motives we have discussed. Systems of religious concepts tend to (1) be comprehensive and well integrated, (2) emphasize the orderliness of the universe, and (3) portray the world as "just" (or, at least, as not morally arbitrary). Religion provides answers to questions that otherwise might seem unanswerable. In short, religion is a major source of meaning. This fact is particularly, though not exclusively, evident in regard to tragic events and crises. In these situations, religion can provide all three of Thompson's (1981) components of meaning by assuring the endurability of future events (e.g., "God wouldn't do this to me unless He knew I could handle it"), providing concomitant positive outcomes (e.g., "God has taught me a valuable lesson"), and defining events as part of a plan (e.g., "God's plan"). We therefore propose the following corollary to Axiom 6:

C6.1.   Systems of religious concepts provide individuals with a comprehensive, integrated meaning-belief system that is well adapted to accommodate and explain events in the world.

A second characteristic of nearly all religions is that they satisfy the need or desire to predict and control events. We suggest that this result can be obtained in one of two ways. First, most religions provide mechanisms whereby individuals can control future outcomes—usually indirectly through God—by means of prayer, execution of prescribed rituals, conformity to certain behavior codes, and the like. We might label this an "instrumental" or "extrinsic" form of control. A second, more "intrinsic" form of control may be exemplified by the belief that if one trusts in God and has faith, everything will turn out well. In other words, although no attempt is made to predict or control future events by religious means, the need or desire for control is suspended in the belief that God is in control and therefore all is (and will continue to be) right with the world. In either case, the result is confidence about the future, as evidenced in the interviews quoted by Bulman and Wortman (1977) and Taylor (1983). We therefore propose:

C6.2.   Systems of religious concepts satisfy the individual's need or desire to predict and control events, either through mechanisms for directly influencing future outcomes (extrinsic form) or through suspension or relinquishing of the need for direct control (intrinsic form).

Religious belief systems also maintain and enhance the self-concept. Shaver and Buhrmester (1983) have identified two general need-satisfying "provisions" offered by interpersonal relationships and social groups that counter feelings of loneliness and low self-esteem: (1) "psychological intimacy," involving unconditional positive regard (love) distributed according to a norm of equality, and (2) "integrated involvement," involving conditional positive regard distributed according to a norm of equity. Religions may enhance the feeling of unconditional regard through the belief that, for example, "God loves me (and all human beings)," and back feelings of conditional regard through recognition for church activities, being an especially moral person, and so forth. In addition, most religious systems offer various means for spiritual development, "reaching toward the ultimate" (Tillich 1957), and other forms of psychological growth and self-enhancement. We therefore propose:

C6.3.   Systems of religious concepts possess a variety of means for the maintenance and enhancement of self-esteem, including unconditional positive regard, conditional positive regard, and opportunities for spiritual growth and development.

Determinants of Religious and Nonreligious Attributions

It is clear that events can be attributed either to religious or to naturalistic (i.e., nonreligious) causes. An attributional approach to the psychology of religion should explain when and why one kind of attribution is chosen over the other. Our conceptualization of this problem closely parallels that of Alloy and Tabachnik (1984), according to which causal attributions are a function of the interaction of prior expectations and beliefs ("schemata") and environmental influences and cues.

Our point of departure from this model notes that when an attribution is made, the attributor typically has available a number of expectancies about cause-effect relationships, namely, both religious and nonreligious meaning-belief systems. The relative availability of these systems in a given situation (and hence the relative likelihood of using one or the other) is seen as a product of the four major categories of factors identified earlier: (1) the *attributor*, (2) the *attributor's context*, (3) the *event* being explained, and (4) the *event's context*. Each of these categories comprises meaning, control, and self-esteem components; ultimately, it is the interaction of these components that determines whether a religious or a nonreligious attribution will be made in any particular set of circumstances.

It will be useful to briefly summarize our model of the attribution process before discussing its various components in detail. We propose that an attributor enters a situation with a general predisposition toward or against the use of religious attributions for explaining events (which is usually called "religiosity"); the attributor's context then exerts an influence on this propensity in one or the other direction. The outcome is an availability level (Fiske & Taylor 1984; Rholes & Pryor 1982) for each of the meaning-belief systems such that, all else being equal, the system of greater availability will be invoked first to formulate an attribution. The attributor then considers the nature of the event to be explained in conjunction with the context of the event. If the dominant system provides a satisfactory explanation, the attribution chosen will be of this type; to the extent that this system fails to offer an acceptable explanation, the attributor will turn to the other explanatory system. Although we believe that the more common case in our culture is the one in which a naturalistic explanation is more available and hence evaluated first (the "God of the gaps" theology; Gorsuch & Smith 1983), our view can accommodate the alternative case as well.

Characteristics of the Attributor

It is obvious that people differ in their propensity to use religious or naturalistic explanations, a fact particularly evident when one considers those at the pro- and anti-religious extremes of the religiosity continuum (Ritzema 1979). In general, the relative availability of religious and naturalistic meaning-belief systems is a function of various social influences. There is considerable evidence for a connection between early religious socialization, on the one hand, and church attendance, knowledge of one's faith, the probability of having religious experiences, the strength of religious beliefs, and the likelihood of conversion, on the other (Clark 1929; Coe 1900; Starbuck 1899; Wilson 1978). One aspect of this relationship has to do with the personal availability of a religious language. For example, Laski (1961) and Bourque and Back (1971) have shown that people with a religious language tend to describe their experiences in religious terms; in Bernstein's (1964) words, "Language marks out what is relevant affectively, cognitively and socially, and experience is transformed by what is made relevant" (p. 117).

Of course, the religious and naturalistic meaning-belief systems of different attributors vary in kind as well as in strength. Gorsuch and Smith (1983), for example, found that attributions to God varied as a function of differences on the dimensions of "Fundamentalism" and "Nearness to God." Moreover, the tendency of people to make dispositional attributions is hypothesized to hold for attributions to God: That is, they will differ in the references they make to God's personality, motives, desires, and so on. Research on images of God (e.g., Gorsuch 1968; Spilka, Armatas, & Nussbaum 1964) has revealed that God is conceived as ranging from loving, forgiving, and merciful, on the one extreme, to arbitrary, punitive, and threatening, on the other. It also appears that the image a person finds plausible is related to family background and self-concept (Spilka, Addison, & Rosensohn 1975).

A second dispositional dimension involves the attributor's beliefs about the relative efficacy of religious and nonreligious mechanisms for controlling and predicting outcomes. Research has shown that people tend to make attributions that provide a sense of control over similar events in the future; they should therefore make more religious attributions, for example, to the extent that they perceive secular efforts as ineffective. In a highly influential monograph, Rotter (1966), focusing primarily on naturalistic causes of events, distinguished between internal (personal) and external (environmental) causes and found that individuals differ reliably in their tendency to attribute events to one kind of cause or the other. Levenson (1973) later expanded this scheme to include "chance" and "powerful others," and Kopplin (1976) added "God control," in the first explicit attempt to investigate locus of control from a religious perspective. In our view, empirical findings with the God-control scale are interpretable in terms of a general disposition toward making religious attributions.

Finally, the propensity toward using religious versus naturalistic attributions is determined in part by the relative importance of these factors in maintaining the individual's positive self-concept. According to Shaver and Buhrmester (1983), social influences on self-esteem involve both conditional and unconditional components of positive regard; as discussed earlier, such regard might be attained by making either religious or naturalistic attributions. To the extent that one's self-concept is dependent on religious sources of self-esteem, this type of attribution is likely to be preferred.

Intrinsic and Extrinsic Religiosity. Current perspectives on religiosity generally agree that these concepts are multidimensional. The most thoroughly researched framework is that of Allport (1959, 1966; Allport & Ross 1967), which distinguishes between intrinsic and extrinsic religiosity. Intrinsic faith involves a total commitment to religion that places living religiously above other considerations. Extrinsic faith is utilitarian and oriented toward the attainment of nonreligious goals, including personal security in the face of threats.

The literature suggests that intrinsically oriented people view God as a source of unconditional love and support (e.g., Spilka & Mullin 1977). This orientation seems to go along with feelings of both personal control and God control and with high self-esteem (Flakoll 1974; Silvestri 1979; Spilka & Schmidt 1982). In contrast, extrinsic religionists have harsher images of God, more often feel threatened, and have lower self-esteem (Spilka & Mullin 1977). They seem to make attributions to God more conditionally, such as when God's help seems likely to get them through an immediate crisis (Spilka & Schmidt 1982). In general, then, intrinsic and extrinsic orientations toward religion can be viewed as sets of particular meaning, control, and self-esteem components that frequently co-occur and are manifested in religious expressions.

The fact that benevolent God images are related to a supportive family background and to high self-esteem and that all of these are related to intrinsic religiosity and certain kinds of control attributions suggests that all are causally interconnected in some way. The attribution perspective suggests why: 1) Several of these variables—God image, intrinsic religiosity, and control attributions—are part of the same system of religious attributions, and 2) the belief that events are generally meaningful, controllable, and beneficial, and that the self and others (including God) are reasonable, trustworthy, and caring seems to reflect previous social experience, possibly including parental affection and trustworthiness. Whether or not this particular line of reasoning proves correct, the attributional perspective encourages researchers and theorists to cut across existing conceptual and methodological boundaries to ask: What do these variables, concepts, and frameworks have to tell us about individuals relying on attributions or explanations of particular kinds?

The preceding discussion is formally summarized in the following derivation from Axiom 5 and Axiom 6 (and its corollaries):

> D1. The likelihood of choosing a religious rather than a non-religious attribution for a particular experience or event is determined in part by dispositional characteristics of the attributor such as (1) the relative availability to that person of religious and naturalistic meaning-belief systems, (2) beliefs about the relative efficacy of religious and naturalistic mechanisms for controlling events, and (3) the relative importance of religious and naturalistic sources of self-esteem.

Context of the Attributor

The notion of "availability" is based on the fact that human beings are limited-capacity information processors. Only a handful of concepts or ideas can be available at a given moment. As a result, people frequently make decisions on the basis of information that psychologically is most easily and quickly accessible at the time (Fiske & Taylor 1984; Nisbett & Ross 1980). The attributor's context is therefore important to the attribution process to the extent that it stimulates or limits various cognitive processes, including the relative availability of various explanations. If religious interpretations are salient and available, that kind of attribution is more likely to be made.

One obvious example arises when the attributor is in an inherently religious setting (e.g., church) or a clearly nonreligious setting (e.g., an experimental psychology laboratory). It has been found that two-thirds to three-fourths of religious experiences occur while people are involved in religious activities (Bourque 1969; Spilka, 1980). The mere presence of one or more highly salient religious stimuli in a nonreligious setting may have a similar, though perhaps less pronounced, effect on attributions; manipulations that focus the attributor's attention on a potential cause influence subsequent causal assessments (e.g., Taylor & Fiske 1975, 1978). This context effect is probably responsible for the consistent failure of social psychologists to encounter religious attributions in the laboratory, even when working with religious research participants. Not only is the psychology laboratory understood by subjects to be a "scientific" setting, but questionnaires and other devices used in psychological research rarely provide religious response alternatives that would enhance the salience of potential religious attributions.

Another setting feature affecting the relative availability of meaning systems is the extent to which other people in the setting directly or indirectly encourage or discourage the use of religious attributions (Lofland 1966; Lofland & Stark 1965). Proudfoot and Shaver (1975) discussed several examples of the effects of group pressure on the attribution process, for example, during the testimonial portion of certain religious ceremonies.

We have argued that the perceived efficacy of religious and nonreligious control/prediction mechanisms influences the propensity to use one or the other kind of attribution. It thus stands to reason that contextual factors are likely to affect the attribution process in much the same way. An obvious example occurs where the attributor has already attempted to control outcomes using either religious or nonreligious means; in such cases, a new attributional strategy may be adopted because it affords a greater sense of control. To wit, a highly religious person who normally shuns medicine and doctors might adopt naturalistic attributions after various religious attempts at controlling a serious illness fail. The reverse is also observed; that is, a generally nonreligious person resorts to prayer in order to be rid of an illness that naturalistic medicine is unable to cure.

This context effect on perceptions of controllability is not limited to the attributor's own control efforts. Indeed, it seems entirely likely that recent observation of another person's control efforts would lead to similar implications for the attribution process. Religious attributions are likely to be viewed as more viable and plausible immediately following attendance at a successful faith-healing event, whereas naturalistic explanations might be sought after witnessing a positive outcome of medical treatment.

A similar line of reasoning leads us to believe that situational factors that temporarily alter the religious and naturalistic components of a person's self-esteem should influence attributional choices in a manner parallel to dispositional differences in self-esteem. Such fluctuations might be initiated by a context in which the attributor feels incompetent or unintelligent (naturalistic) or immoral and sinful (religious). In the latter case, the direct threat to the religious component of self-esteem may dispose the attributor against seeking religious attributions for other—especially—negative events. Under these circumstances, one's self-concept may be best served by temporarily "turning off" the religious meaning-belief system until self-esteem is restored via other means.

Certain aspects of social coercion might also be included here. When attributors believe that other people will like them more if particular attribution is made, they will be more likely to adopt that attribution strategy. In general, a particular attribution is likely to be chosen to the extent that the attributor feels it will boost (or prevent a decrease in) self-esteem; one way in which this may occur is through the approval of others in the immediate situation. These influences are summarized in a second derivation:

> D2. The attributor's context influences the relative likelihood of a religious rather than a nonreligious attribution by temporarily altering (1) the relative availability of the two meaning-belief systems, (2) the attributor's perception of the efficacy of religious versus naturalistic control mechanisms, or (3) the relative salience of these competing sources of self-esteem.

Characteristics of the Event

A widely recognized principle that permeates psychology is that people are more likely to assimilate new information into existing cognitive structures than to alter firmly held beliefs to accommodate contradictory information (e.g., Nisbett & Ross 1980). For those with highly available religious and naturalistic meaning-belief systems, this task is expedited because they have a choice of two sets of beliefs into which new data may be assimilated. Moreover, religious belief systems are generally well adapted for explaining apparently incongruous information: For example, practically any event can be interpreted as an example of "God working in mysterious ways."

Given the state of the attributor's meaning-belief systems, different kinds or "domains" of events (Spilka & Schmidt 1983) will be more or less explainable by such systems. For example, certain experiences are widely held to be religious in nature (e.g., "speaking in tongues") and hence are more likely to be viewed religiously. For events that are interpretable either way, the knowledge the attributor has about that type of event will influence the perceived plausibility of potential religious and nonreligious reasons for its occurrence and therefore will affect the choice of explanation. As mentioned previously, a nonreligious person might choose a religious attribution to explain an event in the medical domain about which that person has little naturalistic knowledge (Fichter 1981; O'Brien 1982). In contrast, religious individuals might choose a naturalistic explanation of that which is incongruous with an image of God as loving and powerful (Spilka, Spangler, & Nelson 1983).

Events that have important implications for the attributor's future are likely to receive attributions that make these outcomes seem more predictable or controllable. It is not surprising, then, that people make more religious attributions under threats to life and security (Fichter 1981; Gray 1970). Such explanations provide a greater sense of control—or simply more faith that the outcome will be satisfactory—than do naturalistic attributions. Other examples of this sort of control bias are plentiful in the research literature. For example, self-blame for a serious accident may sometimes increase one's sense that similar future catastrophes can be avoided (Bulman & Wortman 1977). Similarly, the cause of a cancer may be attributed to diet, a physical blow, or other natural causes that can be avoided in the future (Taylor, Lichtman, & Wood 1984). In general, whichever type of attribution promises more control over the event in the future is more likely to be invoked as an explanation.

When events occur that have significant implications for self-esteem, attributions are likely to be chosen that effectively restore self-esteem to a more comfortable level. The most obvious instances are those in which an event actually happens to the attributor. Bulman and Wortman (1977) reported, for example, that highly religious people were more likely than less religious people to blame themselves for their serious accidents, perhaps because attributions to God would have implied that they had fallen from God's favor, had been sinful or wicked, and so forth. Those that did make God attributions, in contrast, frequently pointed out that God had chosen them because they were special in some way (e.g., able to handle the stress in an exemplary fashion), and often they reported that they had become a better person as a result of the experience. However, attributions to God for highly desirable outcomes could be quite ego enhancing for the religious person who interprets the incident as evidence of being deserving in God's eyes.

This line of reasoning leads to some interesting hypotheses with respect to intrinsic-extrinsic differences in religiosity. Intrinsically religious people may gain the most in self-esteem by attributing positive outcomes to God. That they may see themselves as favored in God's eyes has far stronger implications for self-esteem than if they took all the credit personally. Extrinsics, on the other hand, would be expected to display typical self-enhancing biases by attributing positive outcomes to the self and negative outcomes to external factors. This discussion of event characteristics leads to a third derivation:

> D3. Characteristics of events that influence the choice between religious and nonreligious attributions include (1) the degree to which the event to be explained is congruent with the individual's meaning-belief systems, (2) the degree to which religious and naturalistic mechanisms for controlling similar events are seen to be effective, and (3) the degree to which religious and naturalistic explanations represent potential sources of self-esteem.

Context of the Event

Although it may be reasonable to think of event context as one way in which events vary, it is useful to consider context separately. First, knowledge that an event occurred in an inherently religious setting, for example, can increase the salience of religious explanations and therefore the likelihood of such attributions. Second, given the availability of religious and naturalistic meaning-belief systems when explanations are needed, the context of the event influences the relative plausibility of both types of explanations. Thus, having a sudden, unexpected heart attack might be interpreted differently depending on whether it occurred in a synagogue or on a golf course.

Context may also influence the implications an event has for one's sense of control. For example, it may suggest that prayer averted a disaster or that an actor's failure on a task was or was not determined by environmental constraints. More important, such information is relevant for determining whether certain kinds of control efforts will be efficacious in the future with respect to similar events. Event context also has implications for the degree to which various attributions influence self-esteem. If a person with a health problem runs into an old friend who recommends a particular doctor, this may be interpreted differently depending on whether it follows a session of praying for a cure. If it does, the person who receives the cure may feel that God has responded favorably to a request, which can be expected to raise self-esteem. And if the informant is one of several acquaintances with the same health problem, all of whom have been praying but only a few of whom have recovered, a person is especially likely to feel chosen or favored.

In summary:

> D4.   The context in which a to-be-explained event occurs influences the likelihood of religious versus naturalistic attributions by (1) affecting the relative plausibility or availability of various explanations, (2) providing information about the efficacy of various mechanisms for potentially controlling similar events, or (3) influencing the degree to which the event impacts on the attributor's self-esteem.

DISCUSSION AND RECOMMENDATIONS

One of the benefits of adopting an attributional approach to the psychology of religion is that it increases the likelihood of fruitful interaction between the psychology of religion and other subfields of psychology, especially social psychology.

Such diverse phenomena as intrinsic religiosity, scores on a God-control scale, and explanations of achievements, accidents, and illnesses fit comfortably within a single conceptual framework adapted from recent research. It is worth mentioning that attribution researchers have developed and tested a wide range of research paradigms and psychometric procedures that can easily be employed in the study of religion.

Much of the existing attribution literature concerns the role of attributions in social interaction. This suggests the possibility of conceptualizing a person's relationship with God as similar to various kinds of interpersonal relationships that have already been studied. Jones and Pittman (1982), for example, have analyzed social influence processes from an attributional perspective and argue that the goal of much social behavior is to induce interaction partners to adopt certain desirable explanations of our behavior. Ingratiating behavior, for instance, is intended to elicit an attribution of likability and appears in such forms as other-enhancement (e.g., flattery) and doing favors. In another self-presentational strategy, supplication, influencers advertise their helplessness and dependence in order to elicit sympathy and assistance. It is easy to see how these ideas might be applied to the process of prayer, in which the petitioner often heaps praise on the deity and offers various concessions (ingratiation), and might be used to reaffirm personal inferiority and dependence while entreating God for help and guidance (supplication).

It is important to note that the more restrictive attribution theories discussed by Proudfoot and Shaver (1975), which are primarily concerned with personal experiences, can be subsumed by the more general theory outlined here. Proudfoot and Shaver discussed the example of Stephen Bradley, a man who experienced heart palpitations after returning home from a religious revival and interpreted his condition as "being moved by the Spirit" (p. 322). In the language of this essay, the *event* is the heart palpitations, the *event context* includes the immediately preceding revival, the *attributor* is Bradley (who was obviously familiar with religious concepts and language), and the *attributor's context* includes Bradley's home environment and the fact that he was alone. The interpretation of physiological arousal as a religious experience represents just one application of a general attribution process that includes explanations of avalanches, answered prayers, and stock market fluctuations as well.

Although our discussion has focused largely on the effects on attributions of event characteristics, the attributor's context, and so on, the attribution process is clearly an interactive one. For example, success on a task (the event) under rather difficult conditions (event context) may elicit quite different explanations from, say, intrinsic and extrinsic religionists. Specifically, intrinsics may gain more in self-esteem by sharing credit with God for their good fortune (and viewing themselves as favored in the deity's eyes), whereas extrinsics might be more self-congratulatory about having defied the odds. In contrast, task failure would likely produce a quite different pattern of results. Thus, we see the interaction of event characteristics, attributor characteristics, and event context that leads to a particular attribution.

It has been our goal to construct and describe an attribution theory for the psychology of religion that is not only general but will prove empirically fruitful as well. We hope others will join us to test, revise, and expand the theory in an attempt to better understand religious beliefs and religious behavior.

13

RELIGION-AS-SCHEMA, WITH IMPLICATIONS FOR THE RELATION BETWEEN RELIGION AND COPING

DANIEL N. MCINTOSH

Religion is more than an organization of beliefs. It is broader in that it exists in the form of texts, symbols, and traditions, and it is narrower in that it appears in the form of individuals' rites, habits, and other behaviors (Spilka, Hood, & Gorsuch 1985; Spiro 1987a). However, at one level religion can be viewed as cognitive in that every religious system includes a set of propositions held to be true (Spiro 1987b). One way to conceptualize how these beliefs function and are organized is to consider religion to be a cognitive schema. Viewing religion as such has heuristic value and serves to explain some of the psychological reality of what religion is and how it functions in people's lives. Recently, Janoff-Bulman (1989) examined the relation between people's unquestioned assumptions about the world and the stress of traumatic events, with the view that these assumptions are schematic in nature. Her work made two important contributions. She used the notion of cognitive schema to understand how people's assumptions function, and she addressed the relation between these assumptions and coping with aversive events. The present chapter expands this framework to include not just individual assumptions but also broader systems of beliefs—specifically, religion. Viewing religion as a cognitive schema has advantages for both the psychology of religion and coping research, because it connects these fields to the wealth of find-

Reprinted and edited with permission of author and publisher from *The International Journal for the Psychology of Religion, 5* (1995), 1–16.

ings and perspectives about beliefs developed recently in social psychology (cf. Fiske & Taylor, 1991).

RELIGION-AS-SCHEMA

What Is a Schema?

Definition. A *schema* is a cognitive structure or mental representation containing organized knowledge about a particular domain, including a specification of the relations among its attributes (Fiske & Linville 1980; Gardner 1985; Taylor & Crocker 1981). Schemas are built via encounters with the environment and can be modified by experience (Bartlett 1932; Neisser 1976). People have schemas for many things, not only for objects (Neisser 1976) but also for events, roles, individuals, and the self (Fiske & Linville 1980; Markus 1977; Taylor & Crocker 1981). A God schema might include, for example, assumptions about the physical nature of God, God's will or purposes, God's methods of influence, and the interrelations among these beliefs.

Cognitive schemas operate at various levels of generality, with broad, abstract schemas usually having more specific ones embedded within them (Neisser 1976; Taylor & Crocker 1981). For example, a schema for God might be part of a larger, more abstract schema for religion—which might also include schemas for death, morals, and so forth. Work on schemas has not often dealt with the most abstract schemas that are least subject to reality testing (Janoff-Bulman 1989). However, because schematic processing appears to occur in approximately the same fashion at each level of abstraction (Taylor & Crocker 1981), knowledge about the functioning of lower-level schemas can help us understand more abstract-level schemas, such as religion.

One consistent finding about schemas is their propensity for stability. During the constant barrage of stimuli, the tendency is toward adapting data to an existing schema (assimilation) rather than the reverse (accommodation; Neisser 1976). Also, schemas constantly change, usually through small modifications (Bowlby 1969; Horowitz 1976). For example, people tend to persist in maintaining theories they have formed in the laboratory, even when this evidence is later described as false (Anderson, Lepper, & Ross 1980; Ross, Lepper, & Hubbard 1975; see also Bowlby 1980; Parkes 1975). Similarly, people may continue to believe "theories" learned in a church or temple class even when later faced with contradictory or inconsistent information.

Function. The notion of schema is connected with how schemas are seen as functioning. Schema research was stimulated by findings that people bring to situations certain knowledge that influences how they perceive and understand the situation (see Fiske & Linville 1980, for a review, and Bartlett 1932, as an example).

To begin with, schemas influence what is perceived. Neisser (1976) wrote that people notice "only what they have schemas for, and willy-nilly ignore the rest" (p. 80). Further, because relations among schema elements are imposed on the stimulus configuration, schemas influence how people understand what they perceive (Bartlett 1932; Bruner 1957b; Taylor & Crocker 1981). They arrange their environment to reflect the organization of relevant schemas. For example, subjects who possess a masculine self-schema (i.e., consider themselves highly masculine and view masculinity as very important to themselves) perceive a video of everyday behavior in terms of masculinity to a greater degree than those without such a masculine self-schema (Markus, Smith, & Moreland 1985). Similarly, a religious schema can provide a framework for understanding events and, therefore, can influence how the perceiver evaluates the events. Generally, if a series of events is ambiguous, someone with a religious schema is more likely than a person without such a schema to impose a religious interpretation on the events. Further, those with a particular religious schema may understand events much differently than those without that schema. An example of how a specific religious schema causes different understandings of an event was reported by Gorer (1965). He noted that the Spiritualists and Christian Scientists in his sample denied completely the importance of death and, therefore, did not experience grief. To the Spiritualists and Christian Scientists, the situation does not call for grief. Put in more schematic terms, the datum of someone's death is assimilated into the Spiritualist or Christian Scientist religious schema, and with this schema, death is not viewed as important and worthy of grief.

Similarly, schemas allow people to go beyond the information given by providing elements to fill in missing pieces of what is perceived (Bruner 1957a; Rumelhart & Ortony 1977). On hearing a fellow bus passenger mention that she has just donated some clothes to Deseret Industries and is going home to read her "triple combination," those having a Mormon schema will be able to infer that the speaker is Mormon. Note that if the perceiver's schema does not, in reality, match the situation, the perceiver may *in*correctly fill in missing information. Two passersby might make different inferences when seeing one person dunk another into a river (e.g., baptism or homicide); both schemas allow the observers to go beyond the information given (i.e., the actions of the people in the river), but only one of them can be correct.

Related to this, schematic conceptions of how the world works may help create the reality that people anticipate even in the absence of objective environmental bases (Taylor & Crocker 1981). To wit, if a person whose religious schema includes a belief in faith healing sees a once terminally ill person healthy, he or she may assume, even without further information, that someone had prayed for that person's healing. The datum of the person's cure is easily and quickly assimilated into the faith-healing schema. The cure is then connected to beliefs about healing in ways defined by the person's schema (e.g., prayer must have been involved). This person will thus have created an example of the power of prayer; someone with another schema may have understood the stimulus (the cured person) much differently—perhaps relating it to beliefs about "doctors being quacks." As another example, one person may incorrectly infer from his or her religious schema that a second person is religious, from cues such as hairstyle or dress. Based on this assumption, a theological discussion may take place. Even if the second person is not religious, the discussion may be politely continued. This will help confirm the first person's inference. In addition, the discussion itself may make the second person more religious. In this example, the first person's view of reality, based on his or her schema, created a situation that made that person more certain of the assumption (the second person discussed theology) and may potentially have changed reality (the second person's religiousness).

A benefit of conceptualizing religion as a schema is that research on the effects of schema on the processing of information can be applied to religion. Several of these functions are described later. Because schemas allow people to fill in gaps in input or knowledge, they allow individuals to employ heuristics or shortcuts that simplify and shorten the process of problem solving (Taylor & Crocker 1981). When a problem has cues that activate a schema, people can use that schema to assist in solving the problem. Taylor, Crocker, and D'Agostino (1978) found that problems with schema-relevant cues were solved faster than problems with schema-irrelevant cues. Perhaps individuals with religious schemas can employ heuristics to solve problems that are relevant to the religious domain (e.g., finding meaning in misfortune, explaining seemingly "unnatural" occurrences).

Relatedly, Taylor and Crocker (1981) reported that a large number of studies show faster cognitive processing for schema-relevant versus schema-irrelevant material. For example, Markus (1977) found that students who had schemas about themselves for being either dependent or independent responded faster to schema-relevant information than students who did not possess schemas in these domains. Related to religion, individuals with religious schemas have significantly shorter response latencies than those without such schemas when asked to indicate if a religious adjective describes them (Spencer & McIntosh 1990). Taylor and

Crocker (1981) pointed out, however, that some studies find *longer* processing times for schema-relevant stimuli. One reason for this may be the centrality of the stimuli. "Information that is highly redundant and/or central to the schema might be processed faster than schema-irrelevant material, whereas information that has novel implications for the schema and/or is peripheral to the schema might be processed more slowly" (Taylor & Crocker 1981:102). In the realm of religion, this suggests, for example, that an individual whose religious schema includes an explanation for why good things happen to bad people will be able to process information about the successes of a "bad" person more quickly than a person for whom the instance would be novel or not included in the schema.

The complexity of a schema also has implications for the processing of information. Tesser (cited in Taylor & Crocker 1981) suggested that schemas provide criteria for evaluation and that people with highly developed schemas make confident and extreme evaluations more quickly than people without schemas. Similarly, people are faster and more confident in predicting the future if they have a schema for the stimulus domain (Markus 1977). Those who possess a complex religious schema should be able to evaluate the religious significance of stimuli more quickly and would be more confident when predicting future religious outcomes (e.g., what will happen to church-state relations if the Supreme Court makes this ruling?) than those without a complex religious schema.

In short, schemas enable people to identify stimuli quickly, fill in information missing from the stimulus array, and select a strategy for obtaining the information or solving a problem (Taylor & Crocker 1981). Schemas frame the way information is perceptually organized, stored, retrieved, and processed. Schemas sort the myriad stimuli, make them meaningful, and facilitate their processing.

How Does the Schema Construct Relate to Previous Work?

The idea that beliefs about the physical or metaphysical universe influence how one views events or novel information is not new to psychology in general or to the psychology of religion in particular. Previous scholars have discussed schemas and schemalike constructs. For example, Bowlby (1969, 1980) presented the idea that individuals have inner *working models* of the world. Hall (1986) discussed *cosmologies*, defined as belief systems based on viewing the universe as an orderly system involving complex interacting processes of energy or life force. Ball-Rokeach, Rokeach, and Grube (1984) suggested that a person's value-related attitudes toward objects and situations and organization of values and beliefs about the self form a comprehensive belief system that provides a cognitive framework, map, or theory. Glock and Piazza (1981) saw people as structuring reality in causal terms—such as what or who has power to influence events. What Parkes (1975) termed the *assumptive world* is a strongly held set of assumptions about the world and the self.

Schemalike functions for belief systems have also been discussed. Just as schemas are built through experience, so previous experience constructs systems of beliefs (e.g., Bowlby 1969; Parkes 1975). Ball-Rokeach et al. (1984) saw belief systems as relatively enduring, yet able to undergo change as well. Harvey, Hunt, and Schroder (1961) proposed that they provide a network of relations that give people an orientation and ties to the world. This supplies people with linkages to the surrounding world through which reality is read (see also Luckmann 1967). The framework described by Ball-Rokeach et al. (1984) enables the person to engage in cognitive activity related to "selective remembering and forgetting, information processing, decision-making, conflict resolution, ego defense, denial, withdrawal, judging, intending, trying, praising and condemning, exhorting, and persuading—and doing" (p. 27). Bowlby (1969) stated that people have maps of the environment that influence reactions to changes in the environment. Parkes (1975) indicated that a view of reality is "maintained and used as a means of recognizing, planning, and acting" (p. 132).

More specific to the psychology of religion, the schema construct can be tied to Allport's conception of intrinsic religiosity (Allport 1966; Allport & Ross 1967). He indicated that for individuals with an intrinsic orientation, religion serves as the framework within which they live their lives; he conceived intrinsic religiousness as relating to all of life and as being integrative and meaning-endowing (Donahue 1985a). These attributes can be seen as functions of having and using a developed religious schema. Some part of being "intrinsically religious" may be possessing such a schema.

How Does the Schema Construct Help the Psychology of Religion?

If previous scholars have worked with concepts similar to the schema construct, what reason is there to adopt the idea of religion-as-schema? There are several.

It is a virtue of the schema construct that it does not conflict with previous work. Whatever bit of reality the other frameworks have tapped may be shared by viewing religion as a schema. One advantage of adopting the schema notion is that it combines previous work into a unified framework. For example, Allport's (1966; Allport & Ross 1967) religious framework can be combined with Bowlby's (1969) idea that working models are built via experience and with the notion of Harvey et al. (1961) that belief systems affect how people structure their understanding of the world. Thinking of religion as a schema allows us to integrate much previous work into a consistent framework.

More important, adopting the schema concept links research by cognitive and social psychologists on thinking and information processing to work on systems of beliefs in general and religion in particular. It is more probable that the way people's minds function is consistent across content areas than that the way the mind works relative to religion is different from, say, how it works relative to astronomy.

The processing of religious information has already received attention. Lipson (1983) considered religious background as providing children with religious schemas. She gave Catholic and Jewish children neutral and religion-specific readings. Each group recalled more text-based propositions, generated more implicit recall, made fewer recall errors, and spent less time reading the schema-relevant passage than the schema-irrelevant passage. Religious knowledge strongly affected their perception or memory, or both. Using a cognitive psychology approach in examining memory for religious messages, Pargament and DeRosa (1985) evaluated the effects of students' beliefs about whether God or people control people's lives on memory for three sermonlike messages, each advocating a particular combination of God and personal control. Results supported the view that students' religious schemas affected their memory or perception of the speeches. This influence is likely to occur in other domains as well (e.g., news reports).

Lechner (1990) applied work on cognitive schemas to his study of people's God concepts. A well-delineated concept of God was associated with integration of religious beliefs into daily life. Being religious can thus be seen as involving, in part, more elaborate schemas in the religious domain and more overlap between that domain and others.

In his description of Christian evangelism, Ingram (1989) provided an example of how viewing religion as a schema integrates both psychological and sociological perspectives on religion. Using Goffman's (1974) notion of frames (a type of schema), Ingram (1989) indicated that proselytizers use an evangelical schema to interpret the events of a witnessing encounter and try to shift the potential convert's interpretation of the situation—and life—to an evangelical frame. Thus, religious schemas can both be introduced from the outside (by society, peers, missionaries, and so on) and, once possessed by an individual, can influence both perceptions of events and actual behavior.

One domain in which a cognitive-schematic understanding of religion has been constructive is in examining the relation between religion and coping.

RELIGION AND COPING

Treating religion as a cognitive schema is useful in investigating how religion can influence the coping process and outcome and also in exploring how traumatic events can affect faith. To explore these questions, we must first consider from a cognitive standpoint what happens when an individual experiences a stressful event. When a life change occurs (e.g., relocating to a new place, the death of a loved one), people must make the event, which has occurred in external reality, real inside the self (Horowitz 1976; Parkes 1975). This involves integrating the data of the occurrence with prior assumptions (Janoff-Bulman 1989). Hastie (1981) noted that any specific event can be evaluated as congruent, incongruent, or irrelevant with regard to a particular schema. How a particular event relates to one's religious schema is likely to have an impact on coping and adjustment. A major coping task of people experiencing potentially stressful life changes is assimilating their experiences into their extant cognitive schemas or changing their basic schemas about themselves and their world (accommodation), or both (Horowitz 1976; Janoff-Bulman 1989).

Many major life events (e.g., births, transitions to adulthood, marriages, deaths) have historically been linked to religion and are often given religious significance (Spilka, Hood, & Gorsuch 1985). This may cause religious schemas to be cued when such events occur. In addition, people dealing with major life events often indicate that they use religion as part of coping (e.g., Balk 1983; Friedman et al. 1963; Koenig, George, & Siegler 1988). Religious schemas are therefore likely to be activated when people are coping. Thus, attributes of individuals' religious schemas may have an impact on how they deal with such events. Of course, not everyone has a religious schema, and many people's religious schemas may be peripheral and undeveloped. Some probably have other schemas that fulfill the same functions that a religious schema can. These are individual-difference variables that can be examined in the religion-as-schema perspective.

How might a religious schema influence coping with an event? Two particular functions of schemas seem applicable here: (1) increased speed of processing domain-relevant information, and (2) assimilation of stimuli to a form congruent with an extant schema. The first function may expedite cognitive processing of the event, and the second may facilitate the finding of meaning in the event.

Cognitive Processing

Recall that possessing a schema in a domain of interest enables the person to process schema-relevant information more quickly and efficiently and that the perceiver may be able to employ shortcuts or heuristics that simplify and shorten the process. If religious people do possess a cognitive structure that includes ways of thinking about traumatic events, such a schema should facilitate faster cognitive processing of such events.

Faster processing may also be related to better adjustment to aversive events. Recall that people must integrate data from traumatic events with extant beliefs. Being able to cognitively process a negative event quickly and efficiently could facilitate the integration of the event. Having a well-developed religious schema may be analogous to having a closer match between the event and one's schema. Instead of having to fumble around inventing or modifying a less developed schema after the event occurs, one can just plug the event into the extant schema and begin processing. Thus, processing is likely to occur more quickly and more smoothly. Parkes (1975) claimed that a successful transition from an old situation to a new one is more likely if the person has a relatively realistic model of the new situation. Processing "on the fly" is likely to be more sloppy and hazardous than processing according to established plans. To the extent that religious beliefs promote the latter type of processing, religion should relate to better adjustment.

McIntosh, Silver, and Wortman (1993) evaluated the role of religion in parental coping with the loss of a child to sudden infant death syndrome (SIDS). SIDS death was studied because it provides a good arena in which to examine ideas about the impact of traumatic occurrences. The death of one's child is certainly one of the most traumatic events that can occur (Palmer & Noble 1986), and the nature of SIDS does not allow the bereaved time to cognitively prepare for the crisis. McIntosh et al. (1993) found that the more important religion was to respondents, the more cognitive processing (e.g., intentional and unintentional thinking about the baby and its death) was evident immediately after the loss. To the degree that those for whom religion is more important also possess a more developed religious schema, this is consistent with the notion that having a religious schema can facilitate thinking about the death of a loved one. More cognitive processing immediately after the loss is linked to greater well-being and potentially less distress eighteen months later. Thus, religion is associated with an important part of the coping process, and this was predicted by viewing religion as a cognitive schema.

Finding Meaning

Taylor (1983) proposed that the search for meaning (i.e., finding a purpose for or an understanding of the event) is one of three important themes in the coping process (see also Rothbaum, Weisz, & Snyder 1982; Silver & Wortman 1980). A number of studies reported that meaning is often sought during crises (e.g., Bulman & Wortman 1977; Dollinger 1986; Glick, Weiss, & Parkes 1974; Sanders 1980) and that finding meaning in misfortune is associated with effective adjustment (Silver, Boon, & Stones 1983; Thompson 1991; but see Dollinger 1986 for evidence of an attribution-distress link).

Religion may well be able to provide this meaning (Allport 1950; Clark 1958; Spilka, Hood, & Gorsuch, 1985; Wuthnow, Christiano, & Kuzlowski 1980). Sherrill and Larson (1987) maintain that among burn patients, the meaning supplied by religious commitment is an important and understudied part of coping. In fact, religion-as-schema does relate to this process. Recall that schemas influence how people understand what they perceive. A schema may shape the individual's reality to be in line with the schema, even without objective foundation (Taylor & Crocker 1981). For example, Bartlett (1932) found that subjects frequently added causal ties, ignored unusual information, and revised the plot of a non-Western-style Indian folktale until the story resembled a Western schema for folktales. In a similar fashion, a person whose religious schema already includes an understanding of traumatic events may better be able to fit such an event to an extant schema, perhaps imposing understanding and meaning (see Wuthnow et al. 1980). McIntosh et al. (1993) found in their study of religion's role in parental coping after losing a child to SIDS that greater importance of religion was associated with parents' finding more meaning. Having found meaning, a person may be more likely to experience better adjustment to the event. Indeed, McIntosh et al. (1993) reported that the finding of meaning is associated with less distress and more feelings of well-being immediately after the loss and less distress eighteen months later. Viewing religion as a schema allows us to understand *how* religion can impose meaning on traumatic events and *why* religious beliefs might be helpful when dealing with a crisis.

Schemas not only affect how people respond to incoming events and information (and thus how they cope with traumatic events), but schemas themselves are influenced by events and information. Thus, viewing religion as a schema also assists in making predictions about how religious beliefs will change in response to traumatic events.

Religious Change from Trauma

Trauma has been proposed as a cause of religious conversion (e.g., Ullman 1982) as well as a generator of religious doubts (e.g., Friedman et al. 1963). Traumatic events can challenge generally unquestioned and unchallenged fundamental beliefs (Janoff-Bulman 1989; Janoff-Bulman & Frieze 1983; Parkes 1975); sometimes radical changes occur in people's belief systems (Bowlby 1969). Janoff-Bulman and Frieze (1983:7; Janoff-

Bulman 1989) seemed to assume that everyone's basic beliefs will be "shattered" by victimization. However, as reported by Janoff-Bulman (1989), multiple victimizations do not continue to generate change in a person's assumptive world or belief system. Thus, once one is victimized, further victimizations do not necessarily destroy one's beliefs and do not require the same reorganization as an initial victimization. This leaves the door open to the existence of those who do not experience a radical adjustment of beliefs as a result of the initial victimization. Janoff-Bulman and Frieze (1983) wrote that the number of assumptions affected depends on the individual. Perhaps some have developed schemas prior to any victimization that allows them to bypass any dramatic reorganization.

Considering differences in religiosity as differences in elaboration of a religious cognitive schema may allow us to predict who will experience religious change after a crisis. For example, because those who have an elaborated belief system that incorporates understandings of a particular event (e.g., death) should have less of a need to modify or reject their schema when confronted by such events, those people who are most religious at the time of the trauma may experience less religious change. This gains some support by Cook and Wimberley's (1983) findings that there is little evidence that adjustment to the death of one's child produces stronger adherence to religion for those having a religious commitment already—those who already have a framework do not appear to change.

Using a panel of parents who had lost a child to SIDS, McIntosh, Silver, and Wortman (1989) tested hypotheses about religious change derived from viewing religion as a cognitive schema. Because a more developed or elaborated religious schema might be able to assimilate the event better and thus obviate the need for change, McIntosh et al. (1989) predicted that the most religious respondents—those assumed to have the most complex schemas—would experience the least actual change in religion between three weeks after the loss and three months after the loss. Further, a comparison of absolute change supported the hypothesis; pairwise comparisons of differences between group means revealed that absolute change for those who indicated at three weeks after the loss that religion was "not very important" through "very important" did not differ from each other, but each was greater than the absolute change found in those who indicated religion was "extremely important." That this difference is not due to a ceiling effect is inferred from open-ended responses on the effect of the loss and the small number relative to the other groups of those originally in the "extremely important" group who showed a decrement in importance of religion. These findings suggest that those who possess an elaborate or complex religious schema prior to a traumatic event change this schema less—perhaps because the power of the schema reshapes the event rather than vice versa.

FUTURE DIRECTIONS

Viewing religion as a cognitive schema is consistent with previous psychological investigations of beliefs and religion. Further, it has proven useful in understanding how people comprehend and remember religious messages, in the relation between religiousness and people's concept of God, in the process of public evangelism, and in how religion and coping with trauma are related.

These studies exemplify what can be done when viewing religion as a cognitive schema. One area that needs further work is the direct examination of religious schemas. How many people have them? What areas of perception or processing do they influence? What are different ways in which they are formed and organized? Understanding how religious schemas function in general can provide insight into a number of questions.

Psychologists of religion long ago put aside the notion that religion was unidimensional, with people simply varying on how religious they were (Spilka, Hood, & Gorsuch 1985). Thus, if the religion-as-schema view is to be helpful, it must be more than a way to describe "religious" versus "nonreligious" people or people with religious knowledge versus those without it; it must prove useful in dealing with individual differences among religious people. One potential distinction made apparent by viewing religion as a schema is differences in the organization of people's beliefs. Some cognitive organizations of religious beliefs might be highly structured and hierarchical, whereas others might be simple, abstract, and vague. What effect does this individual difference have on the functions of religion in people's lives? Another important difference among people may be in whether their religious schema is salient or central—or whether it is connected to the self (cf. Markus 1977; Spiro 1987a). Two people may have very complex religious schemas. If, for one of them, religion is an important part of the self, then the religious schema is likely to be activated often—perhaps chronically—and thus will have more influence in life than will the other person's schema (cf. Markus 1977).

Another domain in which viewing religion as a schema would be helpful is that of religious experience. For example, certain religious schemas may cause individuals to interpret ambiguous stimuli as religious or mystical in nature. Relatedly, knowing what stimuli or environmental cues activate religious schemas could be used to understand the structure and function of individuals' religious beliefs.

Finally, as suggested by both work on evangelism (Ingram 1989) and on the effect of trauma on religion (McIntosh et al. 1989), considering religion as a schema can be helpful in studying religious change and conversion.

Viewing religion as a cognitive schema is conceptually rich and empirically useful. Whenever an investigator is interested in not only the content of religious beliefs but also their organization, relation to other beliefs, role in problem solving, and effects on perceiving, evaluating, and remembering stimuli, the researcher could consider conceptualizing and applying what psychology knows about the structure and functions of a schema. Psychologists of religion have long known that religion can powerfully affect the way people perceive and understand the world. They have also long known that the world can influence religious beliefs. Religion is more than a cognitive schema, but thinking of it as such provides a useful way to analyze these relations and to understand religious beliefs themselves.

14

TOWARD AN ATTITUDE PROCESS
MODEL OF RELIGIOUS EXPERIENCE

PETER C. HILL

The cognitive revolution has affected most areas of investigation that interest psychologists. To date, however, there has been little research on cognitive processes in the psychological study of religion. Neglect of this dimension is surprising, given that religious behavior is generally rooted in a belief system. Similarly, a void involving the general study of affect (Hill 1995) appears in the psychology of religion despite William James's insistence to be "bent on rehabilitating the element of feeling in religion and subordinating its intellectual part" (1902:492). This chapter addresses this dearth of research on cognition and affect by investigating the promising role that the attitude concept has for the psychology of religion.

I focus specifically on what has been dubbed the "mediational" (Cooper & Croyle 1984) or "process" (Chaiken & Stangor 1987; Fazio 1986) model. Of special interest is an adaptation of the process model offered by Fazio (1986, 1989). This perspective attempts to capture an interaction of cognitive and affective processes that underlie attitudes.

RELIGIOUS EXPERIENCE AS ATTITUDES

Attitudes are central to religious experience. Hill and Bassett (1992) point out how the spiritual and mental aspects of humanity are incomplete

Reprinted and edited with permission of author and publisher from *Journal for the Scientific Study of Religion*, 33 (1994), 303–314.

unless the concept of attitude is included. Viewing religion in terms of attitudes generally does not conflict with extant models. Rather, an attitude approach may complement these other models by examining more precisely the underlying attitudes embedded within the models' major constructs, thus preserving and potentially expanding the truths found therein. For example, an attitudinal approach augments both Allport's (1950) conception of intrinsic-extrinsic religious orientation and Rokeach's (1960) theory of the open and closed mind. The attitude process model promoted suggests that the accessibility of a religious attitude at a given moment may have important implications for measuring religious experience, such as in determining how central or important religion is to a person.

One of the reasons the concept of attitude has not often been used is the considerable historical disarray found in attitudinal research. Abelson (1988) suggests that a primary reason for this disarray is that researchers may not have devoted "enough attention to those attitudes that make a difference to people and society, attitudes that people hold with some degree of conviction" (p. 267). By arguing that the strong belief has much to offer, Abelson recommends religion as one of the most important, yet heretofore overlooked, domains for attitudinal research.

Abelson's (1988) use of the term "conviction" is but one way of conceptualizing attitude importance. A relatively new and provocative attitude model (Fazio 1986, 1989) shares Abelson's view by stressing that the accessibility of an attitude should offer much to the psychology of religion.

Two Foundational Issues

Attitude Accessibility

Social psychologists commonly agree that an attitude involves categorizing an object along some sort of good-bad evaluative dimension. This perspective led Fazio (1986) to the following definition: "An attitude is essentially an association between a given object and a given evaluation" (p. 214). Both "object" and "evaluation" are to be understood in a broad sense: Individuals may have attitudes on almost anything. Similarly, an evaluation is to be viewed on a broad continuum, from that which is strongly affectively based to that which is almost entirely cognitive.

The key construct in Fazio's (1986, 1989) model is *attitude accessibility*, which is conceptualized in terms of the strength of the association between an object and its evaluation. Fazio's associationist orientation suggests that strong attitudes are more readily available with surer applicability when an issue arises that calls for their expression.

Automatic and Controlled Processes

One particular element of the cognitive component of attitude is the distinction between automatic and controlled processes. Shiffrin and Dumais (1981) support this two-process view, suggesting that controlled processing "requires attention and decreases the system capacity available for other processing. Automatic processing does not necessarily demand processing resources, freeing the system for higher level processing and alternative control processing" (p. 111). In reality, most cognitive processes contain some sort of mixture of automatic and controlled components.

Schneider and Shiffrin (1977) and Schneider and Fisk (1980) suggest that the two most distinguishing characteristics between automatic and controlled processing are *capacity* and *control*. With regard to capacity, controlled cognitions require active attention, thereby utilizing resources from the limited cognitive capacity of the individual. Shiffrin and Dumais (1981) not only support this claim but also imply that automatic processing does not decrease processing capacity. Thus, an individual may engage in automatic processes (and may be influenced by the object of such processes) without interfering with other cognitive activities.

The second distinguishing characteristic, control, is especially relevant in applying the attitude process model to the psychology of religion. Here, "control" refers to the degree of regulation an individual may have over a given cognitive process. Again citing prior research, Schneider and Shiffrin (1977), Schneider and Fisk (1980), and Shiffrin and Dumais (1981) characterize as automatic any process that requires attention despite the efforts of the individual to prevent the attention system from being engaged, suggesting a lack of cognitive control. A key feature of automatism, then, is its inescapability.

An Attitude Process Model: Representation in Memory

When we experience an object, any previously stored assessment toward it will highly influence our evaluation of that object. Among the factors involved in how memories are stored, those moderating variables that have been empirically established as contributors to attitude importance will be the focus here.

Moderating Variables

Considerable research (Brent & Granberg 1982; Krosnick 1988) has compared important attitudes (i.e., attitudes that involve an issue or object about which the person cares deeply) and unimportant attitudes on a number of topics. The most relevant findings are that attitudes of greater importance are more accessible in memory (Krosnick 1989) and are characterized by stronger associations between an object and its evaluation. Krosnick has suggested that attitude accessibility and importance are functions of at least three important factors: *frequency of activation* (Yankelovich, Skelly, & White 1981), *saliency* or *distinctiveness* (Krosnick 1986), and *linkage with other constructs* (Wood 1982). Therefore, more important attitudes are likely to be more frequently activated, relatively distinct, and highly linked to related constructs.

Object-Evaluation Association

Some attitudes are strong in the sense that they result from closely linked associations between an object and its accompanying evaluation, whereas the more divorced object-to-evaluation relationship defines a weak attitude. The attitude process model predicts that the associative strength of the evaluation to the object is a major determinant of whether the attitude is expressed automatically or as a controlled process. A strong object-evaluation relationship is necessary for the spontaneous automatic attitude that is relatively easy to access.

However, if the attitude results from controlled cognitive processing, then one has to either actively retrieve a previously stored assessment or create an entirely new evaluation. Such an attitude requires greater effort and is more difficult to access than an attitude that is automatically activated. Such processing occurs when there is a weak object-evaluation relationship (i.e., a weak attitude).

Whether an attitude is strong or weak, it will involve certain beliefs, affect, and values (BAVs). Gorsuch's (1986) extension of Fishbein and Ajzen's (1975) "reasoned action" model of attitudes and behavior suggests that the relationship between attitudes and their guiding beliefs is mediated through both affect (understood as personal feelings engendered by perceived consequences) and values (defined as views of an ultimate end desirable for all people under all circumstances), thus making the model of particular relevance to the psychology of religion. Gorsuch's BAV model is somewhat limited, however, to BAVs, attitudes, and behavior that are construed as a product of "reasoned action." Gorsuch recognizes this limitation and recommends that unconscious decisionmaking models for the psychology of religion also be developed. Though not *explicitly* discussed in detail here, unconscious processes characterize automatic attitude activation far more than controlled activation (Shiffrin & Dumais 1981).

Associative Networking

The associate network theory of memory and emotion is highly regarded and has been the focus of considerable research (see Anderson 1983; Bower 1981). A proposition (which links two or more concepts or images, e.g., "Mary kissed me on the Ferris wheel") is processed by a "spreading activation" to related concepts and propositions through associative linkages. Thus, remembering that Mary kissed me on the Ferris wheel (a proposition), which produces from memory various emotions (e.g., excitement), is an event that becomes affiliated with other events that produce the same emotion(s). Many aspects of the emotion (autonomic patterns, expressive behaviors, evoking appraisals, verbal labels, and so on) are collected together that help strengthen the linkage with the associated event from memory (Bower 1981).

Consistent with the notion of spreading activation, Judd, Drake, Downing, and Krosnick (an unpublished study reported in Tesser & Shaffer 1990) found that the response time of one's evaluation of an issue was faster when it had been primed by an attitude response to a related issue than by a response to an unrelated issue. These same authors also noted that responses on one issue tend to polarize subsequent attitudes, but only on related issues.

Associative networking may occur for both automatic and controlled attitudes. Under conditions of controlled processes, the individual may recognize additional (and potentially measurable) BAVs that further strengthen expressed attitudes as predicted by the reasoned action models. Of greater interest here is the spreading activation process from automatic attitudes. Such linkages should also increase the perceived importance of the attitude (Higgins & King 1981), enhancing the probability of its subsequent automatic processing and its associated network of related attitudes.

Perception, Situation Definition, and Behavior

By approaching attitudes in terms of their functional significance, one can easily see how they influence perceptions. For example, Lynn and Williams (1990) found that attitudes toward labor unions influence how individuals perceive the validity and extremity of either pro-union or anti-union statements and create bias in causal interpretations of actions. The strength of religious attitudes may create a similar perception bias (Lynn 1987). Lord, Ross, and Lepper (1979) discovered that people with strong attitudes on complex social issues are likely to examine empirical evidence in a biased manner by accepting confirming evidence at face value but subjecting disconfirming evidence to critical evaluation.

Certainly one's perceptions will influence how the situation is defined, which in turn will influence behavioral action (Fazio 1986). Latane and

Darley (1968) demonstrated that of subjects who experienced smoke coming from under a door, only those who defined the event as a possible indicant of fire were willing to report it to the experimenter. Thus, perceptions and interpretations of encountered situations strongly influence behavioral actions.

APPLICATION TO THE PSYCHOLOGY OF RELIGION

The notion that an automatic attitude is immediately activated upon the mere presentation of a corresponding attitude object, regardless of any attempt to ignore it, may describe what a highly religious person experiences toward a religious attitude object. A person with a strong attitude toward a religious object or issue may activate that attitude spontaneously and without conscious control upon mere presentation of the object. In contrast, a less religious person, without a strong religious attitude, may require a more reflective effort to formulate an assessment of a religious object or issue. This effort may include retrieving a previously stored but difficult to access evaluation or may involve active construction of an attitude on the spot. In either case, more time and effort would be involved than for the more religious person using an automatic process (Fazio, Sanbonmatsu, Powell, & Kardes 1986).

It is tempting to equate the distinction between automatic and controlled activation of religious attitudes with that between an affective and cognitive basis of religious belief. Given that automatic activation occurs spontaneously without conscious reflection, an automatic attitude, although strong, may actually be rather superficial. In a similar vein, Batson and Raynor-Prince (1983) reasoned that religious questers (who would more likely use controlled cognitive processes with regard to religious objects) should demonstrate greater cognitive complexity in the religious domain than those with an end (intrinsic) or means (extrinsic) orientation. Indeed, it may often be the case that an affectively based automatic activation of a religious attitude may not be well thought through.

Caution is, however, necessary. First, automatism in the process model reflects attitude strength, defined as the strength of the association between a given object and its evaluation. A strong attitude is not necessarily an attitude without prior thought. Indeed, the attitude may be subjected to considerable reflection before it becomes automated. Thus, mindlessness does not necessarily characterize automatic activation. Second, it is premature to label an automatically activated religious attitude as either immature or mature (or pathological or healthy). To do so confuses the *process structure* of the attitude with its *content*.

Measuring Religious Attitude Strength

The importance of a religious attitude is understood in the process model in terms of the associative strength between a particular religious object (such as the Bible) and its evaluation. The strength of the association can be operationalized for empirical testing by a latency of response measure to an attitudinal inquiry (Fazio et al. 1982; Fazio, Sanbonmatsu, Powell, & Kardes 1986; Powell and Fazio 1984). A relatively fast response indicates a stronger (i.e., more accessible) attitude. Lending support to the validity of this idea, Fazio and Williams (1986) found that response time was inversely correlated with attitude-behavior correspondence.

An initial study investigating religious object-evaluation associations (Hill, Jennings, Haas, & Seybold 1992) supports the response latency technique as a way of measuring religious attitude strength. These associations predicted that although attitude strength of religious and nonreligious people toward religiously neutral objects would be similar, attitude strength toward religious objects should be greater for religious people. This was found. Although not designed to be a definitive test of the attitude process model, this initial empirical study not only suggests the validity of the latency response measure of religious attitude importance, but also provides promising preliminary data about the model itself.

WHAT DOES THE PROCESS MODEL OFFER THE PSYCHOLOGY OF RELIGION?

Many potential benefits can be identified by applying the attitude process model to the study of religious experience. To begin with, it provides an alternative conceptualization of the importance and centrality of religion in the life of a religious believer. Kirkpatrick and Hood (1990) have questioned whether the domination of the intrinsic-extrinsic (I/E) religious orientation paradigm during the past few decades has been good for the psychology of religion. By proposing as central features such concepts as attitude importance, attitude accessibility, and the automatic/controlled attitude distinction, the process model is an attempt to provide a called-for alternative.

Relation to Extant Models

One of the virtues of an attitudinal approach to religion is that it need not conflict with current theoretical models and may increase the utility of such extant models by enhancing our understanding of underlying cognitive and motivational processes.

Religious Orientation. After decades of research on Allport's (1950) conception of mature and immature religion, Kirkpatrick and Hood (1990) lament that there is little understanding of what such terms as *religious orientation, intrinsic,* and *extrinsic* actually mean. They ask, "Is it [religious orientation] about motivation, personality, cognitive style, or something else?" and suggest that "perhaps it is a little of each; but in any case, greater precision in definition is clearly called for from a scientific perspective" (p. 444). They are especially disappointed with the lack of both a conceptual and empirical underpinning of the intrinsic dimension, suggesting that "in the end it seems to measure the important but theoretically impoverished construct of (something like) 'religious commitment'" (p. 448).

Allport's I/E distinction can be traced back to his personality concept of *functional autonomy* of motives, suggesting that religious orientations are essentially motivational in nature (cf. Meadow & Kahoe 1984: 290–299). Nevertheless, the heuristic value of the religious commitment variable (whether conceptualized as intrinsic religion or not) needs further development. What, for example, are the cognitive and affective bases of such a commitment?

In response to Masters's (1991) concerns with their disappointment in I/E research, Kirkpatrick and Hood state that a good theory of religious commitment "should try to show how religious experience crosscuts these various domains [i.e., motivation, cognition, and personality style] in a dynamic and interactive way" (1991:320). An approach to religious experience stressing attitude importance may not only be useful in further conceptualizing religious commitment, but it may also help researchers elucidate some cognitive and affective processes underlying such commitment. As a case in point, rather than relying upon a rather simplistic descriptive typology of "living" or "using" religion, researchers could explore the conditions under which the religiously committed are more likely to use automatic cognitive processes. Such an investigation, in turn, may help explain the extent to which religious beliefs are used to comprehend everyday experiences. Kwilecki's (1991) view of religious development as a process through which perceived "awareness of the supernatural becomes 'chronic' in a life, that is, broadly and consistently functional" (p. 65) is compatible with the religious commitment perspective promoted here. By measuring attitude importance, researchers may also begin to disentangle relations such as what components of religious experience (e.g., ritual, doctrinal, experiential, ethical, and so forth) are typically demanding of (or reflect) religious commitment.

Open- and Closed-Mindedness. Rokeach's (1960) theory of the open and closed mind distinguishes two types of cognitive systems: a highly centralized system with a small number of central "authority beliefs" from which other beliefs emanate, and a relatively decentralized system where authority beliefs are more tentative and less controlling of related beliefs. Both centralized (i.e., closed-minded) and decentralized (i.e., open-minded) belief systems are inherent in disbelief systems as well. That is, central authority beliefs in the closed system say much more about what not to believe than do authority beliefs in the open system. Similarly, changes in authority beliefs in the closed mind (though less likely to occur) have, relative to the open mind, greater repercussions throughout the belief system. Rokeach (1960:4) identified Eric Hoffer's *The True Believer* (1951), a book with a heavy focus on religious belief, as the single major stimulant of his thinking.

Again, the attitude process model may illuminate many of the cognitive and affective processes at work in both open and closed systems. For example, peripheral beliefs in Rokeach's theory (which are often *attitudes* as they are defined here) may be more automatically activated within the context of an authority belief in a closed rather than open system. The lack of reflective effort in accessing the peripheral belief may help explain why contradictory peripheral beliefs can coexist within the closed system, though Rokeach himself (1960:36) explained such coexistence in terms of belief compartmentalization. It is clear that Rokeach has provided the psychology of religion with a helpful *descriptive* model of two general cognitive structures. The attitude process model may provide missing explanatory linkages within Rokeach's theory, thus making it more useful for the study of religious experience.

Other Advantages

Other benefits of the attitude process model for the psychology of religion can be identified. First, it has introduced what may be a valuable unobtrusive measure of religious attitudes, namely, latency of response to an attitudinal inquiry. This may be a fairly good indicator of automatic activation of an attitude toward an object (Fazio, Sanbonmatsu, Powell, & Kardes 1986). Such a measure may be useful as an adjunct to a number of self-report scales designed as measures of either substantive or functional aspects of religion. Attitude researchers are constantly searching for measures other than self-reports, with their well-documented social desirability confounds. Within the scientific study of religion, the social desirability issue has been one focus of many in the debate regarding the validity of measures of intrinsic religion (cf. Batson & Ventis 1982:277–281). This approach provides a means for measuring attitudes without the accompanying social desirability bias.

Second, Fazio, Sanbonmatsu, Powell, and Kardes (1986) suggest that the degree to which an attitude is automatically activated predicts the resiliency of the attitude to counterinfluence. How one processes new information may differ, depending on whether or not the attitude is automatically activated at the presentation of an attitude object. Attitudes automatically activated may make the individual less vulnerable to counterattitudinal information (Wood 1982). People with religious attitudes that are automatically activated may make the individual less vulnerable to countermessages (such as other religious conversion appeals). Thus, the automatic-controlled distinction may be useful in investigating such phenomena as religious apostasy.

Finally, the process model may have important implications for the well-documented attitude-behavior inconsistency. Fazio, Sanbonmatsu, Powell, and Kardes (1986) suggest that automatically activated attitudes more reliably guide behavior than do attitudes governed by controlled processes. They reason that in the case of controlled processes, activation of an attitude may not always occur and behavior toward the object may proceed either without an evaluative consideration of the object or solely on the basis of whatever feature of the object happens to be salient in the immediate situation. Such factors may lead to behavior that is not congruent with one's true attitudes. This hypothesis, if supported, would also apply to the religious domain.

Social psychologists increasingly recognize the theoretical merits and apparent benefits of conceptualizing attitudes in terms of process. Given the central role that attitudes play in religious experience, an attitude process approach also appears worthy of further development by psychologists of religion.

15

IN THE EYE OF THE BEHOLDER: A SOCIAL-COGNITIVE MODEL OF RELIGIOUS BELIEF

ELIZABETH WEISS OZORAK

When everything else has gone from my brain . . . the neighborhoods where I lived, . . . my own name and what it was on earth I sought, . . . and finally the faces of my family—when all this has dissolved, what will be left, . . . the dreaming memory of the land as it lay this way and that. I will see the city poured rolling down the mountain valleys like slag, and see the city lights sprinkled and curved around the hills' curves, rows of bonfires winding . . . When the shining city, too, fades, I will see only those forested mountains and hills, and the way the rivers lie flat and moving among them.

—Dillard, 1987

With these words Annie Dillard begins the prologue to her autobiography, *An American Childhood.* They provide the perfect metaphor for religious faith: an emotional landscape of primordial strength and simplicity upon which we erect structures of reasoned belief. Those structures reflect the tastes and habits of our time and culture. Some fit better into the landscape than others, and some are sturdier than others. They may be remodeled, may fall into decay, or may be obliterated by fire or storm;

Original contribution, edited with permission of author.

the lay of the land itself changes little, except in the rare event of an earthquake.

The fundamental premise of this model is that the individual never approaches religious experience as a tabula rasa. Some relevant inclinations seem to be genetically predisposed (Waller et al. 1990). Many are provided through our earliest experiences, especially those involving authority figures about whom we care deeply. These inclinations take the form of belief frameworks and powerful emotional predispositions. They structure and color our perceptions and our memories of subsequent experiences so as to make them fit within the framework we have already built. As with all deep convictions, the emotional foundation comes first and remains central, with cognitive elaboration occurring gradually (Abelson 1988). A painful lack of fit may cause us to adjust our beliefs away from their early moorings, but the habits of mind and heart we acquired with them are usually evident in the contours of our new ideas. To understand an individual's religious faith, as it is experienced, we must understand these habits.

Psychologists have learned a great deal about how the mind works. We know that we actively construct meaning rather than passively absorb it; our cognitive processes are remarkably efficient, due in part to robust heuristics and biases that lead us to satisfy rather than maximize outcomes; we process positive information better than negative information and tend to ignore disconfirming evidence unless we are tripped up by a bad outcome (Matlin 1994). This knowledge has been applied to a wide variety of real-life settings (see Arkes & Hammond 1986) but has not been extensively applied to religion. Recently, however, there have been calls for more work examining the cognitive processes that underlie religious belief and practice (e.g., Hunsberger 1991). What follows is a description of how some of these processes may function in a religious context.

TOP-DOWN PROCESSING EFFECTS IN PERCEPTION

Top-down, or concept-driven, processing is perception that is preceded and shaped by expectation. We rely heavily on this type of perception to make sense of incomplete or fleeting information—for example, when we use our knowledge about language and journalistic style to skim an article. Sometimes our expectations override the actual information, as when we mistake a stranger for someone we know and are expecting to see. Emotional expectations can influence our reactions in a similar way—for example, when we laugh at an unfunny joke because the source has previously been funny (Wilson, Lisle, Kraft, & Wetzel 1989). Thus, top-down processing includes both a perceptual readiness and, where appropriate, an emotional readiness. The emotional predisposition may also enhance the perceptual.

We often respond emotionally to people, places, and events that remind us of those associated with powerful feelings—the place that is just like home, the person who uncannily resembles an old flame. Recent work (Gillespie 1995) suggests that for many, the experience of the sacred is specifically associated with tears. "You'll have to excuse me," [one of her informants] said, reaching for a Kleenex; "my tear ducts are directly connected with my spirituality" (p. 8).

Louis Pasteur said that chance favors the prepared mind. We might equally well say that the prepared mind favors chance—like the woman described by Hunsberger (1990) who saw the face of Jesus in a billboard spaghetti ad. Note that we need not assume that she was wrong. Our expectations about what we will perceive are often correct. Our emotional hopes and fears are often justified.

However, strong expectations and strong hopes make it difficult to distinguish between correct and incorrect perceptions, especially where there is no educative feedback. In many real-life situations there is no simple way of determining the degree to which our perceptions have been accurate (Gilovich 1991).

This type of processing is one cause of people's tendency to confirm rather than test their beliefs (Snyder & Cantor 1979). People may create de facto selective exposure to confirming information by avoiding sources that are likely to refute their beliefs (Fiske & Taylor 1991). More certainly, people attend selectively to confirming evidence, weight it more heavily than disconfirming evidence, and recall it more readily. They also tend to look for flaws in opposing viewpoints but not in their own (Gilovich 1991). The same set of mixed information can thus cause people on both sides of an issue to become more convinced of their own position.

As we can see, first information plays a disproportionate role in forming attitudes. People also show a desire for evaluative consistency—sometimes called the halo effect. If they like one aspect of something enough, they try hard to like everything else about it; and if they get off on the wrong foot, they find it hard to like anything at all (Wilson, Lisle, Kraft, & Wetzel 1989). Interestingly, if people do change their minds, they generally "rewrite history" to the effect that they have always really thought what they currently think (Hasher, Attig, & Alba 1981). The exception seems to be where there is a clear crisis that effectively explains their change of heart. The overwhelming tendency is to order information to fit within a plausible narrative framework (Pennington & Hastie 1988). Cognitive pressures, like social pressures, are overwhelmingly on the side of consistency in religious belief and commitment. A massive study by the Search Institute (Benson 1990) bears this out; nearly one-half of their subjects reported stable levels of commitment across the life span, whereas nearly all the others reported a gradual, linear increase in commitment to their faith.

SCHEMATIZATION OF MEMORY

Religion is acquired through a combination of direct experience and secondary information. Since it is stored in memory, it is subject to the same biases as other material in long-term memory. It must be structured according to some systematic principles, which will be evident in retrieval as well as encoding. Conceptual frameworks, or schemas, allow us to efficiently organize what we know. Subsequently, we are tempted to trim perception to fit our schemas, and the longer we keep information in memory, the more distorted it becomes (Matlin 1994). Because schemas serve as a kind of filing system, they allow us to retrieve information more easily when it fits the system than when it doesn't. Schemas also allow us, often unconsciously, to fill in gaps in our information in plausible ways. As memories become more distant, we are increasingly likely to engage in this kind of reconstruction. Thus, our memories about religious experiences tend with time to resemble increasingly our expectations for religious experience. Recent evidence that religious experiences conform to expectations (Spilka, Ladd, McIntosh, & Milmoe 1994) probably reflects both perceptual and mnemonic effects of schemas. If the bulk of our experience is increasingly congruent with our beliefs, we will likely become more committed to those beliefs.

Our reliance on what we can remember results in an "availability bias" (Tversky & Kahneman 1973). The more easily we can recall an instance that fits a particular category, the more likely, common, or true we believe that category of instances to be. One result of this bias is that the more we read or hear a statement, the more confident we are of its truth (Hasher, Goldstein, & Toppino 1977), as long as we are not asked to analyze why we believe it (Millar & Tesser 1986a). Religious testimonies of others—or repeated statements of disenchantment—can encourage an individual to invest in a belief system simply because the statements themselves are memorable.

A poster popular in my school years claimed, "If you can imagine it, you can become it." At least, the more easily we can imagine something, the more likely we think it is (Kahneman & Tversky 1982). In addition, having once imagined it, we often cannot distinguish between our memories of real and plausible imagined events, especially if the simulation is elaborate and vivid (Carroll 1978). This tendency increases with age (Johnson et al. 1979), presumably because we have so many more events to keep straight. Even if the experience is real, repeated review and interpretation changes the nature of the memory (Matlin 1994). Belief systems, religious or not, encourage this kind of reinterpretation; and emotional readiness (or lack of it) for certain interpretations prompts further analysis of the events and one's responses to them.

Schema effects are heightened by chronicity, the tendency to be "chronically primed" with respect to certain kinds of information. The newly pregnant woman suddenly sees other pregnant women and women with babies everywhere; the dieter is conscious of everyone's weight and eating habits. Attempts to suppress this awareness generally only make it worse (Wegner 1989). Chronic schemas produce the most efficient processing of information and heighten long-term recall for relevant material (Fiske & Taylor 1991). The person whose religious schemas are constantly primed will notice, remember, and reinterpret religious information more than the person not thus primed. As those chronically primed schemas become more richly elaborated, they also become harder to disconfirm, since they allow for more complex ways of accommodating exceptions.

Interpretation of events is dramatically affected by what Kahneman and Tversky (1984) call cognitive frames. For instance, we can be influenced to accept or reject an option simply by framing the consequences in terms of gains or in terms of losses. People avoid risking gains and seek risks with regard to losses (Rachlin 1989). These effects are puzzlingly resistant to change and retain their appeal even when we are aware that they are misleading us (Kahneman & Tversky 1984). This may explain why people who are unhappy—for example, with their close relationships—are more prone than happy people to change religious beliefs and affiliation; they are gambling with losses rather than with gains (Ozorak 1989).

SOCIAL-COGNITIVE EFFECTS ON ATTITUDES AND BEHAVIORS

The above effects are precipitated by individuals as a consequence of the way the mind works. However, people don't typically think in isolation (Resnick 1991). In what ways—other than outright pressure to comply— might others influence a person's beliefs?

First of all, others may provide the point of departure for the formation of a belief. Parents typically provide the anchor point for a child's religious beliefs (Ozorak 1989). Whereas many people move away from their parents' beliefs and values, they do not generally adjust far enough to obscure the effect of the original anchor point. What is more, whether commitment is high or low, adjustment is often in the direction of the original tendency. This phenomenon, called polarization, is apparently due to two factors: information sharing and social comparison (Isenberg 1986).

For any issue, there exists a pool of relevant arguments. An individual will have thought of some, but not all, of these arguments; therefore, the more people who share their thoughts, the larger the sample of arguments that will be aired. If the pool, or the selection of individuals sampling from it, is biased, the result will be a disproportionate number of arguments in favor of the person's original position, thus strengthening the person's commitment to that position. Given people's tendency to confirm prior beliefs, we can guess that the sample is often biased in this way. In fact, just reviewing the arguments in favor of one's position can cause polarization when the individual is already committed to that position.

The other root of polarization is the belief we all cherish that we are better than average. Interaction with others and comparison of our views and behaviors with theirs allow us to evaluate the extent of our virtue, whether it is defined as obedient piety or as hard-headed questioning. If we find ourselves wanting, it is tempting to become more extreme. Furthermore, if we are not sure which virtue to adopt, we are safest in choosing those manifested by people whom we admire for other reasons (Brown 1986). Thus, social comparison is partly responsible for the emotional nature of religious cognition. An emotional struggle ensues when those we admire and care about espouse virtues that we find ourselves unable to endorse—for example, when the child of fundamentalist parents becomes convinced through personal experience that their beliefs are wrong (Ozorak 1988).

Such wholesale rejections of parental beliefs and values are atypical. One reason already discussed is the confirmatory bias. Another is the transactive nature of memory (Wegner 1986) and thinking (Resnick 1991); we rely on other members of our social groups to help us remember and reason. We may also shape reality to conform to our expectations (Snyder & Swann 1978). People often respond to our perceptions of them by acting accordingly and may continue to act out our view of them with others. In this way, our expectations become self-fulfilling prophecies. Those who expect a religious group to support them emotionally may elicit nurturing behavior, whereas skeptics and deviant believers can elicit rejection. People who expect to gain strength from prayer and worship may act in ways that cause important changes in their social experiences. For example, joining a covenant group, volunteering at the local soup kitchen, or consciously being more patient and loving with others may provide new opportunities for social support and positive feedback.

Members of especially intense and demanding religious groups may experience the sunk cost effect. That is, when a person has made a heavy public investment in something, there is tremendous resistance to cutting one's losses even if the original promise has not been realized (Arkes & Blumer 1985). This seems to be due partly to our aversion to sure losses, discussed earlier, but is probably also a result of not wanting to appear misguided. Furthermore, in order not to feel misguided, the person may decide that the investment has paid off after all and reinterpret the nature of the loss, becoming more committed in the process. Disconfirmation effects like these have been well documented among publicly committed religious believers (Batson 1975; Festinger, Riecken, & Schachter 1956).

Outcome and Interpretation

People try to interpret events as supporting their existing commitments and may unwittingly cause outcomes that provide such support. They may also experience confirming outcomes solely because they expect to— in other words, they experience a kind of placebo effect. The psychological state of belief creates a different physical state. Such effects have been documented for hypnosis, although recent studies (see Wagstaff 1981) indicate that suggestion alone suffices to produce them.

Scientists are trained to try to exclude such effects, but in practice they are enormously important. If, for example, my migraine headaches disappear because I have been hypnotized, or have visited a faith healer, or have taken an inert pill, I have been cured just as surely as if I had taken an active drug. This is fully compatible with the practice of modern medicine. Physicians rightly take advantage of placebo effects when they convince their patients of the miracle qualities of new treatments. Likewise, if a person prays and subsequently finds that it becomes easy to solve previously intractable problems, that person has been helped by faith. It may be theologically pertinent to ask whether God intervened to produce the result, but in practical terms the answer is irrelevant: The result itself is indisputably real. Moreover, useful effects from any one source (prayer, psychological suggestion, or physiological intervention) need not preclude useful effects from the others: One may trust in Allah but still tether the camel.

Wise religion and wise science are those that identify appropriate areas of likely help. Scientology, for example, originally claimed to be able to eliminate colds; but such claims were easily falsified (Bainbridge 1980).

Embarrassments of this kind are not limited to religion. Medicine itself provides many examples of misplaced confidence in potentially harmful procedures (Gilovich 1991; Nolen 1987). In science and faith alike, sincerity may be necessary, but it is not sufficient.

The fact remains that some consequences are easier to assess than others because they pertain to a well-defined event, whereas others have multiple end-points or outcomes that are ambiguous or subjective. A person either does or does not get a cold; a critically ill person dies or lives; a child gets a coveted bicycle for Christmas or not. Health is much trickier to specify (So you think you're healthy? But maybe you could be in even better shape), and emotional well-being is subjective as well as hard to define. Even concrete events may occur in an indefinite time frame, which makes it hard to tell what has influenced their occurrence. A couple trying to conceive a child may seek both physical and spiritual aid over an extended period—which in itself may increase the likelihood of conception—so that if they succeed, it is difficult to know what made the decisive difference. Highly religious individuals are more likely than nonreligious individuals to pray for emotional or subjective outcomes (Ozorak & Kosiewicz 1994); it stands to reason that they will be more likely to feel that their prayers are answered.

Of course, outcomes are not always favorable, not by any stretch of positive thinking. As Spilka, Hood, and Gorsuch (1985) suggest, unexpected events that challenge feelings of personal control or threaten self-esteem are especially likely to cause a reappraisal of religious beliefs and commitment. The individual will try to restore coherence to the belief system but is also powerfully motivated to minimize the likelihood of further upheavals. As Pargament (1987) put it, we want answers, and we also want to stay psychologically together. We can use religion to help us understand events or as a path for action in the face of events, or both.

Given the emotional nature of religion and our vulnerability in crisis, satisfactory paths for action are probably the greater need in restoring our sense of order. Meaning often derives from action and is probably not always necessary. Wulff (1991b) describes an alternative to the traditional dichotomy of belief and unbelief in which a person appreciates, is moved by, and participates in a faith without literal belief in its doctrine. In his description, I recognize cosmopolitan Jewish friends who see no intrinsic evil in cheeseburgers but who nevertheless derive spiritual satisfaction from keeping kosher dietary laws and Catholic friends who are comforted by reciting Hail Marys despite intellectual doubts about the virgin birth. Because religious beliefs are often "hot cognitions," anchored in emotional experiences and associations, we may not be able to describe them and their effects on our behavior accurately. However, the emotional underpinnings will continue to drive our behavior (Wilson, Dunn,

Kraft, & Lisle 1989). We then interpret and reinterpret the resulting experiences to check for goodness of fit with existing beliefs.

Ritual enactments and sacred texts may be construed as mythic and performative rather than literal—true in an active emotional sense rather than a descriptive one. This doesn't make them inaccessible to disagreement, but it changes the nature of the debate (McClendon & Smith 1994). Both ritual and text also serve as means of identifying oneself with a community and family. Abrupt changes in faith are often associated with ruptures in the fabric of family or community (Ozorak 1993). As William James (1902) noted nearly a century ago, reason alone is rarely a match for compelling emotional experience. There is an important convictional difference between what we know and what we merely know about.

Truth and Consequences

The fact that our perceptions are unreliable, our memory faulty, and our emotions self-protective with regard to faith says no more about the realness of the divine than about all the other things we misperceive, misrecall, and misjudge: It simply offers a perspective beyond our verbal reports. It may be that those very biases allow us to set aside a mindset that would otherwise seal us off from the divine. A colleague of mine once grumbled, "You psychologists with your empirical methods—you'll never understand religion. Ask the mystics." He might have cited James (1902):

> It must always remain an open question whether mystical states may not possibly be . . . superior points of view, windows through which the mind looks out upon a more extensive and inclusive world. The difference of the views seen from the different mystical windows need not prevent us from entertaining this supposition . . . [In that case] we should be liable to error just as we are now; yet the counting in of that wider world of meanings, and the serious dealing with it, might, in spite of all the perplexity, be indispensable stages in our approach to the final fullness of truth. (pp. 385–386)

James's criteria for truth were pragmatic. The consequences, or "fruits," of faith must justify it, personally and socially. His own belief is articulated in just these terms: "God is real since he produces real effects" (p. 461). Modern data on the effects of religious belief are less tidy and, perhaps, less heartening. Modest relations are often found between religiousness and personal well-being or socially approved behavior, but since these studies are typically correlational, they can't tell us much about causation. Such studies often use narrow measures of religiousness (church attendance or belief orthodoxy) or restricted subject pools (white middle-class Christians). In one of the few studies that attempted to alter the participants' behavior, Darley and Batson (1973) found that allusions to the parable of the Good Samaritan had no effect on seminarians' helping behavior. There was no relation between self-reported religiousness and helping; and worse, the highest rate of helping was only 63 percent. Good weather seems to be a more reliable predictor of altruism than does religious faith (Aronson, Wilson, & Akert 1994).

My guess is that research itself will have to get messier before generating the kinds of powerful studies that will illuminate the justifiability of human religious convictions. With McClendon and Smith (1994), I think that convictions can be shown to be justifiable, but we need to attain a better understanding of what the personal and social bases of justification ought to be. Should they include James's (1902) "solemn, serious and tender . . . glad[ness]," his "love of life, at any and every stage of development" (p. 50, 453)? Is theology really, as Chopp (1994) and Bondi (1995) would have it, "about saving lives" (Bondi 1995:11)? We know that behavior does not always reflect attitudes, but that some prediction from one to the other is possible (Fiske & Taylor 1991). To return to the metaphor at the start of this chapter, I think we need to get a much clearer picture of the shape of the spiritual landscape if we hope to predict how experience will flow over it. We are not beyond needing James's careful attention to minute details of religious experience in individual cases, adding perhaps a richer conception of the communal context in which they arise, plus the dimension of change over time in the same individuals. In order to understand what James calls the wider self, we too may need to become wider selves.

James would surely have endorsed the following exhortation from Henry David Thoreau (1854):

> We must learn to reawaken, and keep ourselves awake, not by mechanical aids, but by an infinite expectation of the dawn, which does not forsake us in our soundest sleep (p. 78) . . . Only that day dawns to which we are awake. There is more day to dawn. The sun is but a morning star (p. 293).

That is Thoreau's appeal to emotional and perceptual readiness. It stands also as a fitting challenge to psychologists of religion.

Commentary: Believing Is Seeing —
How Religion Shapes Our Worlds

This section focuses on how religious beliefs shape what we perceive, recall, and think. Each chapter extends recent and influential work in social and cognitive psychology to understanding religion. The starting point is religion as beliefs. These theories do not, however, hold that religion is merely this. All point to social and contextual influences on religious cognition and to behavioral outcomes from these cognitive processes.

The first two chapters highlight the explanatory function of religion and how this ties in with attribution theory in social psychology. As Proudfoot and Shaver indicate in Chapter 11, people often explain internal states and external events by attributing their source to something other than the genuine cause or at least weighing the different possibilities in a nonveridical manner. As noted in Chapter 12 by Spilka, Shaver, and Kirkpatrick, religion is universally available as a source of potential causes. In both these chapters, the authors specify factors (e.g., religious cues) that may contribute to whether it will be used. Note that this approach is neutral as to the truth of religious explanations. Its principles can be applied equally well to a person who underestimates divine influence as to one who overestimates it. What it suggests are questions to think about when considering whether people will perceive religious involvement. One research task is to ascertain which of these have how much influence, for whom, and under what circumstances. This seems a prime area for the type of experimental approaches advocated by Batson (Chapter 1). Can the findings from other areas of psychology extend to religious attributions? Does the presence of clergy or religious symbols change the weights individuals assign to particular causes? Can we generate religious emotions or experiences by altering the psychologically available causes? Do people make differing types of attributions to the divine if they consider it to be personlike rather than not (see Spilka, Shaver, and Kirkpatrick's C1.2 and C1.3)? Do those for whom religion is a key contributor to self-esteem show different patterns of attributions compared to those for whom religion is relatively unrelated to the self? Empirical demonstrations of such effects would bolster the claim that these theories provide a true explanation of real-life religious phenomena.

Chapters 13, 14, and 15 deal with more specific cognitive structures and processes. One way to view them is as specifications of what the person brings to the attributional task and how it affects the process. There is more to be taken from these, however. In Chapter 15, Ozorak lays the groundwork with her survey of the social cognition literature, discussing how it applies to religious phenomena.

Hill's focus in Chapter 14 is more specific; by examining religion as an attitude process, he makes clear and specific predictions and suggests a number of interesting directions. In Chapter 13, McIntosh concentrates on the schematic nature of religion. He demonstrates how considering religion from this standpoint can lead to insights into how it functions in real-life domains. Although utility is a necessary criterion in evaluating a cognitive approach, it is not enough to demonstrate the veridicality of this approach. Studies need to be done to explore the specific nature of religious cognitive structures.

These articles allow us to consider what it means to be "religious" from a potentially different perspective. As Hill notes, individual differences in religion likely exist separately in the content and the cognitive processes or structures associated with the content. It may not be the endorsement of particular doctrines or beliefs that makes one religious but may rather be their accessibility (Hill), their connection to the self-schema (McIntosh), or their degree of chronic activation that determines this (McIntosh, Ozorak). A person may believe fully and unquestionably in the resurrection of Christ, but unless he or she thinks about this often, connects it to or uses it in understanding various life events, this person may not appear—or be?—any more religious than a person who has no such belief. Not all beliefs are equal in influence, and these approaches tell us how and why this may be. Empirically, it suggests that we may wish to operationalize degree of religiousness by accessibility of religious attitudes (from Hill) or according to whether someone is self-schematic for religion (see McIntosh), for example.

These theoretical approaches point out that there is much that is *not* unique about religion and that this commonality with topics studied in other areas of psychology provides a cornucopia of findings, methods, and explanations that help us understand the psychology of religion. Can what is distinctive about religious beliefs, behavior, and emotion be productively addressed by such borrowed theories? Confirming whether these approaches can be generalized to religious phenomena *is* one empirical task. Hill points out that extending these theories to religion may be helpful to their development, as religious attitudes are held with much more conviction than those typically studied in the social psychology laboratory. McIntosh notes that schemas of the level of abstraction of religion are much less studied than others. Research carefully evaluating how well these notions hold in the domain of religion are needed.

However, more must be done for these to be more than trivial extensions of social cognitive work to the religious domain. Proudfoot and Shaver note that the psychology of religion has a plenitude of post hoc explanations. Can these theories allow us to predict and manipulate religious phenomena? Hill's discussion of automaticity suggests that under stress, people will rely on automatic processing. Combined with Ozorak's statement that religious cognitions may be laid down early, this is consistent with McIntosh's consideration of the importance of religion in the stress process. Perhaps this is why religious beliefs are key in coping contexts. One way of evaluating the first premise is by examining the effect of cognitive load on the religious versus nonreligious cognitions. Can we *cause* religious thinking in this way? Doing so would help us understand why people rely on it more in some circumstances and would likely lead to a more precise understanding of individual differences.

PART 6

The Experience of Religion

16

A Taxonomy of Religious Experience

RODNEY STARK

The study of religious experience provides an example of those strange discontinuities that beset social science. At the turn of the century, religious experience was a major concern of a number of eminent scholars. The next generation of scientists failed to pursue these promising beginnings, and in subsequent decades almost nothing has been added to our understanding of religious experience.

If the quest is to be taken up again, the initial task is conceptual. The term "religious experience" covers an exceedingly disparate array of events—from the vaguest glimmerings of something sacred to rapturous mystical unions with the divine or even to revelations. Some basic elements must be systematically extracted from these diverse phenomena if theory and empirical investigation are to be carried much further. I attempt here to develop some basic subtypes and ordering dimensions for organizing the variety of experiences to which people attach religious definitions.

The conceptual scheme has been informed by data from a sample of Protestant and Roman Catholic church members. These data include both quantifiable and qualitative information on the religious experiences of respondents. They indicate the relative frequency of different

Reprinted and edited with permission of author and publisher from *Journal for the Scientific Study of Religion*, 5 (1965), 97–116.

forms of religious experience and illustrate how people perceive such experiences.

Following previous writers, I suggest that the essential element characterizing religious experience, which distinguishes it from all other human experience, is *some sense of contact with a supernatural agency*. Or, as it has been well put by Glock, religious experiences are "those feelings, perceptions, and sensations which are experienced by an actor or defined by a religious group or a society as involving some communication, however slight, with a divine essence, i.e., with God, with ultimate reality, with transcendental authority" (Glock 1959:26–27).

Various events or feelings are only "religious experiences" if a person *defines* them as such. Obviously many of the events I shall be discussing are most often not given religious definitions these days. I am not, then, concerned with such events in themselves, only when someone attaches to them some sense of contact with the supernatural.

All religious experiences are therefore occasions defined by those experiencing them as an encounter between themselves and some supernatural consciousness. For analytic purposes, these are treated as inter-"personal" encounters, and an important dimension along which these encounters can be ordered is the sense of intimacy between the two "persons" involved. By conceiving of the divinity and the experiencing individual as a pair of actors involved in a social encounter, some configurations of relations between them may be specified that can be ordered in terms of social distance. We initially sketch four such possible configurations of inter-actor relations: (1) The human actor simply notes (feels, senses, and so on) the existence or presence of the divine actor; (2) Mutual presence is acknowledged; the divine actor is perceived as noting the presence of the human actor; (3) The awareness of mutual presence is replaced by an affective relationship akin to love or friendship; (4) The human actor perceives himself or herself as a confidant of or as a fellow participant in action with the divine actor.

As in normal human affairs, encounters of the former types are more frequent than those of the latter—one has many more acquaintances than friends. Similarly, any more intimate relationship has likely passed through less intimate previous states. This order coincides with the frequency with which various kinds of religious encounters are distributed within a general population and with the frequency of different kinds of divine encounters in the career of a single individual.

Although the majority of religious experiences seem to consist, at the sensory level, of feelings or other emotional states, these may also be accompanied by visual and auditory phenomena usually referred to as *visions* and *voices*. We may now consider whether these simple inter-actor configurations are adequate to organize and classify the remarkably varied phenomenon of religious experience.

THE CONFIRMING EXPERIENCE

The most general kind of religious experience, and the one most frequently reported in America, shall be called the *confirming* experience. Such experiences provide a sudden "feeling," "knowing," "intuition," and so forth that the beliefs one holds are true, that one's weltanschauung provides an accurate interpretation of the ultimate meaning of reality. What is meant here is a sudden intensification of this conviction—a special occasion of certainty induced by an experience of the presence of sacred influence. Confirming experiences may be divided into two subtypes on the basis of the specificity of the perception of divine presence.

1. The first of these subtypes will be called a *generalized sense of sacredness*. Here are diffuse, ill-defined, emotional experiences of reverence, awe, or solemnity that lie on the borderline between the sacred and profane. These are the least spectacular occurrences that people will label as religious experiences. Typically, these are instances of special ritual or emotional significance that are accompanied by a mild quickening of faith and a sense of surrounding holiness. Often, such experiences are associated with sacramental acts such as Communion or Baptism or with other special church occasions.

Another common association of general senses of sacredness is with major life-cycle milestones, for example, as with a great sense of sacredness invested in such moments as marriage ceremonies or the death of loved ones. Although these encounters clearly have deep meaning and impact for those who experience them, they are very general and unspecified feelings and are described primarily in terms of an emotional state.

2. This more focused subtype of confirming experience will be referred to as a *specific awareness of the presence of divinity*, akin to what James called the "something there" experience (James 1902). The characteristic feature of these experiences is the perception that divinity in a specific sense (e.g., God, Jesus, a creator, and so on) is present in a special way (close at hand, in the room, and the like), as opposed to a general sense that the divine is present everywhere. I must emphasize that the present divinity is *not* perceived as specifically acknowledging the presence of the individual. Such feelings commonly occur in response to what strikes individuals as empirical confirmation of the validity of their religious perspective. For example, the wonders of nature commonly elicit confirming experiences among Christians, often during a visit to the forest or countryside by an

urbanite unaccustomed to these sights. Some reported a sense of God's close presence when awed by an especially nice sunset or by other phenomena that indicated to them that the world testifies to God's handiwork.

Whatever their origins, confirming experiences are relatively common among members of American churches. Forty-five percent of the Protestants in our sample responded that they were "sure" they had experienced "a feeling that [they] were somehow in the presence of God." Forty-four percent of the Roman Catholics were also sure. These experiences were much more common among fundamentalist groups than among mainline bodies.

These perceptions of divine presence may lead to more complex religious experiences. However, many people who go this far go no further.

THE RESPONSIVE EXPERIENCE

The next most common type of religious experience may be called *responsive*. Where the confirming experience indicates only an awareness of the existence or presence of divinity, the responsive refers to occurrences when a person feels that this awareness is mutual, that the divine has also taken specific notice of the individual's existence.

These responsive experiences may be further subdivided into the three basic modes by which the divine may be interpreted as taking notice of an individual: *salvational, miraculous,* and *sanctioning* experiences.

1. The *salvational* subtype denotes states in which individuals feel that the divine has chosen to count them among his own, sealing their election into eternal reward. It is in this category that the vast body of literature on Christian "conversion," at least in the "twice-born" sense, belongs. Belief in a judging God who rewards or punishes eternally gives special salience to this particular kind of religious experience and leads to expectations concerning salvation, which probably accounts for this experience being so widespread. Denominational differences among Protestants varied from 9 percent of the Congregationalists to 93 percent of the Southern Baptists. However, these differences reflect the degree to which salvational experiences are encouraged by fundamentalist and liberal churches in America. Such activity is at best unseemly among the liberal denominations, whereas it is highly esteemed by their more conservative brethren.

Thus, it is no surprise that church bodies have developed well organized and institutionalized mechanisms to generate and channel predispositions for salvational experiences. And their "saved" members have a well-developed rhetoric concerning how one best seeks this experience, which reveals that this is typically a consequence of building up a sense of sin and guilt that is triggered by the pleading and urging of preacher, congregation, and often close friends during prayer meetings specifically intended for "saving souls."

Indeed, this engrossment with sin as the dynamic of salvation led Starbuck (1899) to define "conversion" as *"a process of struggling away from sin, rather than of striving toward righteousness"* (p. 87). Salzman (1953) argues that such conversions are likely to be "regressive" and "psychopathological," typically occurring "during attempts to solve pressing and serious problems in living, or to deal with extreme, disintegrating conflicts . . . It is a pseudo-solution and is likely to occur in neurotic, prepsychotic, or psychotic persons" (pp. 177–179). Given this preoccupation with guilt and its role in salvational experiences, it is no wonder that the common theme in accounts of such experiences is cleansing and purification.

It must be emphasized that although I have drawn heavily on traditional Christian salvation experiences, I do not mean to limit the salvational type to this narrow range of events. Rather, I mean to classify here all occasions when individuals sense that the divine has turned attention to them, acknowledged special interest in them, and extended some verification of their special status in his eyes.

2. The *miraculous* subtype of responsive experiences is less a thing of the spirit than of the flesh. It denotes instances when people feel that the divine has taken note of them during a period of crisis and difficulty and has actively intervened in the processes of the physical world on their behalf. A common incident is the healing miracle.

A second common variety of miraculous experiences involves escapes or rescues from danger. A number of respondents cited unexpected survival of auto accidents as instances of miraculous intervention by God.

Another common event attributed to divine intervention was a good turn in economic affairs. Many respondents reported getting jobs, finding lost letters, getting new appliances, and so forth as a direct result of divine action in their behalf.

The prototype of the miraculous, however, is probably the healing or life-sparing intervention and thus could be called a "foxhole" variety of religious encounter. Like the salvational, it is based on emotional strains, typically fear, but unlike salvation, it does not commonly occur in specially prepared social situations. Lacking the reinforcement such situations provide, the miraculous is probably much less likely than the salvational to have long-lasting consequences for religious commitment. Although some turn to a deep religious involvement in gratitude for an apparent response to their emergency prayers, as did Luther after he survived the thunderstorm, they perhaps more commonly behave like the scared soldier in Hemingway's vignette, who promised to tell the world about Jesus if he lived through the shelling, but who never told anybody.

3. The miraculous has been characterized as perceptions of divine intervention in the material world to the advantage of the individual. However, the divine may be felt to intervene in negative ways, that is, to interfere in temporal affairs to punish or deflect the individual from his goals. We shall call this genre of divine response the *sanctioning* experience.

People who undergo sanctioning experiences often report that it was for their own good, that although God sent them apparent misfortune, this prevented them from further harm.

Some people report a less indirect linkage between sanctioning experiences and a valued outcome: God simply made them aware of his displeasure toward them for certain acts or attitudes, and they ceased their "sinning," thus becoming happier directly.

THE ECSTATIC EXPERIENCE

The third type of religious experience is designated the *ecstatic*. This involves all the components of the two less intimate types—an awareness of the divine and a sense that awareness is returned—and in addition, denotes a deepening of this sense of mutual awareness into an affective personal relationship. If the confirming experiences are like knowing of God's presence, and the responsive are like being introduced to God, then the ecstatic are comparable to the intimacy of friendship or, perhaps, even courtship. Indeed, a heavily sexual motif runs through the ecstatic writings of Catholic monastics, past and present, and similar reports of physical sensations and exhilaration dominate Protestant and non-Christian ecstasies as well.

The dominance of this sexual theme led Leuba (1925) to argue convincingly that sexual frustration and preoccupation were major psychological sources of the religious ecstasies of the "Grand Mystics" of the Middle Ages. Observation of religious ecstasy among more ordinary people in recent times reaffirms this impression of a close linkage between religious ecstasy and sexual arousal.

The prototype of this kind of religious encounter is a physical and psychological upheaval of intense proportions, similar to orgasm, intoxication, or seizures—an overpowering of the senses by divine "touch." In this category we may classify such occurrences as "visitations of the Holy Spirit," often expressed by jumping, shaking, screaming, and speaking in other tongues as the Holy Spirit gave utterance.

Physical sensations associated with ecstatic experiences are perhaps the most common feature of such experiences reported by cloistered nuns. Similar sensations of being touched by electric current, X-rays, radar, and so on are common features of the delusional systems of psychotics.

It is clear that the distinction between ecstatic and responsive experiences of the salvational variety is somewhat difficult to draw. Clearly, there is a sense of intimacy between the human and divine actors during encounters marked by the divine designation of the person as chosen for divine approval. But such intimacy, likely to be a once-in-a-lifetime encounter, falls short of what we call ecstasy. Ecstasy denotes a sense of union and distinct involvement between the actors. It is not difficult to distinguish ideal examples of the salvational and ecstatic from one another—a sense of being marked and chosen is contrasted to a sense of being engulfed by divine love, usually accompanied by extraordinary sensory manifestations and psychic states akin to loss of consciousness, seizures, and so forth. The difficulty lies in deciding the status of borderline encounters—the extremely intense salvation or the relatively mild ecstasy. Here, for now, we can only suggest focusing on the emphasis given to being chosen as against being embraced, noting, too, that salvational experiences may directly lead into ecstatic experiences during a single divine encounter.

THE REVELATIONAL EXPERIENCE

The fourth, and least common, type of religious experience is the *revelational*. Here, the person has not only been taken into the bosom of the divine, but has become a confidant of the divine. The recipient is given a message concerning divine wishes or intentions. Upon occasion, the divine may give such messages through signs or symbols, and some have even claimed the divinity sent them written messages, but typically revelations are spoken. This raises the issue of visions and voices as characteristics of religious experiences, which I have postponed until now.

Visions—occurrences that individuals define as visually beholding the divinity—may accompany any or all of the types of religious experiences previously discussed, although they are probably more common during the more intimate varieties. However, even confirming experiences can take the form of a vision—the divinity is seen but does not acknowledge the presence of the viewer.

Voices, on the other hand, by definition cannot be part of a confirming experience, since if the divine speaks to you he acknowledges your presence—you might say he has given you a message. Yet, the revelational becomes a messy category indeed if all experiences accompanied by a voice are included. The criteria for classifying voice-accompanied religious encounters can be taken from the content of what was said. If the voice simply acknowledged the person's existence, summoning a person to salvation, urging comfort, or giving directions on how to solve problems or escape trouble, and the like, then it may be classified as part of a responsive experience. If the voice speaks primarily of love, blessing, affection, and so on, then it is likely to be part of an ecstatic experience. However, if the voice imparts *confidential information about the future, divine nature,* or *plans,* then it must be considered to be revelational.

Having excluded a variety of divine messages from consideration as revelations, we are still faced with an extraordinarily heterogeneous genre of religious experience. The revelational applies equally to persons receiving divine instructions to grow a beard and to those presented with new theologies. For this reason, I shall introduce three further distinguishing characteristics that, if treated dichotomously, would generate an eightfold typology of revelational experiences. I shall not attempt systematically to consider the cells of the typology here but shall limit discussion to the variables and sketch some of the more interesting combinations.

1. Perhaps the most crucial distinction to be drawn is between revelations that are *orthodox* and those that are *heterodox.* By orthodox, I refer to divine messages that are consonant with existing interpretations of divine nature, will, and desires and that, at most, simply elaborate what is already accepted as true. This is best illustrated by saintly and papal revelations. Most revelations are probably orthodox, since cultural innovation is a relatively uncommon human activity. However, the aspect of revelational activity that makes it fraught with disruptive potential for existing religious institutions (and secular institutions sanctioned by prevailing theology) is the possibility that the information imparted by the divinity will be heterodox, that is, contradict and challenge prevailing theological "truths."

We need only think of Jesus Christ for a classic example of the devastating role revelations may play in the career of religious institutions. This threatening characteristic of revelations has led such institutions to develop strict controls on revelational activity and often to ban it entirely. Foremost among these controls in Western society have been means for distinguishing "true" from "false" revelations. The standard employed has been orthodoxy, the argument being made that since no true revelations could be heterodox, heterodox revelations are self-impeaching and false by definition.

This distinction between "good" and "evil" spirits closely relates to notions of black and white magic and in the Catholic tradition is complemented by the practices of canonization and anathematization. But despite these controls and the many other mechanisms that have been employed to preclude or channel revelational activity, people continue to bring back new and heretical versions of eternal truth from their encounters with divinity. Even the contemporary American scene, for all its secularization, abounds in messiahs, prophets, and messengers bearing new revelations and often acknowledging new gods. Hence, the distinction between orthodox and heterodox revelations remains of both historical and current use for classifying and investigating religious experience.

2. A further division in revelational experiences may be made between *enlightenment* and *commission*. The former indicates that aspect of divine communiqués that provides information concerning ultimate truths and instructions to take particular actions to further divine designs. The divine may be perceived as simply offering information or may commission the recipient to play a divinely inspired role in human affairs. These two varieties of revelations are analytically distinct, but it should be noted that they often occur together, and indeed, commissions are perhaps most commonly combined with enlightenment, although the reverse is less true.

Enlightenment itself proves amenable to subdivision into what I will call the *prophetic* and the *theological* types. The prophetic designates enlightenment concerning future events and states in the empirical world, whereas the theological refers to enlightenment on eternal verities (e.g., the nature of divine will and character). Either variety of enlightenment may or may not be combined with a commission. The prophets of the Old Testament offer classic instances of revelations that commissioned people to act on the basis of their foreknowledge of impending events. Typically, it would seem, prophesy foretells calamity, often the imminent destruction of society or even of the material world. Such revealed prophetic visions remain potent social forces in the modern world.

3. The third distinction concerns the scope of the revelation's application. Perhaps most often, revelations have significance only for the recipient or for some personal associates. For example, many prophetic revelations foretell the death of loved ones or provide other intimate foresights. Commissions, too, may only concern the personal behavior; however, sometimes the message has relevance for all people or for large groups, such as in the case of new theologies, eschatological prophesies, or commissions to launch social reforms. I shall only speak of those with individual relevance as *personal revelations* and of the latter as *general revelations*.

Having elaborated the specific subtypes in this taxonomy, criteria of order must be considered. The presentation of the types was governed by an order of analytic complexity—simple to elaborate—and it was also suggested that they represent discrete stages through which individuals pass in developing greater intimacy in their contacts with divinity.

This is not to suggest that the less complex and less intimate types are always experienced prior to more complex and intimate contacts, but this is probably the course of passage. It may also be true that several stages could occur in one spiritual encounter, the incident beginning with a simpler state and passing shortly into the next more complex type. However, it is *not* suggested that having attained a more complex type marks the end of less complex experiences. In fact, indications are that the more intimate contacts one has, the more often the less intimate contacts are experienced, too. For example, nuns who have had ecstatic experiences report voluminously on daily or even hourly confirming experiences. Some of the West Coast millenarians who had confirming responsive experiences as often as several times a day commonly had ecstatic experiences once a week or more and had revelational experiences fortnightly. This suggests that not only does this ordering of types of religious experience indicate their frequency within a population, but it also indicates their frequency for those who manifest all four types.

Besides being ordered on the basis of increased intimacy and decreased frequency, this succession of the types reflects the degree to which they are encouraged or discouraged by religious institutions as well as by secular norms. While confirming experiences are strongly supported by most churches, responsive experiences are encouraged by fewer churches, ecstatic experiences are favored by even fewer, and revelational experiences are even opposed by the vast majority of religious institutions. Secular society values religious experiences in the same order, and the public definition of these types ranges from "pious" to "nuts." It has been truly said that many who were canonized during the Middle Ages would be in asylums today.

Thus far, I have discussed only experiences that constitute encounters with "good" divinity; however, voluminous reports of satanic encounters suggest that, historically, "evil" and "good" supernatural forces have been about equally common. Simply to keep these two kinds of contact separate, they may be called *divine* and *diabolic* religious experience. Because it seems reasonable to assert that diabolic contacts have played nearly as important a role as the divine in Western religious life, any attempt to provide a classificatory scheme for religious experiences should address both kinds of supernatural contacts.

Since the same elements are involved in diabolic contacts as in the divine—encounters of increasing intimacy with what is defined as a supernatural consciousness—it is possible to directly adapt the types just presented to the "evil" experiences. Because this adaptation is relatively simple and because remarks made about divine experiences also apply to the diabolic, I shall only briefly sketch the taxonomy of diabolic experiences.

The Confirming

Corresponding to the generalized sense of sacredness discussed previously, the vaguest and most ill-defined diabolic experiences can be described as a *generalized sense of evil*. Here such events are classified as individuals experiencing the presence of evilness or sinfulness. The more focused confirming experiences with the diabolic, like those with the divine, are viewed as *a specific awareness of the special presence of an evil supernatural being or force*.

The Responsive

This refers to encounters during which the supernatural actor acknowledges the presence of the individual. This may take three forms.

1. *The temptational:* occasions when the evil being specifically beckons one to sin and evil to draw away from divine grace, which is the diabolic counterpart of the salvational experience.

Data indicate that temptational experiences are nearly as common as salvational experiences among Protestants and considerably more common than salvation among Catholics. Thirty-two percent of the former were "sure" they had experienced "a feeling of being tempted by the Devil," whereas 36 percent of the Catholics were "sure." Again variation among Protestant groups was great: from 11 percent of the Congregationalists to 76 percent of the Southern Baptists.

2. The *damnational* corresponds to the miraculous. Here, evil supernatural forces are seen as intervening to reward "sin" and thwart "righteousness." The folk saying, "The Devil helps his own" captures the essence of this experience. The damnational experience differs from the temptational primarily by being an unexpected intervention in time of trouble or need rather than a holding out of inducements to act.

3. The *accursed* is the diabolic counterpart of the *sanctioning* and refers to instances when the evil being is seen as intervening in the material world to bring misfortune to individuals who have rejected sinfulness.

The Terrorizing

This refers to highly emotional encounters with diabolic agencies during which the individual feels horrified, and terrified, by a specific sense of being intimately assaulted by an evil being.

The Possessional

Whereas the revelational indicates messages from the divine being and perhaps coparticipation in action, the possessional refers to similar relations with the diabolic. Here are perceptions of being given satanic messages and confidences and even feeling oneself taken over as an agent of Satan and lending assistance to him. Such possessional experiences may also be distinguished on the basis of the three variables introduced to classify revelational experiences.

Although possessional experiences may seem outlandish in these relatively unbedeviled days, they are historically common and, indeed, may still be found. After all, many of the wretches burned during the witch hunts of the Middle Ages actually believed themselves to be in league with the Devil. The West Coast cultists frequently explained away behavior, such as fits of temper or violations of religious prohibitions, in terms of having been taken over by Satan and, hence, not being personally responsible for these acts. They also frequently identified outsiders—including, eventually, the sociologists who observed them—as conscious agents of Satan.

In summary, I show that religious experiences, both diabolic and divine, can be analytically broken down into four general types and into several further subtypes on the basis of the configuration of relationships between the divine and human actor during any spiritual encounter. Moreover, I argue that these four general types may be similarly ordered on the basis of complexity; intimacy of the inter-actor relationship; frequency, both in their distribution within populations and occurrence for individuals; and variation in the degree to which they are encouraged or discouraged by both religious and secular norms. Further, I suggest that this order represents a developmental model and that individuals pass from the less complex to the more complex during the career of their religious encounters.

In conclusion, a word should be said about the utility of, and the criteria for assessing, conceptual schemes such as this in scientific inquiry. Any phenomenon, or cluster of phenomena, can be characterized in a great many different ways. Aside from clarity, there is no compelling intrinsic reason any particular way ought to be preferred. Yet any conceptualization of a phenomenon requires some assumptions that certain aspects of it are its essence and other things about it are trivial or irrelevant. When we ask, "Irrelevant to what or to whom?" we come to the underlying character of all scientific definitions or formulations. The answer is this: irrelevant to the tasks of predicting the occurrence of this phenomenon and other phenomena to which we think it is related. Scientific concepts are essentially utilitarian, as is the scientific definition of truth itself. The test of scientific concepts, then, lies in their usefulness in making predictions about various events. It is on the basis of how well they suit such tasks that we speak of them as true. Indeed, from the scientific perspective, one does not even ask whether they are "real," for there is no other acceptable sense in which such concepts are believed to exist.

Although the taxonomy elaborated in this chapter seems appropriate for classifying the reports written by respondents, any final judgment of its worth can only come when its utility is evidenced in empirical investigations of religious experiences. If it is to be useful, the assumption that these types of religious experience represent a *developing sequence* of felt encounters with the supernatural must be verified by empirically finding that the data scale in this manner. If this proves to be the case, then the various theoretical considerations presented here will enhance our understanding of the data and ought to point out some beginnings for predicting the occurrence of religious experiences.

17

THE EMPIRICAL STUDY OF
MYSTICISM

RALPH W. HOOD, JR.

One can divide empirical research in the contemporary psychology of mysticism into two extreme camps. Although such dichotomies always court danger, including that of oversimplification, they also focus on strategies that guide research.

One camp argues for "getting respect" (Batson 1986) by directing the psychology of religion into the mainstream of current academic psychology. The intent of this camp is clear: the psychology of religion can be made both theoretically and empirically more meaningful when its concepts and methods are derived from the psychological mainstream. Current proponents of this view have focused upon attribution theory (Spilka & McIntosh 1995), attachment theory (Kirkpatrick 1995), and helping behavior (Batson, Schoenrade, & Ventis 1993).

In the other camp are those who find that some of the ideas central to the psychology of religion can profitably be found within the academic study of religion. For these scholars it is psychology that gains respect from incorporating into its discourse concepts and methods intrinsic to religion. One central thesis emerges: Social scientists have been unable to account for the totality of the sense of God within concepts once considered definitive as explanations of religion (Bowker 1973; Preus 1987). As such, a psychology of religion is enhanced rather than diminished to the extent it shares a common discourse with religious studies. This is the position I wish to argue in the presentation of a psychology of mysticism

Original contribution, edited with permission of author.

that is both empirically based and yet guided by ideas derived from both religious studies and psychology.

To realize this aim, I shall first focus on recent critical assessments of mainstream psychology that broaden the horizon of empirical study. I will then examine the conceptualization and measurement of mystical experience and then survey reports on the facilitation, expression, and evidential value of religious experience. In each instance I will suggest empirical research possibilities. My goal is to move from mainstream social psychology to empirical work that is legitimated by contemporary postmodern reconceptualizations of methodology and theory construction (Gergen 1991; Parker 1989; Parker & Shotter 1990; Roseneau 1992).

A PHILOSOPHICAL CAVEAT

A caution is in order here to remind the skeptical reader that there exists a vast literature critical of mainstream psychology, especially social psychology. Whether one begins with critiques of a too-narrow empirical emphasis (Harre & Secord 1972) or the admission of postmodern discourse into criticisms of social psychology (Gergen 1991), the outcome is the same: Claims to methodologically privileged avenues to scientific knowledge are indefensible. Within a postmodern perspective, mainstream social psychology is itself problematic (Parker 1989; Parker & Shotter 1990). At a minimum, any appeal to absolute methodological criteria as normative for the social sciences in general, or social psychology in particular, is suspect. Psychologists need not be unduly sensitive about this. As Ravetz (1981) has noted, the claim that advancements in science are methodologically driven is less historical fact than cultural image: "For, ever since the time of Galileo, Descartes and Bacon, the dominant image [of science] has involved their claim that there exists a correct Method that leads to Truth" (p. 200).

Within postmodern discourse, methodological claims to truths are themselves dubious. Neither measurement (Gorsuch 1984) nor experimentation (Batson, 1986; Batson, Schoenrade, & Ventis 1993), nor indeed any single methodology (Roth 1987), can be the criterion for judging social science. Although most journal articles are written as if theories are in some sense tested as empirical hypotheses to be either verified in a classic positivist sense (Carnap 1966) or falsified in a more contemporary Popperian sense (1959), advancements in the philosophy of science such as the Duhem-Quine thesis (Robinson 1981) make it apparent that no single study or set of studies falsifies or verifies theory-based empirical research. Indeed, the debate from Kuhn on, centering on the omnipresent yet ever-rejected notion of "paradigm," has raised the possibility of the incommensurability of evidence and the entirely suspicious nature of the social sciences (Hood 1994; Kuhn 1970, 1977; Lakatos & Musgrave 1970; Laudan 1977). Most striking is the growing appreciation of the irrational bases by which scientists select among methodological and theoretical options. Feyerabend (1975) has made the philosophical case most forcefully, but his views are echoed in less extreme form in critical histories of psychology, particularly dynamic psychology (Ellenberger 1970).

The complex issues involved in this debate suggest a broader context within which to place the empirical study of mysticism. This caveat should remind readers that what constitutes empiricism, and an empirically derived theory, is in no sense resolved. As such, the present proposal regarding the empirical study of mysticism, utilizing concepts and ontological claims from the domain of religion, is not as radical as it might appear to those unfamiliar with contemporary critical debates regarding the philosophical foundations of the social sciences. As empiricists we must still gather and assess our data, but precisely what this process is must be evaluated with an open-minded ecumenical spirit perhaps more characteristic of contemporary religious studies than the social sciences.

Empirical Identification of Mystical Experience

Mysticism is regarded here as a way of life that acknowledges the validity of personally experienced mystical states. This may apply to personal experiences or to those of others. Nothing in such states requires religious interpretation. However, when mystical experience becomes part of one's ultimate concern, it becomes religious mysticism (Jones 1986). Mysticism, of course, need not be defined as an essential aspect of any religion. Still, where it is an ultimate concern, such an experiential claim implies the centrality of mysticism to the understanding of religion (Katz 1983). An empirical corollary of these claims is that mystical experience can occur both within and outside of religious traditions. A second corollary is that wherever it occurs, it can be expected to affect lives, as it is perceived to be an experience of reality about which one is ultimately concerned. A final corollary is that the nature of mystical experiences ought to have identifiable empirical consequences.

In other words, as one experiences ultimate reality in personal terms, metaphors like "love of God" become operative; reality experienced impersonally suggests other metaphors such as submission or acceptance of "what is."

Embedding the study of experiences in a longitudinal context permits the empirical study of variations over time in the meaning of such events to an individual. These understandings are often guided by the growth of knowledge within particular faith traditions (Katz 1983).

CONCEPTUALIZING AND
MEASURING MYSTICISM

It is now possible to operationalize and measure the report of mystical experience. Operational definitions, however, become meaningful when they are theoretically based. Our concern with mysticism is founded upon the phenomenological work of Stace (1960), in which two forms of mysticism are delineated: introvertive and extrovertive. Although criticisms of Stace abound (see Katz 1978), his analyses of mysticism remain central to the philosophical literature on mysticism. Although conceptually challenged, his distinctions are often supported in independent studies (Hood 1994; Jones 1986). In addition, Stace's phenomenological work is the basis for the most frequently cited scale that empirically measures the report of mystical experience, the M-Scale (Hood 1975; Doblin 1990).

Two aspects of Stace's conceptualization of mysticism are most relevant to measurement efforts. To begin with, Stace argues for a distinction between experience and its interpretation, a matter that has dominated current debates on mysticism and religious experience (Hood 1985; Proudfoot 1985; Spickard 1993). Basically, this polemic centers on the extent to which interpretation dominates any claim to minimally based mediated experience. The gist of these arguments is that any claim to experience is itself interpretive. Thus, mystical claims to unmediated experience are either wrong, meaningless, or seriously compromised. Although the debate cannot be detailed here, an empirical corollary is that factor analyses of mysticism measures ought to identify an interpretative factor or factors relatively independent of a more fundamental experience factor. Such treatments of the M-Scale identify at least (1) a minimal interpretive phenomenological factor, and (2) an interpretive factor. Several factor analytic studies suggest the adequacy of a two-factor solution readily perceived as mystical experience and its interpretation (Caird 1988; Hood 1975; Reinert & Stifler 1993). However, both Caird (1988) and Reinert and Stifler (1993) suggest the possibility of a three-factor solution in which two interpretive factors emerge, one religious and the other not. These studies confirm a stable structure for the M-Scale, reflecting Stace's unity criterion of mysticism, plus an interpretative factor or factors. However, all of these studies lack sufficient subject (Ss) to item ratios to be definitive (Tabachnick & Fidell 1983).

The conceptual literature on mysticism identifies two discrete experiences of union as central to mysticism, one sense-based and the other not

(Hood 1985, 1989a; Stace 1960). Measurement ought to identify both of these experiences. Stace (1960) refers to them as extrovertive and introvertive mysticism. The first refers to a perceptual unity among a multiplicity of objects. Introvertive mysticism refers to a non-sense awareness of unity devoid of all content. Stace (1960) feels that the extrovertive denotes a lower form of mysticism likely to lead to introvertive mysticism; I believe the opposite is true (Hood 1989a). Empirical investigation of the relation of these two mysticisms requires longitudinal studies to identify possible developmental patterns. However, until recently, factor analysis of the M-Scale failed to identify these two forms as independent factors. Again, in most analyses, the ratio of Ss to items was too small for adequate treatment. Recently, an analysis with a more adequate sample size produced introvertive, extrovertive, and interpretative factors with acceptable reliabilities (Hood, Morris, & Watson 1993).[1]

It is recommended that these three scales be employed in future research. Given the centrality of the two mysticisms in the conceptual literature, we can now suggest several empirical corollaries based on their operationalization. First, different processes are likely to be involved in each form, since one involves sense perception and the other either does not or minimally involves such activity. Second, the intensity of extrovertive mysticism ought to be a function of the number of sense items integrated or seen as "one" in the experience. A more intense extrovertive experience will integrate more sense objects. The obverse of this should hold for introvertive mysticism—the more sense percepts abandoned the greater the intensity of the introvertive experience. Third, introvertive mysticism is traditional, usually cultivated by various meditative and religious traditions and hence may be more susceptible to voluntary attainment. The rich literature on meditation supports this contention (Goleman 1977; Naranjo & Ornstein 1971). Lastly, extrovertive mysticism should be spontaneously reported. However, it also can be cultivated.

A further suggestion is that extrovertive mysticism is similar in process to concept formation where discreet items are integrated under a broader rubric. The retort to "One cannot compare apples and oranges" is to talk about fruits. Still, extrovertive mysticism is more perceptual than conceptual; to talk about it necessitates reflection. Although research on both language and perception is relevant to reports of extrovertive mysticism, it has yet to influence empirical work in the psychology of religion. Fruitful progress has been made in the related area of altered states and transpersonal psychology (Tart 1969, 1975).

---

1. The items for these scales may be obtained from the book editors or from Dr. Hood.

Survey Reports of Mystical Experience

Surveys of mystical experience consistently indicate that this phenomenon is common and not restricted to pathological groups (Hood 1985; Spilka, Hood, & Gorsuch 1985). Further, about one-third of randomly sampled Americans and Europeans report such events. Unhappily, few studies intercorrelate the various indices of mystical experience used in survey research, so precisely what is measured is in doubt. At face value, most survey questions are similar to M-scale items (Spilka, Hood, & Gorsuch 1985). Although reports of mystical experience correlates positively with socioeconomic class, education, and age (Hardy 1979; Hay & Morisy 1978), the most consistent finding involves gender; females claim higher and more frequent experiences.

Even though the precise role of language in the report of mystical experience is debated, it is rarely a focus of research (Hood 1994; Proudfoot 1985; Spickard 1993). Empirical studies suggest that a simple constructionist view of language in the report of mystical experience is not adequate (Hood 1994; Spickard 1993). Three studies are particularly relevant here.

First, Thomas and Cooper (1978) found that individuals responding positively to a question commonly used in survey studies revealed a variety of identifiable experiences, predominantly psychic, faith, and consolation experiences. Only 2 percent were codifiable as mystical in the sense of unity and other criteria compatible with Stace's analysis. This suggests that samples variously identify experiences as mystical. Without specific measurement standards, a variety of incidents are affirmed as mystical that have minimal conceptual relevance to the concept as developed by Stace and Hood. Yet further analysis cannot rule out even some psychic and faith experiences as also mystical (Hood 1989a). Different language may or may not reflect similar experiences in contexts that are made relevant only by the investigator's interest and concerns.

Second, Hood and Morris (1981) have shown, using the widest possible criteria of mysticism employed in research, that individuals equally knowledgeable about the criteria for identifying mysticism differentially report having such episodes. Hence, people do not simply equate knowledge about mysticism with a personal *mystical* experience.

Finally, using physiologically assessed voice analysis, stress was shown to differentiate among persons affirming or denying mystical events. Some claim experience when they in fact have not had such, whereas others deny having experience that in fact they apparently have had (Hood 1978). Thus, no simple relation between language and experience is adequate to handle the complexity of precisely what the referent is when descriptions of mystical experience are given or what roles language plays other than descriptive in the discourse of mysticism in specific or religious experience in general (Keller 1978; Ramsey 1957).

These studies suggest several empirical propositions worthy of investigation: (1) Individuals with appropriate language are more able and hence more likely to report mystical experiences; this can include both false positives and negatives; and (2) the report of mystical experience is not simply linguistically determined. Language may serve to identify an encounter as an instance of mysticism rejected by others even though the experience is the "same." Measurement criteria can be used to identify "sameness" in these cases, but such claims are bounded by the conceptualization that guides their use. Furthermore, experiences identified as identical by given measurement criteria still leave unmeasured differences. Theory must denote what constitutes irrelevant differences.

Finally, the role of language in experience links psychology to literary criticism (Parker & Shotter 1990). Reports of mystical experience need not be descriptive. As with mystical literature, they can be aphoristic, biographical, performative, evocative, dialogical, or merely commentary (Katz 1992; Keller 1978). What is done when individuals speak of mysticism needs sophisticated empirical study (Brown 1994). For example, studies failing to differentiate contemplative and institutionalized psychotic populations from normals on the M-Scale (Stifler et al. 1993) indicate that further contextualization is needed to understand why M-scale scores do not differentiate among these groups. There is nothing inherent in reports of mystical experience that determines the obviously different social psychological fates of such groups. The reaction to and exploration of a mystical experience determines its social psychological relevance. Hence, studies of mysticism must embed their measurements in longitudinal, developmental contexts, both for individuals and groups, so that the wide variety of consequences of mystical experience can be fruitfully explored empirically.

The Facilitation of Mystical Experience

Mystical episodes can be facilitated. Although many see these occurrences as sudden and unanticipated, other accounts follow specific practices, religious and nonreligious. My recent review of quasi-experimental studies utilizing psychedelic drugs, set and setting stress incongruities, and solitude reveal that all stimulate mystical experience (Hood 1995). Another vast literature on meditation suggests its role in expediting mystical experience (Almond 1982; Goleman 1977; Naranjo & Ornstein 1971).

These studies lead to several empirical propositions. First, cultivated mystical experiences probably follow belief commitments to traditions that value and legitimate mysticism. Such institutions have beliefs and practices that identify experiences considered legitimately mystical. The empirical investigation of how this is done is crucial and has just begun. Preston's (1988) work on Zen practice is a noteworthy example. Second, mystical experience incorporated into meaningful belief systems is unlikely to influence one's life. If such events are not seen as inherently meaningful (Rosegrant 1976) and when they are not so interpreted, they may be regarded as incidental. Third, no particular consequences need follow from mystical experiences. How mystical episodes are contextualized in groups (if they are) and internalized personally (if they are) are the empirical predictors of their effects. Although these events have often been identified in the conceptual literature as unanticipated and evocative of new beliefs (O'Brien 1965), they may also be predicted and confirm one's prior beliefs (Spilka, Brown, & Cassidy 1992). Furthermore, they can lead to more esoteric interpretations of mundane doctrines among those who stay within traditions after personal mystical experiences (Katz 1983; Tiryakian 1974). This latter fact accounts for the vast literature within every tradition that suggests an inner, "esoteric" meaning to otherwise more "exoteric" and literal doctrines (Tiryakian 1974). As Jacobs (1995) has emphasized, Judaism has both its rabbinical tradition rooted in the Torah and its mystical tradition based on the Cabala. It can safely be said that no faith tradition exists without esoteric interpretations of otherwise exoteric doctrines proffered by those claiming a deeper experiential understanding. The empirical study of how traditions shape such esoteric understandings is crucial.

The Evidential Value of Mystical Experience

A vast conceptual literature claims that mystical experience has an ontological relevance that contributes to its psychological importance (Burhenn 1994; Copleston 1982; Davis 1989; Hood 1995; Katz 1978). While not denying constructionist claims to social reality, empirical research can benefit from hypotheses derived from the evidential value of religious experiences in general and from mystical experiences in particular. The language of mysticism, whether expressed in terms of God or ultimate reality, suggests that an ontological claim is made. Perhaps most instructive, because they are so far removed from psychology, are the many publications, both popular and critical, relating mysticism to such claims compatible with modern physics (Capra 1983; Jones 1986; LeShan 1966; Talbot 1980; Zukav 1979). This debate parallels our own position that mystical experiences are evidential in an inductive sense (Berger 1980; Hood 1995). If such events are empirically valid, then the language of their expression may require broader considerations that are essentially metaphysical in nature, as James noted (Hood 1992; James 1902). Mystical experience is noetic and its ontological claims, although not privileged, must be taken seriously. Furthermore, they are capable of empirical investigation (Schoen 1985). To refuse to confront mystical claims as descriptive of reality is to miss an important aspect of the psychological investigation of mysticism. Without arguing metaphysical issues, the above philosophical caveat suggests that an a priori refusal to admit the possibility of the descriptive validity of mystical experiences is unwarranted.

Two additional points are made in this regard. First, insofar as extrovertive mystical experience is sense based, it makes claims to reality that must be taken as significant perceptual experiences. That they may be about phenomena more conceptually legitimated within religious discourse than in psychology is not to rule out their reality status for the psychologist. As Swinburne (1981) has succinctly put the issue: "Unless we take perceptual claims seriously, whatever they are about, we shall find ourselves in an epistemological Queer Street. Religious perceptual claims deserve to be taken as seriously as perceptual claims of any other kind" (p. 195). Second, despite the apparent appeal to a nonsensory experience, introvertive mysticism must be considered a reality claim. As Jones (1986) has noted: "Invoking Occam's Razor to disallow reference to factors other than sensory observables ones is question-begging in favor of one metaphysics building up an ontology with material objects as basic" (p. 225).

The inductive approach to the evidential value of religious and mystical experiences suggests propositions certain to enliven research on mysticism. First, it makes the study of mystical experience decidedly empirical but in a manner that requires experience and not a priori metaphysical and ontological propositions to rule out relevant data in advance. Second, despite wide variations in descriptions of mystical experience, the inductive strategy demands that we thoughtfully regard linguistic elaborations and identify the experiences that make them meaningful. Such events are empirically identifiable either in the lives of the describers or in those within their tradition to whom such occurrences are important (James 1902). The discourse of any tradition must be appreciated, but it is no more privileged than any other discourse. However, as Reich (1994) has recently shown, perhaps language common within religious discourse gains significance only when certain forms or levels of thought are achieved that themselves can be empirically identified. Third, description must be taken seriously, as empirical reality claims with ontological and metaphysical relevance. That God exists, that one can be absorbed in the Void, that all is One, are claims to be investigated under the possibility that they are true and affect experience. Perhaps mystical experiences reveal the "that-ness" of the world and not necessarily the "how-ness" of the world explored by science (Jones 1986). But that the world is, is as empirical as how the world is.

Religious reality claims are in principle analogous to scientific claims. The experiencer must (1) be sensitive to reality, (2) be conceptually sophisticated in what is to be perceived, and (3) be committed to canons of truth that demand an openness to experience within which reality is revealed. As perceptions of the scientist are corrected and modified by conceptual concerns linked to reality, so too are mystical claims. Theories of the transcendent are no more "troublesome," to use Garrett's (1974) term, than any other. One could argue that all scientific theories reference some aspect of transcendence. Kuhn's much-maligned arguments concerning the role of paradigm in scientific knowledge affirm the necessity of tradition as a source of knowledge both of and about the transcendent.

Advancements occur within traditions by those knowledgeable in how the tradition explains reality, what it defines as problematic, and the nature of what is transcendent. Thus, as Ravetz (1981) has noted, a Kuhnian view of science affirms the link between tradition and knowledge. Thus, religion and science share in the affirmation of tradition-based knowledge claims. Problems are as much defined by traditions as they are resolved within them. Perhaps this accounts for the fact that most mystics have stayed, however troubled, within a tradition (Katz 1983). As with science, there is a craftsmanship there in which one knows more than can be said (Polanyi 1958). Empirical research needs to denote the procedures within traditions by which mystical practices expand awareness of the ineffable as they articulate what it is that can be voiced. Ineffability is itself paradoxically capable of articulation (Scharfstein 1993). Faith is a craft. Mystics must learn this craft and learn how their world is to be experienced as a form of life (Wittgenstein 1967). To paraphrase Wittgenstein (1971), how mystical language games are played is empirical, not simply that they are played (see Sherry 1977).

If psychologists would abandon the limited constraints of attempting to study mysticism only with concepts derived from its own mainstream discourse, the empirical study of mysticism would be broadened, as would the horizon of those who explore it. One may (but need not) follow Staal's (1975) recommendation that the investigators of mysticism themselves be mystics. The crucial point is that mystical experience be considered for what it claims both psychologically and ontologically. The two are not independent. Mystical experiences carry inductive weight even for nonmystics. As Swinburne (1981) notes: "If it seems to me I have a glimpse of Nirvana, or a vision of God, that is good grounds for me to suppose that I do. And, more generally, the occurrence of religious experience is prima facie reason for all to believe in that of which the experience was purportedly an experience" (p. 190).

Introvertive mysticism, minimally sense-based, cannot be fruitfully studied by analogy to discreet relationships between an object and its being sensed. The recovery of experience as a topic of empirical research requires recognition of an encounter between reality and a person capable of its apprehension. Such a person must also be capable of both having and understanding the encounter, of knowledgeably feeling himself or herself in the episode, and of linguistically engaging this awareness. This broader view of experience eschews the language of subject and object in favor of a transsubjectivity that incorporates both (Berger & Luckmann 1966; Smith 1968).

The reality claims of the mystic stand as authoritative as any other and as open to correction and extension as knowledge has always been within traditions, whether scientific or religious. The empirical study of these claims, including the linguistic realities constructed by those who believe from experience (firsthand or otherwise), is part of what faith traditions are about. This is what a social psychology of religion must empirically be about as well.

COMMENTARY: THE EXPERIENCE OF RELIGION

In Chapter 16, Stark has offered us a valuable taxonomy of religious experience, yet we must first ask, "Has this ever been followed up?" To the best of our knowledge, it hasn't. Our initial question might concern why these different experiential avenues are chosen. For explanation, three domains beckon: (1) personality, (2) development, and (3) a social-psychological realm. Relative to personality, probably the only theory that has explicitly said anything about religious experience is the psychoanalytic, though formulations from Jungian analytical psychology may be pertinent. We do, however, need research-directed conceptualizations, and the attachment perspective presented by Kirkpatrick in Chapter 10 offers such an approach. Hood's various writings seem to us to locate experience in a personality–social psychological transaction, allowing for flexible movement in either direction. Cutting across both personality and social psychology and worthy of a closer look with an eye toward research are a variety of possibilities—self-concept theory, control-helplessness theories, coping theory, the humanistic growth-actualization views of Maslow, Rogers, and so on. Close examination of some trait positions such as that taken by Cattell might be fruitful.

A modern developmental understanding of experience is likely to involve both personality and social psychology, and this rapidly brings us back to the attachment outlook. Still, for general development, one gets the impression that religious and mystical experience has been overlooked. Here is virgin territory to expand positions such as those espoused by Fowler and by Oser and Gmünder. In a more traditional personality-structured view, the ego development theory of Loevinger merits a detailed investigation. That there is a paucity of rigorous developmentally focused studies of religious experience and mysticism is almost an understatement. If ever there was a research area wanting of inquiry and analysis, this is it.

Current social psychological thinking is also very worthy of exploration in particular, via social cognition such as is illustrated in this volume—by attitude process, attribution, and schema approaches. Awaiting study are other promising views that look on experience relative to expectancy theory, consistency, and dissonance and further as interpersonal action and communication, as is explicated in Chapter 6 by Holm. This is a rich province in which to immerse experience as structured by Stark.

A major breakdown advanced by Stark is the divine-diabolic distinction. Considering our religious heritage, is the latter an expression of positive or nega-

tive choice? Next, of course, we have the various forms within each of these patterns. Considerations of psychopathology cannot be dismissed. As one goes from
confirming to revelational expressions, the probability of serious reality disturbances involving delusions and hallucinations seems to increase. There is a philosophical problem here of psychology passing judgment on religion; however,
even religious traditions do not define their adherents as immune to mental dis-
order.

In part, Stark's taxonomy can clash with Hood's (Chapter 17) open position,
and Hood's conceptual history is not congenial to identifying abnormality with
religious experience and mysticism. To date, Hood has not explicitly dealt with a
scheme such as Stark's, which will undoubtedly bring perspectives from various
religious traditions to the forefront. Hood is a brilliant "idea" man, and any coordination he might effect with Stark's framework would be research productive.

In part, Hood does our job for us. He points explicitly to many research possibilities concerning mysticism, not the least of which is establishing possible forms
and interpretations in this sphere of the psychology of religion. If a sharp divid-
ing line can be established between religious experience and its forms and mysticism and its expressions, an avalanche of ideas for possible studies that would
compare and contrast the two can be imagined. What is the role of deity images
in the variant types of mysticism and experience? How do these relate to broader
life factors such as background and present circumstances? What are the empirical consequences of such events in general and their specific forms in particular?
Hood's call for longitudinal research adds an entirely new dimension to this
realm. What doors does this open relative to experience within the family, the personality, the social situation, and so on?

Hood speaks of introvertive and extrovertive types and separates the issue of
interpretation from these. Again, we have a panorama of possible researches that
speak to individual differences, social patterns, and social structural variables in
the broadest sociological sense. We must first back up and detail possible subtypes
of the three mystical provinces discussed. Hood points to the linguistic domain as
necessitating investigation. He cites its relativity to religious traditions, and its ties
to culture have long been known. Language as a determiner of the experiential
context is not to be taken lightly. Witness the referenced work of Bourque and
Back (1971).

These chapters by Stark and Hood call for research and offer many avenues to
such work for the serious reader.

REFERENCES

Abelson, R. P. (1988). Conviction. *American Psychologist, 43,* 267–275.

Ainsworth, M. D. S. (1969). Object relations, dependency, and attachment: A theoretical review of the infant-mother relationship. *Child Development, 40,* 969–1025.

Ainsworth, M.D.S. (1972). Attachment and dependency: A comparison. In J. L. Gewirtz (Ed.), *Attachment and dependency* (pp. 97–137). Washington, DC: Winston.

Ainsworth, M.D.S. (1982). Attachment: Retrospect and prospect. In C. M. Parkes & J. S. Hinde (Eds.), *The place of attachment in human behavior* (pp. 3–30). New York: Basic.

Ainsworth, M.D.S. (1985). Attachments across the life span. *Bulletin of the New York Academy of Medicine, 61,* 792–812.

Ainsworth, M.D.S., Blehar, M. C., Waters, E., & Wall, S. (1978). *Patterns of attachment: A psychological study of the strange situation.* Hillsdale, NJ: Lawrence Erlbaum.

Åkerberg, H. (1975). *Omv-ndelse och kamp.* Lund, Sweden: Studia psychologiae religionum lundensia 1.

Aldwin, C. M. (1994). *Stress, coping, and development: An integrative perspective.* New York: Guilford.

Allen, R. O., & Spilka, B. (1967). Committed and consensual religion: A specification of religion-prejudice relationships. *Journal for the Scientific Study of Religion, 6,* 191–206.

Alloy, L. B., & Tabachnik, N. (1984). Assessment of covariation by humans and animals: The joint influence of prior expectations and current situational information. *Psychological Review, 91,* 112–149.

Allport, G. W. (1937). *Personality: A psychological interpretation.* New York: Holt.

Allport, G. W. (1950). *The individual and his religion.* New York: Macmillan.

Allport, G. W. (1958). *The nature of prejudice.* Garden City, NY: Doubleday.

Allport, G. W. (1959). Religion and prejudice. *The Crane Review, 2,* 110.

Allport, G. W. (1960). *Personality and social encounter.* Boston: Beacon.

Allport, G. W. (1963). Behavioral science, religion, and mental health. *Journal of Religion and Health, 2,* 187–197.

Allport, G. W. (1966). The religious context of prejudice. *Journal for the Scientific Study of Religion, 5,* 447–457.

Allport, G. W., & Ross, J. M. (1967). Personal religious orientation and prejudice. *Journal of Personality and Social Psychology, 5,* 432–443.

Almond, P. C. (1982). *Mystical experience and religious doctrine*. Berlin: Mouton.

Anderson, C. A., Lepper, M. R., & Ross, L. (1980). Perseverance of social theories: The role of explanation in the persistence of discredited information. *Journal of Personality and Social Psychology, 39*, 1037–1049.

Anderson, J. R. (1983). *The architecture of cognition*. Cambridge, MA: Harvard University Press.

Antonovsky, A. (1979). *Health, stress, and coping*. San Francisco: Jossey-Bass.

Arend, R., Gove, F., & Sroufe, L. A. (1979). Continuity of individual adaptation from infancy to kindergarten: A predictive study of ego-resiliency and curiosity in preschoolers. *Child Development, 50*, 950–959.

Argyle, M., & Beit-Hallahmi, B. (1975). *The social psychology of religion*. London: Routledge & Kegan Paul.

Arkes, H. R., & Blumer, C. (1985). The psychology of sunk cost. *Organizational Behavior and Human Decision Processes, 35*, 124–140.

Arkes, H. R., & Hammond, K. R. (1986). *Judgment and decision making*. New York: Cambridge University Press.

Aronson, E., Wilson, T. D., & Akert, R. M. (1994). *Social psychology: The heart and the mind*. New York: HarperCollins.

Aust, C. F. (1990). Using the client's religious values to aid progress in therapy. *Counseling and Values, 34*, 125–129.

Ayim-Aboagye, D. (1993). *The function of myth in Akan healing experience. A psychological inquiry into two traditional Akan healing communities*. Uppsala, Sweden: Acta universitatis upsaliensis, Psychologia et sociologia religionum, 9. Stockholm: Almqvist & Wiksell International.

Bainbridge, W. S. (1980). Scientology: To be perfectly clear. *Sociological Analysis, 41*, 128–136.

Baker, M., & Gorsuch, R. (1982). Trait anxiety and intrinsic-extrinsic religiousness. *Journal for the Scientific Study of Religion, 21*, 119–122.

Balk, D. (1983). How teenagers cope with sibling death: Some implications for school counselors. *School Counselor, 31*, 150–158.

Ball-Rokeach, S. J., Rokeach, M., & Grube, J. W. (1984). *The Great American Values Test*. New York: Free Press.

Bandura, A. (1977). Self-efficacy: Toward a unifying theory of behavioral change. *Psychological Review, 8*, 191–215.

Baron, R. A., & Byrne, D. (1987). *Social psychology: Understanding human interaction* (5th ed.). Boston: Allyn and Bacon.

Bartlett, F. C. (1932). *Remembering*. Cambridge, England: Cambridge University Press.

Basseches, M. (1989). Toward a constructive-developmental understanding of the dialectics of individuality and irrationality. In M. J. Bopp & D. A. Kramer (Eds.), *Transformation in clinical and developmental psychology* (pp. 188–209). Berlin: Springer.

Batson, C. D. (1975). Rational processing or rationalization?: The effect of disconfirming information on a stated religious belief. *Journal of Personality and Social Psychology, 32*, 176–184.

Batson, C. D. (1976). Religion as prosocial: Agent or double agent? *Journal for the Scientific Study of Religion, 15*, 29–45.

Batson, C. D. (1977). Experimentation in psychology of religion: An impossible dream. *Journal for the Scientific Psychology of Religion, 16,* 412–418.

Batson, C. D. (1986). An agenda item for psychology of religion: Getting respect. *Journal of Psychology and Christianity, 5,* 6–11.

Batson, C. D., & Raynor-Prince, L. (1983). Religious orientation and complexity of thought about existential concerns. *Journal for the Scientific Study of Religion, 22,* 38–50.

Batson, C. D., Schoenrade, P., & Ventis, W. L. (1993). *Religion and the individual.* New York: Oxford University Press.

Batson, C. D., & Ventis, W. L. (1982). *The religious experience: A social-psychological perspective.* New York: Oxford University Press.

Baumeister, R. F. (1986). *Identity: Cultural change and the struggle for self.* New York: Oxford University Press.

Bearison, D. J., & Zimiles, H. (Eds.). (1986). *Thought and emotion: Developmental perspectives.* Hillsdale, NJ: Lawrence Erlbaum.

Becker, E. (1973). *The denial of death.* New York: Free Press.

Beit-Hallahmi, B. (1975). Encountering orthodox religion in psychotherapy. *Psychotherapy: Theory, Research, and Practice, 12,* 357–359.

Bellah, R. N. (1970a). *Beyond belief.* New York: Harper & Row.

Bellah, R. N. (1970b). Christianity and symbolic realism. *Journal for the Scientific Study of Religion, 9,* 89–96.

Bem, D. J. (1972). Self-perception theory. In L. Berkowitz (Ed.), *Advances in experimental social psychology* (vol. 6, pp. 1–62). New York: Academic Press.

Benson, P. L. (1990, August). *Development of religious faith and practice across the life cycle.* Paper presented at the Convention of the American Psychological Association, Boston, MA.

Benson, P. L., & Spilka, B. (1973). God image as a function of self-esteem and locus of control. *Journal for the Scientific Study of Religion, 12,* 297–310.

Benson, P. L., & Williams, D. L. (1982). *Religion on Capitol Hill: Myths and realities.* San Francisco: Harper & Row.

Berger, P. L. (1967). *The sacred canopy.* Garden City, NY: Doubleday.

Berger, P. L. (1980). *The heretical imperative.* New York: Anchor.

Berger, P. L., & Luckmann, T. (1966). *The social construction of reality.* London: Penguin Books.

Bergin, A. E. (1980). Psychotherapy and religious values. *Journal of Consulting and Clinical Psychology, 48,* 95–105.

Bergin, A. E. (1983). Religiosity and mental health: A critical reevaluation and meta-analysis. *Professional Psychology: Research and Practice, 14,* 170–184.

Bergin, A. E. (1985). Proposed values for guiding and evaluating counseling and psychotherapy. *Counseling and Values, 29,* 101–115.

Bergin, A. E. (1988a). The spiritual perspective is ecumenical and eclectic (rejoinder). *Counseling and Values, 33,* 57–59.

Bergin, A. E. (1988b). Three contributions of a spiritual perspective to counseling, psychotherapy, and behavior change. *Counseling and Values, 33,* 21–31.

Bergin, A. E. (1991). Values and religious issues in psychotherapy and mental health. *American Psychologist, 46,* 394–403.

Berlyne, D. E. (1960). *Conflict, arousal and curiosity.* New York: McGraw-Hill.

Bernstein, B. (1964). Aspects of language and learning in the genesis of the social process. In D. Hymes (Ed.), *Language in culture and society* (pp. 251–263). New York: Harper & Row.

Berscheid, E., Graziano, W., Monson, T., & Dermer, M. (1976). Outcome dependency: Attention, attribution, and attraction. *Journal of Personality and Social Psychology, 34,* 378–389.

Berzonsky, M. D. (1992). Commentary. *Human Development, 35,* 76–80.

Beutler, L., Crago, M., & Arizmendi, T. (1986). Research on therapist variables in psychotherapy. In S. Garfield & A. Bergin (Eds.), *Handbook of psychotherapy and behavior change* (3d ed., pp. 257–310). New York: John Wiley & Sons.

Bickel, C. O. (1994). *Coping styles and depressive affect.* Unpublished doctoral dissertation. Loyola University at Columbia, MD.

Bindra, D. (1959). *Motivation: A systematic reinterpretation.* New York: Ronald Press.

Blasi, A. (1980). Bridging moral cognition and moral action: A critical review of the literature. *Psychological Bulletin, 88,* 1–45.

Boisen, A. T. (1955). *Religion in crisis and custom: A sociological and psychological study.* Westport, CT: Greenwood Press.

Bondi, R. C. (1995). *Memories of God: Theological reflections on a life.* Nashville, TN: Abingdon Press.

Bornstein, M. H., & Lamb, M. E. (Eds.). (1992). *Developmental psychology: An advanced text* (3d ed.). Hillsdale, NJ: Lawrence Erlbaum.

Bourque, L. B. (1969). Social correlates of transcendental experiences. *Sociological Analysis, 30,* 151–163.

Bourque, L. B., & Back, K. W. (1971). Language, society and subjective experience. *Sociometry, 34,* 1–21.

Bower, G. H. (1981). Mood and memory. *American Psychologist, 36,* 129–148.

Bowker, J. (1973). *The sense of God.* Oxford: Oxford University Press.

Bowlby, J. (1969). *Attachment and loss: Vol. 1. Attachment.* New York: Basic Books.

Bowlby, J. (1973). *Attachment and loss: Vol. 2. Separation: Anxiety and anger.* New York: Basic Books.

Bowlby, J. (1980). *Attachment and loss: Vol. 3. Loss.* New York: Basic Books.

Brandsma, J. M. (1985). Forgiveness. In D. G. Brenner, (Ed.), *Baker encyclopedia of psychology.* Grand Rapids, MI: Baker Book House.

Brehm, J., and Cohen, A. (1962). *Explorations in cognitive dissonance.* New York: Wiley.

Brenner, R. R. (1980). *The faith and doubt of holocaust survivors.* New York: Free Press.

Brent, E. E., & Granberg, D. (1982). Subjective agreement and the presidential candidates of 1976 and 1980. *Journal of Personality and Social Psychology, 42,* 393–403.

Bretherton, I. (1985). Attachment theory: Retrospect and prospect. In I. Bretherton & E. Waters (Eds.), *Growing points in attachment theory and research.* Monographs of the Society for Research in Child Development, *50* (1–2, Serial No. 209), 3–35.

Bretherton, I. (1987). New perspectives on attachment relations: Security, communication, and internal working models. In J. D. Osofsky (Ed.), *Handbook of infant development* (2d ed., pp. 1061–1100). New York: Wiley.

Broen, W. E., Jr. (1957). A factor-analytic study of religious attitudes. *Journal of Abnormal and Social Psychology, 54,* 176–179.

Brown, L. B. (1994, August). Talking and writing about experience: What can we tell? In R. W. Hood Jr. (Chair). *The evidential value of reports of religious experience.* Symposium presented at the Convention of the American Psychological Association, Los Angeles.

Brown, R. W. (1986). *Social psychology: The second edition.* New York: Free Press.

Bruder, E. E. (1947). Some considerations of the loss of faith. *Journal of Clinical and Pastoral Work, 1,* 1–10.

Bruner, J. S. (1957a). Going beyond the information given. In J. S. Bruner, H. E. Gruber, K. K. Hammond, & R. Jessor (Eds.), *Contemporary approaches to cognitions* (pp. 41–69). Cambridge, MA: Harvard University Press.

Bruner, J. S. (1957b). On perceptual readiness. *Psychological Review, 64,* 123–152.

Bulman, R. J., & Wortman, C. B. (1977). Attribution of blame and coping in the "real world": Severe accident victims react to their lot. *Journal of Personality and Social Psychology, 35,* 351–363.

Burhenn, H. (1994). Philosophy and religious experience. In R. W. Hood, Jr., *Handbook of religious experience.* Birmingham, AL: Religious Education Press.

Buss, A. H. (1978). Causes and reasons in attribution theory: A conceptual critique. *Journal of Personality and Social Psychology, 36,* 1311–1321.

Caird, D. (1988). The structure of Hood's Mysticism Scale: A factor analytic study. *Journal for the Scientific Study of Religion, 27,* 122–126.

Campos, J. J., & Stenberg, C. (1981). Perception, appraisal, and emotion: The onset of social referencing. In M. E. Lamb & L. R. Sherrod (Eds.), *Infant social cognition: Empirical and theoretical considerations* (pp. 273–314). Hillsdale, NJ: Lawrence Erlbaum.

Cannon, W. B. (1927). The James-Lange theory of emotions: A critical examination and an alternative theory. *American Journal of Psychology, 39,* 106–124.

Cannon, W. B. (1929). *Bodily changes in pain, hunger, fear, and rage* (2d ed.). New York: Appleton.

Caplovitz, D., & Sherrow, F. (1977). *The religious dropouts.* Beverly Hills, CA: Sage Publications.

Capps, D. (1982a). The psychology of petitionary prayer. *Theology Today, 39,* 130–141.

Capps, D. (1982b). Sundén's role-taking theory: The case of John Henry Newman and his mentors. *Journal for the Scientific Study of Religion, 21,* 58–70.

Capra, F. (1983). *The tao of physics* (2d ed.). Boulder: Shambhala.

Carnap, R. (1966). *An introduction to the philosophy of science.* New York: Basic Books.

Carroll, J. (1978). The effect of imagining an event on expectations for the event: An interpretation in terms of the availability heuristic. *Journal of Experimental Social Psychology, 14,* 88–96.

Cattell, R. B., & Child, D. (1975). *Motivation and dynamic structure.* New York: John Wiley & Sons.

Chaiken, S., & Stangor, C. (1987). Attitudes and attitude change. *Annual Review of Psychology, 38,* 575–630.

Chinen, A. B. (1984). Modal logic: A new paradigm of development and late-life potential. *Human Development, 27,* 42–56.

Chopp, R. (1994). *Saving work: Feminist practices of theological education.* Louisville, KY: Westminster/John Knox Press.

Clark, E. T. (1929). *The psychology of religious awakening*. New York: Macmillan.

Clark, W. H. (1958). *The psychology of religion*. New York: Macmillan.

Coe, G. A. (1900). *The spiritual life*. New York: Abingdon.

Coe, G. A. (1916). *Psychology of religion*. Chicago: University of Chicago Press.

Collins, G. R. (1977). *The rebuilding of psychology: An integration of psychology and Christianity*. Wheaton, IL: Tyndale House.

Collins, G. R. (1980). *Christian counseling. A comprehensive guide*. Waco, TX: Word Publishing.

Cook, J. A., & Wimberley, D. W. (1983). If I should die before I wake: Religious commitment and adjustment to the death of a child. *Journal for the Scientific Study of Religion, 22,* 222–238.

Cooper, J., & Croyle, R. T. (1984). Attitudes and attitude change. *Annual Review of Psychology, 35,* 395–426.

Copleston, F. (1982). *Religion and the One*. New York: Crossroad.

Crafoord, C. (1987). *En bok om borderline*. Stockholm: Natur och Kultur.

Crafoord, C. (1993). *Barndomens återkomst*. Stockholm: Natur och Kultur.

Crowne, D., & Marlowe, D. (1964). *The approval motive*. New York: Wiley.

Curb, R., & Manahan, N. (Eds.). (1985). *Lesbian nuns: Breaking silence*. Tallahassee, FL: Naiad.

Dahrendorf, R. (1959). *Homo sociologicus*. Köln, Germany: Opladen.

Damon, W., & Hart, D. (1992). Self-understanding and its role in social and moral development. In M. H. Bornstein and M. E. Lamb (Eds.), *Developmental psychology: An advanced text* (3d ed., pp. 421–464). Hillsdale, NJ: Lawrence Erlbaum.

Darley, J. M., & Batson, C. D. (1973). "From Jerusalem to Jericho": A study of situational and dispositional variables in helping behavior. *Journal of Personality and Social Psychology, 27,* 100–108.

Davis, C. F. (1989). *The evidential force of religious experience*. Oxford: Clarendon Press.

Deci, E. L., & Ryan, R. M. (1985). *Intrinsic motivation and self-determination in human behavior*. New York: Plenum Press.

Deutsch, A. (1975). Observations on a sidewalk ashram. *Archives of General Psychiatry, 32,* 166–175.

Dewey, J. (1929). *The quest for certainty*. New York: Minton, Balch.

Diener, C. T., & Dweck, C. S. (1978). An analysis of learned helplessness: Continuous changes in performance, strategy, and achievement cognitions following failure. *Journal of Personality and Social Psychology, 36,* 451–462.

Dillard, A. (1987). *An American childhood*. New York: Harper & Row.

Dittes, J. E. (1969). Psychology of religion. In G. Lindsey & E. Aronson (Eds.), *The handbook of social psychology* (vol. 5). Reading, MA: Addison-Wesley.

Doblin, R. (1990). Pahnke's "Good Friday experiment": A long term followup and methodological critique. *Journal of Transpersonal Psychology, 23,* 1–28.

Dollinger, S. J. (1986). The need for meaning following disaster: Attributions and emotional upset. *Personality and Social Psychology Bulletin, 12,* 300–310.

Dombeck, M., & Karl, J. (1987). Spiritual issues in mental health care. *Journal of Religion and Health, 26,* 183–197.

Domes, M. (1993). *Der kompetente Säugling. Die präverbale Entwicklung des Menschen*. Frankfurt/M.: FischerTB 11533.

Donahue, M. J. (1985a). Intrinsic and extrinsic religiousness: The empirical research. *Journal for the Scientific Study of Religion, 24*, 418–423.

Donahue, M. J. (1985b). Intrinsic and extrinsic religiousness: Review and meta-analysis. *Journal of Personality and Social Psychology, 48*, 400–419.

Douglas, M. (1966). *Purity and danger*. London: Routledge and Kegan Paul.

Duke, E. H. (1977). *Meaning in life and acceptance of death in terminally ill patients*. Unpublished doctoral dissertation, Northwestern University, Evanston, IL.

Dunlap, K. (1946). *Religion: Its function in human life*. New York: McGraw Hill.

Durkheim, E. (1893). *De la division du travail social*. Paris: Alcan.

Durkheim, E. (1915). *The elementary forms of the religious life*. London: George Allen and Unwin.

Ebaugh, H., Richman, K., & Chafetz, J. (1984). Life crises among the religiously committed: Do sectarian differences matter? *Journal for the Scientific Study of Religion, 23*, 19–31.

Ebaugh, H.R.F., & Haney, C. A. (1978). Church attendance and attitudes toward abortion: Differentials in liberal and conservative churches. *Journal for the Scientific Study of Religion, 17*, 407–413.

Elkind, D. (1961). The development of quantitative thinking. *Journal of Genetic Psychology, 98*, 37–46.

Elkind, D. (1964). Discrimination, seriation and numeration of size differences in young children. *Journal of Genetic Psychology, 104*, 275–296.

Elkind, D., & Elkind, S. F. (1962). Varieties of religious experience in young adolescents. *Journal for the Scientific Study of Religion, 2*, 102–112.

Ellenberger, H. F. (1970). *The discovery of the unconscious*. New York: Basic Books.

Embree, R. A. (1986, August). *Pro-recreational sex morality, religiosity, and causal attribution of homosexual attitudes*. Paper presented at the Convention of the American Psychological Association, Washington, DC.

Embree, R. A. (1996). Personal Beliefs Scale redux: A model for hypothesis testing. *Psychological Reports, 78*, 195–203.

Embree, R. A., & Embree, M. C. (1993). The Personal Beliefs Scale as a measure of individual differences in commitment to the mind-body beliefs proposed by F. F. Centore. *Psychological Reports, 73*, 411–428.

Entner, P. (1977). Religious orientation and mental health (Doctoral dissertation, Rosemead School of Psychology, 1976). *Dissertation Abstracts International, 38*, 1949B.

Epstein, S. (1984). Controversial issues in emotion theory. In P. Shaver (Ed.), *Review of Personality and Social Psychology* (vol. 5). Beverly Hills, CA: Sage Publications.

Epstein, S. (1991). Cognitive-experiential self-theory: An integrative theory of personality. In R. C. Curtis (Ed.), *The relational self. Theoretical convergences in psychoanalysis and social psychology* (pp. 111–137). New York/London: Guilford.

Erikson, E. H. (1968a). *Identity, youth and crisis*. New York: Norton.

Erikson, E. H. (1968b). Womanhood and the inner space. In *Identity: Youth and crisis* (pp. 261–294). New York: Norton.

Erikson, E. H. (1982). *The life cycle completed*. New York: Norton.

Fazio, R. H. (1986). How do attitudes guide behavior? In R. M. Sorrentino & E. T. Higgins (Eds.), *The handbook of motivation and cognition: Foundations of social behavior* (pp. 204–243). New York: Guilford Press.

Fazio, R. H. (1989). On the power and functionality of attitudes: The role of attitude accessibility. In A. R. Pratkanis, S. J. Breckler, and A. G. Greenwald (Eds.), *Attitude structure and function* (pp. 153–179). Hillsdale, NJ: Lawrence Erlbaum.

Fazio, R. H., Chen, J., McDonel, E. C., & Sherman, S. J. (1982). Attitude accessibility, attitude-behavior consistency, and the strength of the object-evaluation association. *Journal of Experimental Social Psychology, 18,* 339–357.

Fazio, R. H., Sanbonmatsu, D. M., Powell, M. C., & Kardes, F. R. (1986). On the automatic activation of attitudes. *Journal of Personality and Social Psychology, 50,* 229–238.

Fazio, R. H., & Williams, C. J. (1986). Attitude accessibility as a moderator of the attitude-perception and attitude-behavior relations: An investigation of the 1984 presidential election. *Journal of Personality and Social Psychology, 51,* 505–514.

Festinger, L. (1957). *A theory of cognitive dissonance.* Stanford: Stanford University Press.

Festinger, L., & Carlsmith, J. M. (1959). Cognitive consequences of forced compliance. *Journal of Abnormal and Social Psychology, 58,* 203–210.

Festinger, L., Riecken, H., & Schachter, S. (1956). *When prophecy fails.* New York: Harper & Row.

Feyerabend, P. (1975). *Against method: An outline of an anarchist theory of knowledge.* London: NLB.

Fichter, J. H. (1981). *Religion and pain.* New York: Crossroad.

Fillipaldi, S. E. (1982). Zen-mind, Christian-mind, empty-mind. *Journal of Ecumenical Studies, X,* 69–84.

Fishbein, M., & Ajzen, I. (1975). *Belief, attitude, intention and behavior: An introduction to theory and research.* Reading, MA: Addison-Wesley.

Fiske, S. T., & Linville, P. W. (1980). What does the schema concept buy us? *Personality and Social Psychology Bulletin, 6,* 543–557.

Fiske, S. T., & Taylor, S. E. (1984). *Social cognition.* Reading, MA: Addison-Wesley.

Fiske, S. T., & Taylor, S. E. (Eds.). (1991). *Social cognition.* New York: McGraw-Hill.

Flakoll, D. A. (1974, October). *Self esteem, psychological adjustment and images of God.* Paper presented at the meeting of the Society for the Scientific Study of Religion, Washington, DC.

Folkman, S. (1992). Making the case for coping. In B. N. Carpenter (Ed.), *Personal coping: Theory, research, and application* (pp. 31–46). Westport, CT: Praeger.

Forsyth, D. R. (1980). A taxonomy of ethical ideologies. *Journal of Personality and Social Psychology, 39,* 175–184.

Fowler, J. W. (1981). *Stages of faith.* New York: Harper & Row.

Fowler, J. W. (1987). *Faith development and pastoral care.* Philadelphia: Fortress.

Fraas, H.-J. (1992). *Die Religiosität des Menschen. Ein Grundriss der Religionspsychologie.* Göttingen: Vandenhoek & Ruprecht.

Frank, J. D. (1973). *Persuasion and healing.* (Rev. ed.). Baltimore, MD: Johns Hopkins University Press.

Frankl, V. E. (1963). *Man's search for meaning.* New York: Washington Square.

Freiberg, P. (1990, November). Public Interest: AIDS information must confront basic attitudes. *APA Monitor,* p. 27.

Freud, S. (1961). *The future of an illusion.* New York: Norton.

Friedman, S. B., Chodoff, P., Mason, J. W., Hamburg, D. A. (1963). Behavioral observations on parents anticipating the death of a child. *Pediatrics, 32,* 610–625.

Fromm, E. (1950). *Psychoanalysis and religion.* New Haven, CT: Yale University Press.

Fuchs-Ebaugh, H. R., & Haney, C. A. (1978). Church attendance and attitudes toward abortion: Differentials in liberal and conservative churches. *Journal for the Scientific Study of Religion, 17,* 407–413.

Funk, J. D. (1989). Postformal cognitive theory and developmental stages of musical composition. In M. L. Commons, J. D. Sinnott, F. A . Richards, & C. Armon (Eds.), *Adult development, vol. 1. Comparisons and applications of developmental models* (pp. 3–30). New York: Praeger.

Galanter, M. (1979). The "Moonies": A psychological study of conversion and membership in a contemporary religious sect. *American Journal of Psychiatry, 136,* 165–170.

Galanter, M. (1989). *Cults: Faith, healing, and conversion.* New York: Oxford University Press.

Gardner, H. (1985). *The mind's new science.* New York: Basic Books.

Garrett, W. R. (1974). Troublesome transcendence: The supernatural in the scientific study of religion. *Sociological Analysis, 35,* 167–180.

Geertz, C. (1966). Religion as a cultural system. In M. Banton (Ed.), *Anthropological approaches in the study of religion.* London: Tavistock.

Geertz, C. (1973). *The interpretation of cultures.* New York: Basic Books.

Gentner, D., & Jeziorski, M. (In press). The shift from metaphor to analogy in Western science. In A. Ortony (Ed.), *Metaphor and thought* (2d ed.). Cambridge: Cambridge University Press.

Gergen, K. J. (1991). *The saturated self.* New York: Basic Books.

Gibbs, H. W., & Achterberg-Lawlis, J. (1978). Spiritual values and death anxiety: Implications for counseling with terminal cancer patients. *Journal of Counseling Psychology, 25,* 563–569.

Gibbs, J. C., & Schnell, S. V. (1985). Moral development "versus" socialization: A critique. *American Psychologist, 40,* 1071–1080.

Gillespie, J. B. (1995, October). *Tears in articulating spirituality: Non-standard interview methods as mutual empowerment.* Paper presented at the annual meeting of the Society for the Scientific Study of Religion, St. Louis, MO.

Gilovich, T. (1991). *How we know what isn't so.* New York: Free Press.

Glick, I. O., Weiss, R. S., & Parkes, C. M. (1974). *The first year of bereavement.* New York: Wiley.

Glock, C. Y. (1959). The religious revival in America. In J. Zahn (Ed.), *Religion and the face of America* (pp. 26–27). Berkeley, CA: University Extension, University of California.

Glock, C. Y., & Piazza, T. (1981). Exploring reality structures. In T. Robbins & D. Anthony (Eds.), *In gods we trust: New patterns of religious pluralism in America* (pp. 67–83). New Brunswick, NJ: Transaction Books.

Godin, A., & Hallez, M. (1965). Parental images and divine paternity. In A. Godin (Ed.), *From religious experience to a religious attitude* (pp. 65–96). Chicago: Loyola University Press.

Goffman, E. (1974). *Frame analysis.* Cambridge, MA: Harvard University Press.

244   *References*

Goffman, E. (1974). *Stigma: Notes on the management of spoiled identity.* New York: Jason Aronson.

Goldstein, K. (1939). *The organism.* New York: American.

Goleman, D. (1977). *Varieties of meditative experience.* New York: Irvington.

Goody, J. (1961). Religion and ritual: The definitional problem. *British Journal of Sociology, 12,* 142–164.

Gorer, G. (1965). *Death, grief, and mourning in contemporary Britain.* London: Cresset.

Gorsuch, R. L. (1968). The conceptualization of God as seen in adjective ratings. *Journal for the Scientific Study of Religion, 7,* 56–64.

Gorsuch, R. L. (1984). Measurement: The boon and bane of investigating religion. *American Psychologist, 39,* 228–236.

Gorsuch, R. L. (1986, August). *BAV: A possible non-reductionistic model for the psychology of religion.* Paper presented at the meeting of the American Psychological Association, Washington, DC.

Gorsuch, R. L. (1986). Measuring attitudes, interests, sentiments, and values. In R. B. Cattell and R. C. Johnson (Eds.), *Functional psychological testing: Principles and instruments* (pp. 316–333). New York: Brunner/Mazel.

Gorsuch, R. L. (1988). Psychology of religion. *Annual Review of Psychology, 39,* 201–221.

Gorsuch, R. L., & Aleshire, D. (1974). Christian faith and ethnic prejudice: A review and interpretation of research. *Journal for the Scientific Study of Religion, 13,* 281–307.

Gorsuch, R. L., & McPherson, S. E. (1989). Intrinsic/extrinsic measurement: I/E revised and single item scales. *Journal for the Scientific Study of Religion, 28,* 348–354.

Gorsuch, R. L., Mylvaganam, G., Gorsuch, K., Johnson, R., Darvill, T. J., & Danko, G. P. (1991). *Explorations of the intrinsic/extrinsic distinction across cultures.* Paper presented at the annual meeting of the Society for the Scientific Study of Religion and Religious Research Association, Pittsburgh, PA.

Gorsuch, R. L., & Ortberg, J. (1983). Moral obligations and attitudes: Their relationship to behavioral intentions. *Journal of Personality and Social Psychology, 44,* 1025–1028.

Gorsuch, R. L., & Smith, C. S. (1983). Attributions of responsibility to God: An interaction of religious beliefs and outcomes. *Journal for the Scientific Study of Religion, 22,* 340–352.

Gorsuch, R. L., & Venable, G. D. (1983). Development of an "age universal" I-E scale. *Journal for the Scientific Study of Religion, 22,* 181–187.

Gray, J. G. (1970). *The warriors.* New York: Harper & Row.

Greeley, A. M., and McCready, W. C. (1975, January 26). Are we a nation of mystics? *The New York Times Magazine,* pp. 12, 25.

Greenberg, J., Pyszczynski, T., & Solomon, S. (1982). The self-serving attributional bias: Beyond self-presentation. *Journal of Experimental Social Psychology, 18,* 56–67.

Greenwald, A. G. (1980). The totalitarian ego: Fabrication and revision of personal history. *American Psychologist, 35,* 603–618.

Gurin, G., Veroff, J., & Feld, S. (1960). *Americans view their mental health: A nationwide interview survey.* New York: Basic Books.

Habermas, J. (1973). *Kultur und Kritik.* Frankfurt, Germany: Suhrkamp Verlag.

Hall, C. M. (1986). Crisis as opportunity for spiritual growth. *Journal of Religion and Health, 25,* 8–17.

Hall, G. S. (1904). *Adolescence* (2 vols.). New York: Appleton.

Hardy, A. (1979). *The spiritual nature of man.* Clarendon, England: Oxford University Press.

Harre, R., & Secord, P. (1972). *The explanation of social behavior.* Oxford, England: Basil Blackwell.

Harrison, S. M. (1988). Sanctification and therapy: The model of Dante Alighieri. *Journal of Psychology and Theology, 16,* 313–317.

Harvey, O. J., Hunt, D. E., & Schroder, H. M. (1961). *Conceptual systems and personality organization.* New York: Wiley.

Hasher, L., Attig, M. S., & Alba, J. W. (1981). I knew it all along—or did I? *Journal of Verbal Learning and Verbal Behavior, 20,* 86–96.

Hasher, L., Goldstein, D., & Toppino, T. (1977). Frequency and the conference of referential validity. *Journal of Verbal Learning and Verbal Behavior, 16,* 107–112.

Hastie, R. (1981). Schematic principles in human memory. In E. T. Higgins, C. P. Herman, & M. P. Zanna (Eds.), *Social cognition: The Ontario symposium* (vol. 1, pp. 39–88). Hillsdale, NJ: Lawrence Erlbaum.

Hastie, R. (1984). Causes and effects of causal attribution. *Journal of Personality and Social Psychology, 46,* 44–56.

Haun, H. L. (1977). Perception of the bereaved, clergy, and funeral directors concerning bereavement. *Dissertation Abstracts International, 37,* 6791A.

Hay, D., & Morisy, A. (1978). Reports of ecstatic, paranormal, or religious experience. *Journal for the Scientific Study of Religion, 17,* 255–268.

Hazan, C., & Shaver, P. (1987). Romantic love conceptualized as an attachment process. *Journal of Personality and Social Psychology, 52,* 511–524.

Heider, F. (1958). *The psychology of interpersonal relations.* New York: Wiley.

Heiler, F. (1932). *Prayer.* New York: Oxford University Press.

Heller, D. (1986). *The children's God.* Chicago: University of Chicago Press.

Herek, G. M. (1987). Religious orientation and prejudice: A comparison of racial and sexual attitudes. *Personality and Social Psychology Bulletin, 13,* 34–44.

Higgins, E. T., & King, G. (1981). Accessibility of social constructs: Information-processing consequences of individuals and contextual variability. In N. Cantor and J. Kihlstrom (Eds.), *Personality, cognition, and social interaction* (pp. 69–121). Hillsdale, NJ: Lawrence Erlbaum.

Hill, P. C. (1995). Affective theory and religious experience. In R. W. Hood, Jr. (Ed.), *Handbook of religious experience* (pp. 253–377). Birmingham, AL: Religious Education Press.

Hill, P. C., & Bassett, R. L. (1992). Getting to the heart of the matter: What the social-psychological study of attitudes has to offer the psychology of religion. In M. L. Lynn and D. O. Moberg (Eds.), *Research in the social scientific study of religion* (vol. 4, pp. 159–182). Greenwich, CT: JAI Press.

Hill, P. C., Jennings, M. A., Haas, D. D., & Seybold, K. S. (1992, August). *Automatic and controlled activation of religious attitudes.* Paper presented at the meeting of the American Psychological Association, Washington, DC.

Hine, V. H. (1969). Pentecostal glossolalia: Toward a functional interpretation. *Journal for the Scientific Study of Religion, 8,* 211–226.

Hoffer, E. (1951). *The true believer*. New York: Harper & Row.

Hogan, R. (1973). Moral conduct and moral character: A psychological perspective. *Psychological Bulletin, 79*, 217–232.

Holm, N. G. (1976). *Tungotal och andedop*. Uppsala, Sweden: Acta universitatis upsaliensis, Psychologia religionum, 5.

Holm, N. G. (1978). Functions of glossolalia in the Pentecostal movement. In T. Källstad (Ed.), *Psychological Studies on Religious Man*. Uppsala, Sweden: Acta universitatis upsaliensis, Psychologia religionum, 7, 141–158.

Holm, N. G. (1979). *Mystik och intensiva upplevelser*. Åbo, Finland: Publications of the Research Institute of the Åbo Akademi Foundation, no. 51.

Holm, N. G. (1987a). *Scandinavian psychology of religion*. Åbo, Finland: Åbo Akademi University, Religionsvetenskapliga skrifter, nr. 15.

Holm, N. G. (1987b). Sundén's role theory and glossolalia. *Journal for the Scientific Study of Religion, 26*, 383–389.

Holm, N. G. (1991a). Pentecostalism: Conversion and charismata. *International Journal for the Psychology of Religion, 1*, 135–151.

Holm, N. G. (1991b). Sundén's role theory and glossolalia. In H. N. Malony (Ed.), *Psychology of religion. Personalities, problems, possibilities*. (pp. 215–230). Grand Rapids, MI: Baker Book House.

Homans, G. C. (1974). *Social behavior: Its elementary forms* (2d ed.). New York: Harcourt Brace.

Honko, L. (1969). Role-taking of the shaman. *Temenos, 4*.

Honko, L. (1971). Memorat och folktroforskning. In *Folkdikt och folktro*. Lund, Sweden: Gleerups. (1964). Memorates and the study of folk beliefs. *Journal of the Folklore Institute, 1*.

Hood, R. W., Jr. (1975). The construction and preliminary validation of a measure of reported mystical experience. *Journal for the Scientific Study of Religion, 14*, 29–41.

Hood, R. W., Jr. (1978). The usefulness of the indiscriminately pro and anti-categories of religious orientation. *Journal for the Scientific Study of Religion, 17*, 419–431.

Hood, R. W., Jr. (1983). Social psychology and fundamentalism. In A. W. Childs & G. B. Melton (Eds.), *Rural psychology* (pp. 169–198). New York: Plenum.

Hood, R. W., Jr. (1985). Mysticism. In P. Hammond (Ed.), *The sacred in a secular society* (pp. 285–287). Berkeley, CA: University of California Press.

Hood, R. W., Jr. (1989a). Mysticism, the unity thesis, and the paranormal. In G. K. Zollschan, J. F. Schumaker, & C. F. Walsh (Eds.), *Exploring the paranormal* (pp. 117–130). New York: Avery.

Hood, R. W., Jr. (1989b). The relevance of theologies for religious experiencing. *Journal of Psychology and Theology, 17*, 336–342.

Hood, R. W., Jr. (1992). A Jamesian look at self and self loss in mystical experience. *The Journal of the Psychology of Religion, 1*, 1–14.

Hood, R. W., Jr. (1994). Psychology and religion. In V. S. Ramachandran (Ed.), *The encyclopedia of human behavior*. New York: Academic Press.

Hood, R. W., Jr. (1995). The facilitation of religious experience. In R. W. Hood, Jr. (Ed.), *Handbook of religious experience* (pp. 568–597). Birmingham, AL: Religious Education Press.

Hood, R. W., Jr., & Morris, R. J. (1981). Knowledge and experience criteria in the report of mystical experience. *Review of Religious Research, 23,* 76–84.

Hood, R. W., Jr., Morris, R. J., & Watson, P. J. (1993). Further factor analysis of Hood's Mysticism Scale. *Psychological Reports, 73,* 1176–1178.

Hope, D. (1987). The healing paradox of forgiveness. *Psychotherapy, 24,* 240–244.

Horowitz, M. (1976). *Stress response syndromes.* Northvale, NJ: Aronson.

Hunsberger, B. E. (1990, August). *Psychology and religion: Behind the biases.* Paper presented to Convention of the American Psychological Association, Boston, MA.

Hunsberger, B. E. (1991). Empirical work in the psychology of religion. *Canadian Psychology, 32,* 497–504.

Hunt, R. A., & King, M. B. (1971). The intrinsic-extrinsic concept: A review and evaluation. *Journal for the Scientific Study of Religion, 10,* 339–356.

Hutch, R. A. (1983). An essay on psychotherapy and religion. *Journal of Religion and Health, 22,* 7–18.

Hyde, K. E. (1990). *Religion in childhood and adolescence.* Birmingham, AL: Religious Education Press.

Illman, S. (1992). *Vere adest. Religionspsykologisk tolkning av närvarotemat i Olov Hartmans romaner.* Åbo, Finland: Åbo Akademi, Åbo Academy Press.

Imhoff, M., & Malony, H. N. (1979, October). *Physiological arousal, environmental cues and the report of religious experiences: A test of attribution theory.* Paper presented at the convention of the Society for the Scientific Study of Religion, Hartford, CT.

Ingram, L. C. (1989). Evangelism as frame intrusion: Observations on witnessing in public places. *Journal for the Scientific Study of Religion, 28,* 17–26.

Inhelder, B., and Piaget J. (1968). *The growth of logical thinking from childhood through adolescence.* New York: Basic Books.

Isenberg, D. J. (1986). Group polarization: A critical review and meta-analysis. *Journal of Personality and Social Psychology, 50,* 1141–1151.

Jacobs, J. (1995). Judaism and religious experience. In R. W. Hood, Jr. (Ed.), *Handbook of religious experience* (pp. 13–29). Birmingham, AL: Religious Education Press.

James, W. (1890). *The principles of psychology.* New York: Holt.

James, W. (1902). *Varieties of religious experience.* New York: Longmans, Green.

Janoff-Bulman, R. (1989). Assumptive worlds and the stress of traumatic events: Applications of the schema construct. *Social Cognition, 7,* 113–136.

Janoff-Bulman, R., & Frieze, I. H. (1983). A theoretical perspective for understanding reactions to victimization. *Journal of Social Issues, 39,* 1–17.

Jelen, T. G. (1988). Changes in the attitudinal correlations of opposition to abortion, 1977–1985. *Journal for the Scientific Study of Religion, 27,* 211–228.

Jenkins, R. A., & Pargament, K. I. (1988). The relationship between cognitive appraisals and psychological adjustment in cancer patients. *Social Science and Medicine, 26,* 625–633.

Jensen, J. P., & Bergin, A. E. (1988). Mental health values of professional therapists: A national interdisciplinary survey. *Professional Psychology: Research and Practice, 19,* 290–297.

Johnson, M. K., Raye, C. L., Hasher, L., & Chromiak, W. (1979). Are there developmental differences in reality-monitoring? *Journal of Experimental Child Psychology, 27,* 120–128.

Johnson, P. E. (1945). *Psychology of religion.* New York: Abingdon-Cokesbury.

Johnson, P. E. (1959). Conversion. *Pastoral Psychology, 10,* 51–56.

Johnson, S., & Spilka, B. (1991). Religion and the breast cancer patient: The roles of clergy and faith. *Journal of Religion and Health, 30,* 21–33.

Jolley, J. C. (1983, April). *Self-regarding attitudes and conceptions of deity: A comparative study.* Paper presented at the meeting of the Rocky Mountain Psychological Association, Snowbird, UT.

Jones, E. E., Kanouse, D. E., Kelley, H. H., Nisbett, R. E., Valins, S., & Weiner, B. (1971a). *Attribution: Perceiving the causes of behavior.* Morristown, NJ: General Learning Press.

Jones, E. E., & Nisbett, R. E. (1971b). The actor and the observer: Divergent perceptions of the causes of behavior. In E. E. Jones, D. E. Kanouse, H. H. Kelley, R. E. Nisbett, S. Valins, & B. Weiner (Eds.), *Attribution: Perceiving the causes of behavior* (pp. 79–94). Morristown, NJ: General Learning Press.

Jones, E. E., & Pittman, T. S. (1982). Toward a general theory of strategic self-presentation. In J. Suls (Ed.), *Psychological perspectives on the self* (vol. 1, pp. 231–262). Hillsdale, NJ: Lawrence Erlbaum.

Jones, R. H. (1986). *Science and mysticism.* London and Toronto: Associated University Press.

Jones, S. L. (1989). Rational-emotive therapy in Christian perspective. *Journal of Psychology and Theology, 17,* 110–120.

Kagan, J. (1984). *The nature of the child.* New York: Basic Books.

Kahneman, D., & Tversky, A. (1982). The simulation heuristic. In D. Kahneman, P. Slovic, & A. Tversky (Eds.), *Judgment under uncertainty: Heuristics and biases* (pp. 201–208). NY: Cambridge University Press.

Kahneman, D., & Tversky, A. (1984). Choices, values, and frames. *American Psychologist, 39,* 341–350.

Kahoe, R. D. (1974). Personality and achievement correlates of intrinsic and extrinsic religious orientations. *Journal of Personality and Social Psychology, 29,* 812–818.

Kahoe, R. D., & Dunn, R. F. (1975). The fear of death and religious attitudes and behavior. *Journal for the Scientific Study of Religion, 14,* 379–382.

Kakar, S. (1978). *The inner world: A psycho-analytic study of childhood and society in India* (2d ed.). Delhi, India: Oxford University Press.

Källstad, T. (1974). *John Wesley and the Bible.* Uppsala, Sweden: Acta universitatis upsaliensis, Psychologia religionum, 1.

Katz, S. T. (Ed.). (1978). *Mysticism and philosophical analysis.* New York: Oxford University Press.

Katz, S. T. (1983). *Mysticism and religious traditions.* New York: Oxford University Press.

Katz, S. T. (1992). *Mysticism and language.* New York: Oxford University Press.

Kaufman, G. D. (1981). *The theological imagination: Constructing the concept of God.* Philadelphia: Westminster.

Keller, C. A. (1978). Mystical literature. In S. T. Katz (Ed.), *Mysticism and philosophical analysis* (pp. 75–100). New York: Oxford University Press.

Kelley, H. H. (1967). Attribution theory in social psychology. In D. Levine (Ed.), *Nebraska Symposium on Motivation* (pp. 192–238). Lincoln: University of Nebraska Press.

Kelley, H. H. (1971a). Attribution in social interaction. In E. E. Jones, D. E. Kanouse, H. H. Kelley, R. E. Nisbett, S. Valins, & B. Weiner (Eds.), *Attribution: Perceiving the causes of behavior* (pp. 1–26). Morristown, NJ: General Learning Press.

Kelley, H. H. (1971b). Moral evaluation. *American Psychologist, 26,* 293–300.

Kelley, H. H., & Thibaut, J. W. (1969). Group problem solving. In G. Lindzey & E. Aronson (Eds.), *The handbook of social psychology* (vol. 4, pp. 1–101). Reading, MA: Addison-Wesley.

Kildahl, J. P. (1972). *The psychology of speaking in tongues.* New York: Harper & Row.

Kirkpatrick, L. A. (1989). A psychometric analysis of the Allport-Ross and Feagin measures of intrinsic-extrinsic religious orientation. In M. L. Lynn & D. O. Moberg (Eds.), *Research in the social scientific study of religion* (vol. 1, pp. 1–31). Greenwich, CT: JAI Press.

Kirkpatrick, L. A. (1992). An attachment-theory approach to the psychology of religion. *The International Journal for the Psychology of Religion, 2,* 3–28.

Kirkpatrick, L. A. (1995). Attachment theory and religious experience. In R. W. Hood, Jr. (Ed.), *Handbook of religious experience* (pp. 446–475). Birmingham, AL: Religious Education Press.

Kirkpatrick, L. A., & Hood, R. W., Jr. (1990). Intrinsic-extrinsic religious orientation: The "boon" or "bane" of contemporary psychology of religion? *Journal for the Scientific Study of Religion, 29,* 442–462.

Kirkpatrick, L. A., & Hood, R. W., Jr. (1991). Rub-a-dub-dub: Who's in the tub? Reply to Masters. *Journal for the Scientific Study of Religion, 30,* 318–321.

Kirkpatrick, L. A., & Shaver, P. R. (1990). Attachment theory and religion: Childhood attachments, religious beliefs, and conversation. *Journal for the Scientific Study of Religion, 29,* 315–334.

Kirkpatrick, L. A., & Shaver, P. R. (1992). An attachment-theoretical approach to romantic love and religious belief. *Personality and Social Psychology Bulletin, 18,* 266–275.

Klassen, A. D., Williams, C. J., & Levitt, E. E. (1989). *Sex and morality in the U.S.: An empirical enquiry under auspices of the Kinsey Institute.* Middletown, CT: Wesleyan University Press.

Klein, D. C., Fencil-Morse, E., and Seligman, M.E.P. (1974). *Learned helplessness, depression, and the attribution of failure.* Unpublished manuscript, Department of Psychology, University of Pennsylvania.

Knapp, G. (1988). *Narzismus und Primärbeziehung. Psychoanalytisch-anthropologische Grundlagen für ein neues Verständnis von Kindheit.* Berlin: Springer.

Koenig, H. G., George, L. K., & Siegler, I. C. (1988). The use of religion and other emotion-regulating coping strategies among older adults. *The Gerontologist, 28,* 303–310.

Koplowitz, H. (1990). Unitary consciousness and the highest development of mind: The relation between spiritual development and cognitive development.

In M. L. Commons, C. Armon, L. Kohlberg, F. A. Richards, T. A. Grotzer, & J. D. Sinnott (Eds.), *Adult development, vol. 2. Models and methods in the study of adolescent and adult thought* (pp. 105–111). New York: Praeger.

Kopplin, D. (1976, August). *Religious orientations of college students and related personality characteristics.* Paper presented at the convention of the American Psychological Association, Washington, DC.

Krosnick, J. A. (1986). *Policy voting in American presidential elections: An application of psychological theory to American politics.* Unpublished doctoral dissertation, University of Michigan, Ann Arbor.

Krosnick, J. A. (1988). Attitude importance and attitude change. *Journal of Experimental Social Psychology, 24*, 240–255.

Krosnick, J. A. (1989). Attitude importance and attitude accessibility. *Personality and Social Psychology Bulletin, 15*, 297–308.

Kuhn, D. (1988). Cognitive development. In M. H. Bornstein & M. E. Lamb (Eds.), *Perceptual, cognitive and linguistic development* (part 2 of *Developmental psychology: An advanced textbook* [2d ed., pp. 205–260]). Hillsdale, NJ: Lawrence Erlbaum.

Kuhn, T. S. (1970). *The structure of scientific revolutions* (2d ed.). Chicago: University of Chicago Press.

Kuhn, T. S. (1977). *The essential tension: Selected studies in scientific tradition and change.* Chicago: University of Chicago Press.

Kurtines, W. M., Alvarez, M., & Azmitia, M. (1990). Science and morality: The role of values in science and the scientific study of moral phenomena. *Psychological Bulletin, 107*, 283–295.

Kurtines, W. M., Azmitia, M., & Gewirtz, J. L. (Eds.). (1992). *The role of values in psychology and human development.* New York: John Wiley & Sons.

Kurtines, W. M., & Gewirtz, J. L. (Eds.). (1984). *Morality, moral behavior, and moral development.* New York: John Wiley & Sons.

Kwilecki, S. (1991). The relationship between religious development and personality development: A case study. In M. L. Lynn and D. O. Moberg (Eds.), *Research in the social scientific study of religion* (vol. 3, pp. 59–87). Greenwich, CT: JAI Press.

LaBarre, W. (1972). *The ghost dance: The origins of religion.* New York: Dell.

Labouvie-Vief, G. (1992). Mythos und Logos: Komplementäre Ausdrucksformen des menschlichen Geistes. In E. P. Fischer, H. S. Herzka, & K. H. Reich (Eds.), *Widersprüchliche Wirklichkeit: Neues Denken in Wissenschaft und Alltag. Komplementarität und Dialogik* (pp. 165–185). München/Zürich: Piper.

Labouvie-Vief, G., DeVoe, M., & Bulka, D. (1989). Speaking about feelings: Conceptions of emotions across the life span. *Psychology and Aging, 4* (4), 425–437.

Labouvie-Vief, G., Hakim-Larson, J., DeVoe, M., Schoeberlein, S. (1989). Emotions and self regulation: A life-span view. *Human Development, 32*, 279–299.

Lacan, J. (1988). *The seminar of Jacques Lacan, book 1.* Cambridge, England: Cambridge University Press.

Lakatos, I., & Musgrave, A. (Eds.). (1970). *Criticism and the growth of knowledge.* Cambridge, England: Cambridge University Press.

Lamb, M. E. (1978). Qualitative aspects of mother-and father–infant attachments. *Infant Behavior and Development, 17,* 265–275.

Lamb, M. E., Thompson, R. A., Gardner, W., & Charnov, E. L. (1985). *Infant-mother attachment: The origins and developmental significance of individual differences in strange situation behavior.* Hillsdale, NJ: Lawrence Erlbaum.

Lambert, W. W., Triandis, L. M., & Wolf, M. (1959). Some correlates of beliefs in the malevolence and benevolence of supernatural beings: A cross-societal study. *Journal of Abnormal and Social Psychology, 58,* 162–169.

Langer, E. J. (1975). The illusion of control. *Journal of Personality and Social Psychology, 32,* 311–328.

Laski, M. (1961). *Ecstasy.* Bloomington: University of Indiana Press.

Latane, B., & Darley, J. M. (1968). Group inhibition of bystander intervention in emergencies. *Journal of Personality and Social Psychology, 10,* 215–221.

Laudan, L. (1977). *Progress and its problems.* Berkeley: University of California Press.

Lazarus, R. S., & Folkman, S. (1984). *Stress, appraisal, and coping.* New York: Springer.

Lechner, P. L. (1990). Application of theory and research on cognitive schemata to the concept of God. *Dissertation Abstracts International, 50* (11), 5298–5299.

Lehr, E., & Spilka, B. (1989). Religion in the introductory psychology textbook: A comparison of three decades. *Journal for the Scientific Study of Religion, 28,* 366–371.

Lepper, M. R. (1971). *Dissonance, self-perception and honesty in children.* Unpublished manuscript, Department of Psychology, Stanford University, Stanford, CA.

Lepper, M. R., Greene, D., & Nisbett, R. E. (1973). Undermining children's intrinsic interest with extrinsic reward: A test of the "overjustification" hypothesis. *Journal of Personality and Social Psychology, 28,* 129–137.

LeShan, L. (1966). *The medium, the mystic, and the physicist.* New York: Random House.

Leuba, J. H. (1925). *The psychology of religious mysticism.* New York: Harcourt Brace.

Levenson, H. (1973). Multidimensional locus of control in psychiatric patients. *Journal of Consulting and Clinical Psychology, 41,* 397–404.

Levine, M. P., & Troiden, R. R. (1988). The myth of compulsivity. *Journal of Sex Research, 25,* 347–363.

Lieberman, A. F. (1977). Preschoolers' competence with a peer: Influence of attachment and social experience. *Child Development, 48,* 1277–1287.

Liebert, R. M., & Spiegler, M. D. (1990). *Personality: Strategies and issues.* Pacific Grove, CA: Brooks/Cole.

Lindenthal, J. J., Myers, J. K., Pepper, M. P., & Stern, M. S. (1970). Mental status and religious behavior. *Journal for the Scientific Study of Religion, 9,* 143–149.

Linton, R. (1936). *The study of man: An introduction.* New York: D. Appleton-Century.

Linton, R. (1945). *The cultural background of personality.* New York: Appleton-Century-Crofts.

Lipson, M. Y. (1983). The influence of religious affiliation on children's memory for text information. *Reading Research Quarterly, 18,* 448–457.

Little, D., & Twiss, S. B., Jr. (1973). Basic terms in the study of religious ethics. In G. Outka and J. Reeder, Jr. (Eds.), *Religion and morality.* New York: Doubleday.

Little, G. L., & Robinson, K. D. (1988). Moral reconation therapy: A systematic step-by-step treatment system for treatment resistant clients. *Psychological Reports, 62*, 135–151.

Loevinger, J. (1976). *Ego development*. San Francisco: Jossey-Bass.

Lofland, J. (1966). *Doomsday cult*. Englewood Cliffs, NJ: Prentice-Hall.

Lofland, J., & Stark, R. (1965). Becoming a world-saver: A theory of conversion to a deviant perspective. *American Sociological Review, 30*, 862–875.

Long, D., Elkind, D., & Spilka, B. (1967). The child's conception of prayer. *Journal for the Scientific Study of Religion, 6*, 101–109.

Lord, C. G., Ross, L., & Lepper, M. R. (1979). Biased assimilation and attitude polarization: The effects of prior theories on subsequently considered evidence. *Journal of Personality and Social Psychology, 37*, 2098–2109.

Loveland, C. G. (1968). The effects of bereavement on certain religious attitudes. *Sociological Symposium, 1*, 17–27.

Lovinger, R. J. (1984). *Working with religious issues in therapy*. New York: Jason Aronson.

Lovinger, R. J. (1990). *Religion and counseling: The psychological impact of religious belief*. New York: Continuum Publishing.

Luckmann, T. (1967). *The invisible religion*. New York: Macmillan.

Luker, K. (1984). *Abortion and the politics of motherhood*. Berkeley: University of California Press.

Lynn, M. L. (1987, October). *How strong beliefs bias reasoning: An exploratory model*. Paper presented at the annual meeting of the Religious Research Association, Louisville, KY.

Lynn, M. L., & Williams, R. N. (1990). Belief-bias and labor unions: The effect of strong attitudes on reasoning. *Journal of Organizational Behavior, 11*, 335–343.

Maccoby, E. E., & Masters, J. C. (1970). Attachment and dependency. In P. H. Mussen (Ed.), *Carmichael's manual of child psychology* (vol. 2, 3d ed., pp. 73–157). New York: Wiley.

Magnusson, D. (1981). Wanted: A psychology of situations. In D. Magnusson (Ed.), *Toward a psychology of situations* (pp. 9–32). Hillsdale, NJ: Lawrence Erlbaum.

Main, M., Kaplan, N., & Cassidy, J. (1985). Security in infancy, childhood, and adulthood: A move to the level of representation. In I. Bretherton & E. Waters (Eds.), *Growing points of attachment theory and research* (pp. 66–104). Monographs of the Society for Research in Child Development, 50 (1–2, serial no. 209).

Malinowski, B. (1948). *Magic, science, and religion and other essays*. Boston: Beacon.

Malony, H. N., & B. Spilka (Eds.). (1991). *Religion in psychodynamic perspective. The contributions of Paul W. Pruyser*. New York: Oxford University Press.

Marañon, G. (1924). Contribution a l'étude de l'action emotive de l'adrenaline. *Revue Française d'Endocrinologie, 2*, 301–325.

Markus, H. (1977). Self-schemata and processing information about the self. *Journal of Personality and Social Psychology, 35*, 63–78.

Markus, H., Smith, J., & Moreland, R. L. (1985). Role of the self-concept in the perception of others. *Journal of Personality and Social Psychology, 49*, 1494–1512.

Martin, J. E., & Carlson, C. R. (1988). Spiritual dimensions of health psychology. In W. R. Miller and J. E. Martin (Eds.), *Behavior therapy and religion: Integrating spir-*

itual and behavioral approaches to change (pp. 57–110). Newbury Park, CA: Sage Publications.

Maslow, A. H. (1970). *Motivation and personality* (2d ed.). New York: Harper & Row.

Masters, K. S. (1991). Of boons, banes, babies, and bath water: A reply to the Kirkpatrick and Hood discussion of intrinsic-extrinsic religious orientation. *Journal for the Scientific Study of Religion, 30,* 312–317.

Matlin, M. W. (1994). *Cognition* (3d ed.). New York: Holt, Rinehart & Winston.

Maton, K. I. (1989). The stress-buffering role of spiritual support: Cross-sectional and prospective investigations. *Journal for the Scientific Study of Religion, 28,* 310–323.

McClain, E. W. (1978). Personality differences between intrinsically religious and nonreligious students: A factor analytic study. *Journal of Personality Assessment, 42,* 159–166.

McClendon, J. W., & Smith, J. M. (1994). *Convictions: Diffusing religious relativism.* Valley Forge, PA: Trinity Press International.

McDougall, J. (1985). *Theaters of the mind.* New York: Basic Books.

McFarland, S. G. (1989a, October). *Communism as religion.* Paper presented at the meeting of the Society for the Scientific Study of Religion, Salt Lake City, UT.

McFarland, S. G. (1989b). Religious orientations and targets of discrimination. *Journal for the Scientific Study of Religion, 28,* 324–336.

McGuire, W. J. (1973). The yin and yang of progress in social psychology: Seven koan. *Journal of Personality and Social Psychology, 26,* 446–456.

McIntosh, D. N., Silver, R. C., & Wortman, C. B. (1989, October). *Parental religious change in response to their child's death.* Paper presented at the meeting of the Society for the Scientific Study of Religion, Salt Lake City, UT.

McIntosh, D. N., Silver, R. C., & Wortman, C. B. (1993). Religion's role in adjustment to a negative life event: Coping with the loss of a child. *Journal of Personality and Social Psychology, 65,* 812–821.

McIntosh, D. N., & Spilka, B. (1990). Religion and physical health: The role of personal faith and control beliefs. In M. L. Lynn & D. O. Moberg (Eds.), *Research in the social scientific study of religion,* (Vol. 2, pp. 167–194). New York: JAI Press.

Mead, G. H. (1934). *Mind, self and society.* Chicago: University of Chicago Press.

Meadow, M. J., & Kahoe, R. D. (1984). *Psychology of religion: Religion in individual lives.* New York: Harper & Row.

Meyer, M. S. (1988). Ethical principles of psychologists and religious diversity. *Professional Psychology: Research and Practice, 19,* 486–488.

Middleton, R., & Putney, S. (1962). Religion, normative standards, and behavior. *Sociometry, 25,* 141–152.

Millar, M. G., & Tesser, A. (1986a). Effects of affective and cognitive focus on the attitude-behavior relationship. *Journal of Personality and Social Psychology, 51,* 270–276.

Millar, M. G., & Tesser, A. (1986b). Thought-induced attitude change: The effects of schema structure and commitment. *Journal of Personality and Social Psychology, 51,* 259–269.

Miller, D. T. (1976). Ego-involvement and attributions for success and failure. *Journal of Personality and Social Psychology, 34,* 901–906.

Miller, D. T., & Ross, M. (1975). Self-serving biases in the attribution of causality: Fact or fiction. *Psychological Bulletin, 82*, 213–225.

Miller, W. R., & Martin, J. E. (1988). *Behavior therapy and religion: Integrating spiritual and behavioral approaches to change.* Newbury Park, CA: Sage Publications.

Minsky, M. (1985). *The society of mind.* New York: Simon & Schuster.

Moller, H. (1965). Affective mysticism in Western civilization. *Psychoanalytic Review, 52,* 259–274.

Naranjo, C., & Ornstein, R. E. (1971). *On the psychology of meditation.* New York: Viking Press.

Neisser, U. (1976). *Cognition and reality: Principles and implications of cognitive psychology.* San Francisco: Freeman.

Nelson, M. O. (1971). The concept of God and feelings toward parents. *Journal of Individual Psychology, 27,* 46–49.

Nelson, M. O., & Jones, E. M. (1957). An application of the Q-technique to the study of religious concepts. *Psychological Reports, 3,* 293–297.

Newcomb, T. M. (1952). *Social psychology.* London: Tavistock.

Nicholson, H. C., & Edwards, K. (1979, October). *A comparison of four statistical methods for assessing similarity of God concept to parental images.* Paper presented at the meeting of the Society for the Scientific Study of Religion, San Antonio, TX.

Nisbett, R., & Ross, L. (1980). *Human inference.* Englewood Cliffs, NJ: Prentice-Hall.

Noam, G. G. (1990). Beyond Freud and Piaget: Biographical worlds—Interpersonal self. In T. Wren (Ed.) in cooperation with W. Edelstein & G. Nunner-Winkler, *The moral domain. Essays in the ongoing discussion between philosophy and the social sciences* (pp. 360–399). Cambridge, MA: MIT Press.

Nolen, W. A. (1987). Medical zealots. *American Scholar, 56,* 45–56.

Nowell-Smith, P. H. (1967). Religion and morality. In P. Edwards (Ed.), *Encyclopedia of philosophy* (vol. 7, pp. 150–158). NY: Macmillan/Free Press.

Oates, W. E. (1967). A socio-psychological study of glossolalia. In F. Stagg, E. G. Hinson, & W. E. Oates (Eds.), *Glossolalia: Tongue speaking in biblical, historical, and psychological perspective* (pp. 76–99). New York: Abingdon.

O'Brien, E. (Ed.). (1965). *The varieties of mystic experience.* New York: New American Library.

O'Brien, M. E. (1982). Religious faith and adjustment to long-term hemodialysis. *Journal of Religion and Health, 21,* 68–70.

Oser, F. K., & Gmünder, P. (1991). *Religious judgement. A developmental approach.* Birmingham, AL: Religious Education Press.

Oser, F. K., & Reich, K. H. (1987). The challenge of competing explanations: The development of thinking in terms of complementarity of theories. *Human Development, 30,* 178–186.

Oser, F. K., & Reich, K. H. (1992). Entwicklung und Religiosität. In E. Schmitz (Ed.), *Religionspsychologie* (pp. 65–99). Göttingen: Hogrefe.

Oxman, T. E., Freeman, D. H., & Manheimer, E. D. (1995). Lack of social participation or religious strength and comfort as risk factors for death after cardiac surgery for the elderly. *Psychosomatic Medicine, 57,* 5–15.

Ozorak, E. W. (1988). The development of religious beliefs and commitment in adolescence (Doctoral dissertation, Harvard University, 1987). *Dissertation Abstracts International, 48,* 3451B.

Ozorak, E. W. (1989). Social and cognitive influences on the development of religious beliefs and commitment in adolescence. *Journal for the Scientific Study of Religion, 28,* 448–463.

Ozorak, E. W. (1993, August). *Religion and relationships: A projective assessment.* Poster presented at the Convention of the American Psychological Association, Toronto, ON.

Ozorak, E. W., & Kosiewicz, J. D. (1994, November). *The relationship of self-schema to religious schemas and behaviors.* Paper presented at the annual meeting of the Society for the Scientific Study of Religion, Albuquerque, NM.

Packer, M. J. (1992). Toward a postmodern psychology of moral action and moral development. In W. M. Kurtines, M. Azmitia, & J. L. Gewirtz (Eds.),*The role of values in psychology and human development* (pp. 30–59). NY: John Wiley & Sons.

Pahnke, W. (1966). Drugs and mysticism. *International Journal of Parapsychology, 8,* 295–320.

Palmer, C. E., & Noble, D. N. (1986). Premature death: Dilemmas of infant mortality. *Social Casework: The Journal of Contemporary Social Work, 67,* 332–339.

Paloma, M. M., & Gallup, G. H., Jr. (1991). *Varieties of prayer: A survey report.* Philadelphia: Trinity Press International.

Pargament, K. I. (1987, August). *God help me: Towards a theoretical framework of coping for the psychology of religion.* Paper presented at the Convention of the American Psychological Association, New York, NY.

Pargament, K. I. (1990). God help me: Toward a theoretical framework of coping for the psychology of religion. *Research in the Social Scientific Study of Religion, 2,* 195–224.

Pargament, K. I. (1992). Of means and ends: Religion and the search for significance. *International Journal for the Psychology of Religion, 2,* 210–229.

Pargament, K. I. (in press). Religious methods of coping: Resources for the conservation and transformation of significance. In E. Shafranske (Ed.), *Religion and the clinical practice of psychology.* Washington, DC: American Psychological Association.

Pargament, K. I., & DeRosa, D. V. (1985). What was that sermon about? Predicting memory for religious messages from cognitive psychology theory. *Journal for the Scientific Study of Religion, 24,* 119–236.

Pargament, K. I., Ensing, D. S., Falgout, K., Olsen, H., Reilly, B., Van Haitsma, K., & Warren, R. (1990). God help me (1): Coping efforts as predictors of the outcomes to significant negative life events. *American Journal of Community Psychology, 18,* 793–824.

Pargament, K. I., & Hahn, J. (1986). God and the just world: Causal and coping attributions to God in health situations. *Journal for the Scientific Study of Religion, 25,* 193–207.

Pargament, K. I., Kennell, J., Hathaway, W., Grevengoed, N., Newman, J., & Jones, W. (1988). Religion and the problem-solving process: Three styles of coping. *Journal for the Scientific Study of Religion, 27,* 90–104.

Pargament, K. I., & Park, C. L. (1995). Merely a defense? The variety of religious means and ends. *Journal of Social Issues, 51,* 13–32.

Pargament, K. I., Stanick, P., Ishler, K., Friedel, L., Possage, J., Rouiller, R., Ward, M., & Weinborn, M. (1993). *Red flags and religious coping: Identifying some religious warning signs among people in crisis.* Paper presented at the American Psychological Association, Toronto.

Pargament, K. I., & Sullivan, M. (1981, August). *Examining attributions of control across diverse personal situations: A psychosocial perspective.* Paper presented at the convention of the American Psychological Association, Los Angeles, CA.

Pargament, K. I., Van Haitsma, K., & Ensing, D. S. (1995). When age meets adversity: Religion and coping in the later years. In M. A. Kimble, S. H. McFadden, J. W. Ellor, and J. J. Seeber (Eds.), *Aging, spirituality, and religion: A handbook.* Minneapolis: Fortress Press.

Park, C., & Cohen, L. H. (1993). Religious and nonreligious coping with the death of a friend. *Cognitive Therapy and Research, 17,* 561–577.

Park, C., Cohen, L. H., & Herb, L. (1990). Intrinsic religiousness and religious coping as life stress moderators for Catholics versus Protestants. *Journal of Personality and Social Psychology, 59,* 562–574.

Parker, I. (1989). *The crisis in modern social psychology, and how to end it.* New York: Routledge.

Parker, I. J., & Shotter, J. (Eds.). (1990). *Deconstructing social psychology.* New York: Routledge.

Parkes, C. M. (1972). *Bereavement: Studies of grief in adult life.* New York: International Universities Press.

Parkes, C. M. (1975). What becomes of redundant world models? A contribution to the study of adaption and change. *British Journal of Medical Psychology, 48,* 131–137.

Parsons, T. (1951). *The social system.* Glencoe, IL: Free Press.

Parsons, T. (1957) Motivation of religious belief and behavior. In J. M. Yinger, *Religion, Society, and the Individual* (pp. 380–385). New York: Macmillan.

Payne, I. R., Bergin, A. E., Bielema, K. A., & Jenkins, P. H. (1991). Review of religion and mental health: Prevention and the enhancement of psychosocial functioning. *Prevention in Human Services, 9,* 11–40.

Pennington, N., & Hastie, R. (1988). Explanation-based decision making: Effects of memory structure on judgment. *Journal of Experimental Psychology: Learning, Memory & Cognition, 14,* 521–533.

Perrez, M. (1991). The difference between everyday knowledge, ideology, and scientific knowledge. *New Ideas in Psychology, 9,* 227–231.

Perry, W. G., Jr. (1970). *Forms of intellectual and ethical development in the college years: A scheme.* New York: Holt, Rinehart & Winston.

Pettersson, T. (1975). *The retention of the religious experience.* Uppsala: Acta universitatis upsaliensis, Psychologia religionum, 3.

Piaget, J. (1923). *La psychologie et les foi religieuses.* Genève: Labor.

Piaget, J. (1930). *Immanentisme et foi religieuse.* Genève: Robert.

Piaget, J. (1951). *Play, dreams and imitation in childhood.* New York: W. W. Norton.

Piaget, J. (1952). *The child's conception of number.* New York: Humanities Press.

Piaget, J. (1974). *The child and reality.* New York: Viking.

Piaget, J. (1983). Piaget's theory. In P. H. Mussen (Ed.), *Handbook of child psychology, vol. 1. History, theory and methods* (pp. 103–123). New York: Wiley.

Pittel, S. M., & Mendelsohn, G. A. (1969). Situational appraisal inventory: Development and validation of a measure of evaluative attitudes. *Journal of Consulting and Clinical Psychology, 33,* 396–405.

Pittman, T. S., & Pittman, N. L. (1980). Deprivation of control and the attribution process. *Journal of Personality and Social Psychology, 39,* 377–389.

Plog, S. (1965). UCLA conducts research on glossolalia. *Trinity, 3,* 38–39.

Polanyi, M. (1958). *Personal knowledge.* New York: Harper & Row.

Pollner, M. (1989). Divine relations, social relations, and well-being. *Journal of Health and Social Behavior, 30,* 92–104.

Popper, K. R. (1959). *The logic of scientific discovery.* New York: Basic Books.

Powell, M. C., & Fazio, R. H. (1984). Attitude accessibility as a function of repeated attitudinal expression. *Personality and Social Psychology Bulletin, 10,* 139–148.

Pratt, J. B. (1920). *The religious consciousness.* New York: Macmillan.

Preston, D. (1988). *The social organization of zen practice.* Cambridge, England: Cambridge University Press.

Preus, J. S. (1987). *Explaining religion.* New Haven: Yale University Press.

Propst, L. R. (1980). The comparative efficacy of religious and nonreligious imagery for the treatment of mild depression in religious individuals. *Cognitive Therapy and Research, 4,* 167–178.

Propst, L. R., Ostrom, R., Watkins, P., Dean, T., & Mashburn, D. (1992). Comparative efficacy of religious and non-religious cognitive-behavioral therapy for the treatment of clinical depression in religious individuals. *Journal of Consulting and Clinical Psychology, 60,* 94–103.

Proudfoot, W. (1985). *Religious experience.* Berkeley: University of California Press.

Proudfoot, W., & Shaver, P. (1975). Attribution theory and psychology of religion. *Journal for the Scientific Study of Religion, 14,* 317–330.

Pruyser, P. W. (1987). Where do we go from here? Scenarios for the psychology of religion. *Journal for the Scientific Study of Religion, 26,* 173–181.

Pyszczynski, T. A., & Greenberg, J. (1981). Role of disconfirmed expectations in the instigation of attributional processing. *Journal of Personality and Social Psychology, 40,* 31–38.

Rachlin, H. (1989). *Judgment, decision, and choice.* New York: W. H. Freeman.

Ramsey, I. T. (1957). *Religious language.* New York: Macmillan.

Ravetz, J. R. (1981). The varieties of scientific experience. In A. R. Peacocke (Ed.), *The sciences and theology,* (pp. 197–206). Notre Dame, IN: University of Notre Dame Press.

Reed, B. (1978). *The dynamics of religion: Process and movement in Christian churches.* London: Darton, Longman & Todd.

Reese, H. W., & Fremouw, W. J. (1984). Normal and normative ethics in behavioral sciences. *American Psychologist, 39,* 863–876.

Reich, K. H. (1991). The role of complementarity reasoning in religious development. In F. K. Oser & W. G. Scarlett (Eds.), *Religious development in childhood and adolescence* (pp. 77–89), New Directions for Child Development, no. 52. San Francisco: Jossey-Bass.

Reich, K. H. (1992a, July). Cognitive and religious development. Presentation at the symposium *Religion as a Dependent Variable,* Twenty-fifth International Congress of Psychology, Brussels.

Reich, K. H. (1992b). Religious development across the life span: Conventional and cognitive developmental approaches. In D. L. Featherman, R. M. Lerner, and M. Perlmutter (Eds.), *Life span development and behavior* (vol. 2, pp. 145–188). Hillsdale, NJ: Lawrence Erlbaum.

Reich, K. H. (1993). Cognitive-developmental approaches to religiousness: Which version for which purpose? *The International Journal for the Psychology of Religion,* 3, 145–171.

Reich, K. H. (1994). Can one rationally understand Christian doctrines? An empirical study. *British Journal of Religious Education, 16.*

Reilly, B., & Pargament, K. I. (1988). *The ecology of religious coping.* Paper presented at the American Psychological Association, Atlanta, Georgia.

Reinert, D., & Stifler, K. R. (1993). Hood's Mysticism Scale revisited: A factor-analytic replication. *Journal for the Scientific Study of Religion,* 32, 383–388.

Resnick, L. B. (1991). Shared social cognition: Thinking as social practice. In L. B. Resnick, J. M. Levine, & S. D. Teasley (Eds.), *Perspectives on socially shared cognition.* Washington, DC: American Psychological Association.

Rholes, W. S., & Pryor, J. B. (1982). Cognitive accessibility and causal attributions. *Personality and Social Psychology Bulletin,* 8, 719–727.

Richardson, J. T. (1973). Psychological interpretations of glossolalia: A reexamination of research. *Journal for the Scientific Study of Religion,* 12, 199–207.

Ricks, M. H. (1985). The social transmission of parental behavior: Attachment across generations. In I. Bretherton & E. Waters (Eds.), *Growing points of attachment theory and research.* Monographs of the Society for Research in Child Development, 50 (1–2, serial no. 209), 211–227.

Ricoeur, P. (1965/1970). *Freud and philosophy: An essay on interpretation.* New Haven: Yale University Press.

Ritzema, R. J. (1979). Attribution to supernatural causation: An important component of religious commitment. *Journal of Psychology and Theology,* 7, 286–293.

Rizzuto, A.-M. (1979). *The birth of the living God: A psychoanalytic study.* Chicago: University of Chicago Press.

Robinson, D. N. (1981). *An intellectual history of psychology* (rev. ed.). New York: Macmillan.

Rogers, C. R. (1980, January). Healing and growth in the therapeutic relationship. In C. W. Waymon (Chair), *The efficacy of psychotherapy: New perspectives for tomorrow.* Symposium sponsored by The Institute for Social Systems Engineering and The University for Humanistic Studies, San Diego, CA.

Rohner, R. P. (1975). *They love me, they love me not.* New Haven: HRAF.

Rokeach, M. (1960). *The open and closed mind.* New York: Basic Books.

Rokeach, M. (1973). *The nature of human values.* New York: Free Press.

Rosegrant, J. (1976). The impact of set and setting on religious experience in nature. *Journal for the Scientific Study of Religion,* 15, 301–310.

Rosenberg, M. (1962). The dissonant religious context and emotional disturbance. *American Journal of Sociology, 68,* 1–10.

Roseneau, P. (1992). *Post-modernism and the social sciences.* Princeton: Princeton University Press.

Ross, L. (1977). The intuitive psychologist and his shortcomings: Distortions in the attribution process. In L. Berkowitz (Ed.), *Advances in experimental social psychology* (vol. 10, pp. 173–220). New York: Academic Press.

Ross, L., Lepper, M., & Hubbard, M. (1975). Perseverance in self perception and social perception: Biased attributional processes in the debriefing paradigm. *Journal of Personality and Social Psychology, 32,* 880–892.

Ross, M. G. (1950). *Religious beliefs of youth.* New York: Association Press.

Roth, P. A. (1987). *Meaning and method in the social sciences: The case for methodological pluralism.* Ithaca: Cornell University Press.

Rothbaum, F., Weisz, J. R., & Snyder, S. S. (1982). Changing the world and changing the self: A two-process model of perceived control. *Journal of Personality and Social Psychology, 42,* 5–37.

Rotter, J. B. (1966). Generalized expectancies for internal versus external control of reinforcement. *Psychological Monographs, 80* (whole no. 609).

Rumelhart, D. E., & Ortony, A. (1977). The representation of knowledge in memory. In R. C. Anderson, R. J. Spiro, & W. E. Montague (Eds.), *Schooling and the acquisition of knowledge* (pp. 99–35). Hillsdale, NJ: Lawrence Erlbaum.

Rutledge, J. & Spilka, B. (1993, August). *Coping with intimacy: A problem for the single adult Mormon.* Paper presented at the Convention of the American Psychological Association, Toronto.

Sagan, E. (1988). *Freud, women, and morality: The psychology of good and evil.* New York: Basic Books.

Salzman, L. (1953). The psychology of religious and ideological conversion. *Psychiatry, 16,* 177–187.

Sanders, C. M. (1980). A comparison of adult bereavement in the death of a spouse, child, and parent. *Omega, 10,* 303–319.

Sarbin, T. R. (1954). Role theory. In G. Lindzey (Ed.), *Handbook of social psychology* (vol. 1, pp. 223–258). Reading, MA: Addison-Wesley.

Schachter, S. (1964). The interaction of cognitive and physiological determinants of emotional states. In L. Berkowitz (Ed.), *Advances in experimental social psychology* (vol. 1, pp. 49–80). New York: Academic Press.

Schachter, S. (1971). *Emotion, obesity, and crime.* New York: Academic Press.

Schachter, S., & Singer, J. E. (1962). Cognitive, social, and physiological determinants of emotional state. *Psychological Review, 69,* 379–399.

Schaefer, C. A., & Gorsuch, R. L. (1991). Psychological adjustment and religiousness: The multivariate belief-motivation theory of religiousness. *Journal for the Scientific Study of Religion, 30,* 448–461.

Scharfstein, B.-A. (1993). *Ineffability.* New York: State University Press of New York.

Schleiermacher, F. (1893). *On religion.* London: Kegan Paul, Trench & Trubner.

Schmidtchen, S. (1980). Probleme einer Indikation und Integration psychotherapeutischer Verfahren. In S. Schmidtchen & F. Baumgärtel (Eds.), *Methoden der Kindertherapie. Möglichkeiten und Grenzen Ihrer Anwendung* (pp. 162–182). Stuttgart: Kohlhammer.

Schmitt, D. R. (1964). The invocation of moral obligation, *Sociometry, 27,* 299–310.

Schneider, W., & Fisk, A. D. (1980). *Visual search improves with detection searches, declines with nondetection searches.* Human Attention Research Laboratory, University of Illinois (Report 8004), Urbana, IL.

Schneider, W., & Shiffrin, R. M. (1977). Controlled and automatic human information processing: I. Detection, search, and attention. *Psychological Review, 84,* 1–66.

Schoen, E. L. (1985). *Religious language.* Durham, NC: Duke University Press.

Scott, W. (1965). *Values and organizations: A study of fraternities and sororities.* Chicago: Rand McNally.

Seligman, M.E.P. (1975). *Helplessness: On depression, development, and death.* San Francisco: Freeman.

Shaver, K. G. (1975). *An introduction to attribution processes.* Cambridge, MA: Winthrop.

Shaver, P., & Buhrmester, D. (1983). Loneliness, sex-role orientation and group life: A social needs perspective. In P. B. Paulus (Ed.), *Basic group processes* (pp. 259–288). New York: Springer-Verlag.

Shaver, P., Hazan, C., & Bradshaw, D. (1988). Love as attachment: The integration of three behavioral systems. In R. J. Sternberg & M. Barnes (Eds.), *The anatomy of love* (pp. 68–99). New Haven: Yale University Press.

Shaver, P., & Rubenstein, C. (1980). Childhood attachment experience and adult loneliness. In L. Wheeler (Ed.), *Review of personality and social psychology* (vol. 1, pp. 42–73). Beverly Hills, CA: Sage Publications.

Sherrill, K. A., & Larson, D. B. (1987, November). *Recovery in adult burn patients: The role of religion.* Paper presented at The Southern Medical Association Meeting, Section of Neurosurgery and Psychiatry.

Sherry, P. (1977). *Religion, truths and language-games.* New York: Barnes & Noble.

Shiffrin, R. M., & Dumais, S. T. (1981). The development of automatism. In J. R. Anderson (Ed.),*Cognitive skills and their acquisition* (pp. 111–140). Hillsdale, NJ: Lawrence Erlbaum.

Siikala, A. L. (1978). *The rite technique of the Siberian shaman.* Helsinki: Academia Scientiarum Fennica.

Silver, R. L., Boon, C., & Stones, M. H. (1983). Searching for meaning in misfortune: Making sense of incest. *Journal of Social Issues, 39,* 81–102.

Silver, R. L., & Wortman, C. B. (1980). Coping with undesirable life events. In J. Garber & M.E.P. Seligman (Eds.), *Human helplessness: Theory and applications* (pp. 279–340). New York: Academic Press.

Silvestri, P. J. (1979). Locus of control and God dependence. *Psychological Reports, 45,* 89–90.

Simon, W., & Gagnon, J. H. (1986). Sexual scripts: Permanence and change. *Archives of Sexual Behavior, 15,* 97–120.

Skolnick, A. (1985, November). *The ties that bind: Attachment theory and the social psychology of close relationships.* Paper presented at the National Council on Family Relations, Preconference, Dallas.

Smart, N. (1965). Interpretation and mystical experience. *Religious Studies, 1,* 75–87.

Smith, H. (1992). *Forgotten truth. The common vision of the world's religions.* San Francisco: Harper.

Smith, J. E. (1968). *Experience and God*. New York: Oxford University Press.

Smith, J. H., & Handelman, S. A. (1990). *Psychoanalysis and religion*. Baltimore: Johns Hopkins University Press.

Snarey, J., Kohlberg, L., & Noam, G. (1987). Ego development and education: A structural perspective. In Kohlberg, L. et al., *Child psychology and childhood education. A cognitive-developmental view* (pp. 329–391). New York: Longman.

Snook, S. C., & Gorsuch, R. L. (1985). *Religious orientation and racial prejudice in South Africa*. Paper presented at the convention of the American Psychological Association, Los Angeles, CA.

Snyder, M., & Cantor, N. (1979). Testing hypotheses about other people: The use of historical knowledge. *Journal of Experimental Social Psychology, 15,* 330–342.

Snyder, M., & Swann, W. B., Jr. (1978). Behavioral confirmation in social interaction: From social perception to social reality. *Journal of Experimental Social Psychology, 14,* 148–162.

Snyder, M. L., Stephan, W. G., & Rosenfield, D. (1978). Attributional egotism. In J. H. Harvey, W. Ickes, & R. F. Kidd (Eds.), *New directions in attribution research* (vol. 2, pp. 5–34). Hillsdale, NJ: Lawrence Erlbaum.

Spencer, S. J., & McIntosh, D. N. (1990, August). *Extremity and importance in attitude structure: Attitudes as self-schemata*. Paper presented at the meeting of the American Psychological Association, Boston, MA.

Spero, M. H. (Ed.). (1985). *Psychotherapy of the religious patient*. Springfield, IL: Charles C. Thomas.

Spickard, J. V. (1993). For a sociology of religious expense. In W. H. Swatos, Jr.(Ed.), *A future for religion? New paradigms for social analysis* (pp. 109–127). Newbury Park, CA: Sage Publications.

Spilka, B. (1978). The current state of the psychology of religion. *Bulletin of the Council the Study of Religion, 9,* 96–99.

Spilka, B. (1980, April). *Toward a psychosocial theory of religious mysticism with empirical reference*. Paper presented at the convention of the Rocky Mountain Psychological Association, Tucson, AZ.

Spilka, B. (1982, August). *Theory in the psychology of religion*. William James Award presentation at the Convention of the American Psychological Association, Washington, DC.

Spilka, B., Addison, J., & Rosensohn, M. (1975). Parents, self and God: A test of competing theories of individual-religion relationships. *Review of Religious Research, 16,* 154–165.

Spilka, B., Armatas, P., & Nussbaum, J. (1964). The concept of God: A factor-analytic approach. *Review of Religious Research, 6,* 28–36.

Spilka, B., & Bridges, R. A. (1989). Theology and psychological theory: Psychological implications of some modern theologies. *Journal of Psychology and Theology, 17,* 343–351.

Spilka, B., Brown, G. A., & Cassidy, S. A. (1992). The structure of mystical experience in relation to pre- and post experience lifestyles. *The International Journal for the Psychology of Religion, 2,* 241–257.

Spilka, B., Hood, R. W., Jr., & Gorsuch, R. L. (1985). *The psychology of religion: An empirical approach*. Englewood Cliffs, NJ: Prentice-Hall.

Spilka, B., Ladd, K. L., McIntosh, D. N., & Milmoe, S. (1994, November). *The content of religious experience: The roles of expectancy and desirability*. Paper presented at the annual meeting of the Society for the Scientific Study of Religion, Albuquerque, NM.

Spilka, B., & McIntosh, D. N. (1995). Attribution theory and religious experience. In R. W. Hood, Jr. (Ed.), *Handbook of religious experience* (pp. 421–455). Birmingham, AL: Religious Education Press,

Spilka, B., & Mullin, M. (1977). Personal religion and psychosocial schemata: A research approach to a theological psychology of religion. *Character Potential, 8*, 57–66.

Spilka, B., & Schmidt, G. (1982, April). *Attributions as a function of personal faith and locus of control*. Paper presented at the convention of the Rocky Mountain Psychological Association, Albuquerque, NM.

Spilka, B., & Schmidt, G. (1983). General attribution theory for the psychology of religion: The influence of event-character on attributions to God. *Journal for the Scientific Study of Religion, 22*, 326–339.

Spilka, B., Shaver, P., & Kirkpatrick, L. A. (1985). A general attribution theory for the psychology of religion. *Journal for the Scientific Study of Religion, 24*, 1–20.

Spilka, B., Spangler, J. D., & Nelson, C. B. (1983). Spiritual support in life-threatening illness. *Journal of Religion and Health, 22*, 98–104.

Spiro, M. E. (1966). Religion, problems of definition and explanation. In M. Banton (Ed.), *Anthropological approaches to the study of religion* (pp. 85–126). New York: Praeger.

Spiro, M. E. (1987a). Collective representations and mental representations in religious symbol systems. In B. Kilborne & L. L. Langness (Eds.), *Culture and human nature: Theoretical papers of Melford E. Spiro* (pp. 161–184). Chicago: University of Chicago Press.

Spiro, M. E. (1987b). Religion: Problems of definition and explanation. In B. Kilborne & L. L. Langness (Eds.), *Culture and human nature: Theoretical papers of Melford E. Spiro* (pp. 187–222). Chicago: University of Chicago Press.

Spradlin, W. H., & Malony, H. N. (1981, October). *Physiological state deviation, personal religiosity, setting variation and the report of a religious experience*. Paper presented at the Convention of the Society for the Scientific Study of Religion, Baltimore, MD.

Sprinthall, N. A., & McVay, J. G. (1987). Value development during the college years: A cause for concern and an opportunity for growth. *Counseling and Values, 31*, 126–138.

Sroufe, L. A. (1983). Infant-caregiver attachment and patterns of adaptation in preschool: The roots of maladaptation and competence. In M. Perlmutter (Ed.), *Minnesota symposium in child psychology* (vol. 16, pp. 41–81). Hillsdale, NJ: Lawrence Erlbaum.

Sroufe, L. A. (1986). Appraisal: Bowlby's contribution to psychoanalytic theory and developmental psychology; attachment; separation; loss. *Journal of Child Psychology and Psychiatry and Allied Disciplines, 27*, 841–849.

Sroufe, L. A., & Fleeson, J. (1986). Attachment and the construction of relationships. In W. W. Hartup & Z. Rubin (Eds.), *Relationships and development* (pp. 51–71). Hillsdale, NJ: Lawrence Erlbaum.

Sroufe, L. A., & Waters, E. (1977). Attachment as an organizational construct. *Child Development, 48,* 1184–1199.

Staal, F. (1975). *Exploring mysticism: A methodological essay.* Berkeley: University of California Press.

Stace, W. T. (1960) *Mysticism and philosophy.* Philadelphia: J. P. Lippincott.

Starbuck, E. D. (1899). *The psychology of religion.* New York: Scribner's.

Stark, R. (1972). The economics of piety: Religious commitment and social class. In G. Thielbar & S. Feldman (Eds.), *Issues in social inequality.* Boston: Little Brown.

Stark, R., & Welch, K. (n.d.). *IQ and religious commitment.* Unpublished manuscript.

Stifler, K., Greer, J., Sneck, W., & Dovenmuehle, R. (1993). An empirical investigation of the discriminability of reported mystical experiences among religious contemplatives, psychotic inpatients, and normal adults. *Journal for the Scientific Study of Religion, 32,* 366–372.

Stouffer, S. A., Lumsdaine, A. A., Lumsdaine, M. H., Williams, R. M., Smith, M. B., Janis, I. L., Star, S. A., & Cottrell, L. S., Jr. (1949). *The American soldier: Combat and its aftermath.* Princeton: Princeton University Press.

Strickland, B. R., & Shaffer, S. (1971). I-E, I-E, and F. *Journal for the Scientific Study of Religion, 10,* 366–369.

Strickland, F. L. (1924). *Psychology of religious experience.* New York: Abingdon.

Strunk, O. (1959). Perceived relationships between parental and deity concepts. *Psychological Newsletter, 10,* 222–226.

Sundén, H. (1959). *Religionen och rollerna* (4th ed., 1966). Stockholm: Svenska kyrkans diakonistyrelses bokförlag.

Sundén, H. (1966). *Die Religion und die Rollen.* Berlin: Alfred Topelmann.

Sundén, H. (1969). Die Rollenpsychologie und die Weisen des Religions-Erlebens. In C. Hörgl, K. Krenn, & F. Rauh (Eds.), *Wesen und Weisen der Religion.* München, Germany: Max Hueber Verlag.

Sundén, H. (1977). *Religionspsykologi: Problem och metoder.* Stockholm: Proprius förlag.

Sundén, H. (1982). Luther's Vorrede auf den Psalter von 1545 als religions-psychologisches dokument. *Archiv für Religionspsychologie, 15,* 36–44.

Sundén, H. (1987). Saint Augustine and the psalter in the light of role-psychology. *Journal for the scientific study of religion, 26,* 375–382.

Swanson, G. E. (1960) *The birth of the gods.* Ann Arbor: University of Michigan Press.

Swinburne, R. (1981). The evidential value of religious experience. In A. R. Peacocke (Ed.), *The sciences and theology in the twentieth century* (pp. 182–196). Notre Dame, IN: University of Notre Dame Press.

Tabachnick, B. C., & Fidell, L. S. (1983). *Using multivariate statistics.* New York: Harper & Row.

Talbot, W. (1980). *Mysticism and the new physics.* New York: Bantam.

Tamayo, A., & Desjardins, L. (1976). Belief systems and conceptual images of parents and God. *Journal of Psychology, 92,* 131–140.

Tamminen, K. (1991). *Religious development in childhood and youth.* Helsinki: Suomalainen Tiedeakatemia.

Tamney, J. B., & Johnson, S. D. (1983). The moral majority in Middletown. *Journal for the Scientific Study of Religion, 22,* 145–157.

Tart, C. T. (Ed.). (1969). *Altered states of consciousness.* New York: John Wiley & Sons.

Tart, C. T. (1975). *Transpersonal psychologies.* New York: Harper & Row.

Taylor, S. E. (1983). Adjustment to threatening events. A theory of cognitive adaptation. *American Psychologist, 38,* 1161–1173.

Taylor, S. E., & Crocker, J. (1981). Schematic bases of social processing. In E. T. Higgins, C. P. Herman, & M. P. Zanna (Eds.), *Social cognition: The Ontario symposium* (vol. 1, pp. 89–134). Hillsdale, NJ: Lawrence Erlbaum.

Taylor, S. E., Crocker, J., & D'Agostino, J. (1978). Schematic bases of social problem solving. *Personality and Social Psychology Bulletin, 4,* 447–451.

Taylor, S. E., & Fiske, S. T. (1975). Point of view and perceptions of causality. *Journal of Personality and Social Psychology, 46,* 439–445.

Taylor, S. E., & Fiske, S. T. (1978). Salience, attention, and attribution: Top of the head phenomenon. In L. Berkowitz (Ed.), *Advances in experimental social psychology* (vol. 11, pp. 249–288). New York: Academic Press.

Taylor, S. E., Lichtman, R. R., & Wood, J. V. (1984). Attributions, beliefs about control, and adjustment to breast cancer. *Journal of Personality and Social Psychology, 46,* 489–502.

Tesser, A., & Shaffer, D. R. (1990). Attitudes and attitude change. *Annual Review of Psychology, 41,* 479–523.

Thomas, L. E., & Cooper, P. E. (1978). Measurement and incidences of mystical experiences. *Journal for the Scientific Study of Religion, 17,* 433–437.

Thompson, S. C. (1981). Will it hurt less if I can control it?: A complex answer to a simple question. *Psychological Bulletin, 90,* 89–101.

Thompson, S. C. (1991). The search for meaning following a stroke. *Basic and Applied Social Psychology, 12,* 81–96.

Thoreau, H. D. (1854). *Walden.* New York: Peebles Press International.

Thouless, R. H. (1923). *An introduction to the psychology of religion.* New York: Macmillan.

Tillich, P. (1957). *Dynamics of faith.* New York: Harper & Row.

Tiryakian, E. A. (Ed.). (1974). *On the margin of the visible.* New York: John Wiley.

Tschannen, O. (1991). The secularization paradigm: A systematization. *Journal for the Scientific Study of Religion, 30,* 395–415.

Turner, R. H. (1962). Role taking: Process versus conformity. In A. M. Rose (Ed.), *Human behavior and social processes: An interactionist approach* (pp. 20–30). Boston: Houghton-Mifflin.

Tversky, A., & Kahneman, D. (1973). Availability: A heuristic for judging frequency and probability. *Cognitive Psychology, 5,* 207–232.

Tversky, A., & Kahneman, D. (1982). Judgment under uncertainty: Heuristics and biases. In D. Kahneman, P. Slovic, & A. Tversky (Eds.), *Judgment under uncertainty: Heuristics and biases* (pp. 201–208). New York: Cambridge University Press.

Tylor, E. B. (1924/1871). *Primitive culture* (7th ed.). New York: Brentano's.

Ullman, C. (1982). Cognitive and emotional antecedents of religious conversion. *Journal of Personality and Social Psychology 43,* 183–192.

Ullman, C. (1989). *The transformed self: The psychology of religious conversion.* New York: Plenum.

Unger, J. (1976). *On religious experience.* Uppsala, Sweden: Acta universitatis upsaliensis, Psychologia religionum, 6.

Using "faith" as a coping skill. (1990, Fall). *Coping Skills Development (DSC) Newsletter*, p. 1. 124-B Exchange Pl., Lafayette, LA.

van der Lans, J. (1987). The value of Sundén's Role-Theory demonstrated and tested with respect to religious experiences in meditation. *Journal for the Scientific Study of Religion, 26,* 401–412.

Venable, G. D. (1982). *Intrinsic and extrinsic religiosity in developmental perspective.* Unpublished dissertation, Graduate School of Psychology, Fuller Theological Seminary, Pasadena, CA.

Veroff, J. (1983). Contextual determinants of personality. *Personality and Social Psychology Bulletin, 2,* 331–343.

Veroff, J., Kulka, P. A., & Douvan, E. (1981). *Mental health in America: Patterns of help seeking from 1957 to 1976.* New York: Basic Books.

Vitaliano, P. P., DeWolfe, D. J., Maiuro, R. D., Russo, J., & Katon, W. (1990). Appraised changeability of a stressor as a modifier of the relationship between coping and depression: A test of the hypothesis of fit. *Journal of Personality and Social Psychology, 59,* 582–592.

Vivier, L. (1960). *Glossolalia.* Unpublished doctoral dissertation, Johannesburg, South Africa: University of Witwatersrand, Department of Psychiatry and Mental Hygiene.

Wagstaff, G. F. (1981). *Hypnosis, compliance and belief.* New York: St. Martin's Press.

Wallace, A.F.C. (1966) *Religion: An anthropological view.* New York: Random House.

Waller, N. G., Kojetin, B. A., Bouchard, T. J., & Lykken, D. T. (1990). Genetic and environmental influences on religious interests, attitudes, and values: A study of twins reared apart and together. *Psychological Science, 1,* 138–142.

Wallwork, E. (1982). Religious development [according to J. M. Baldwin]. In J. M. Broughton & J. M. Freeman-Moir (Eds.), *The developmental psychology of J. M. Baldwin* (pp. 335–388). Norwood, NJ: Ablex.

Walster, E. (1966). Assignment of responsibility for an accident. *Journal of Personality and Social Psychology, 3,* 73–79.

Wasson, R. G. (1971). The Soma of the Rig Veda: What was it? *Journal of the American Oriental Society, 91,* 169–187.

Waterman, A. S. (1988). On the uses of psychological theory and research in the process of ethical inquiry. *Psychological Bulletin, 103,* 283–298.

Waters, E., Wippman, J., & Sroufe, L. A. (1979). Attachment, positive affect, and competence in the peer group: Two studies in construct validation. *Child Development, 50,* 821–829.

Watson, P. J., Hood, R. W., Morris, R. J., & Hall, J. R. (1985). Religiosity, sin, and self-esteem. *Journal of Psychology and Theology, 13,* 116–128.

Wegner, D. M. (1986). Transactive memory: A contemporary analysis of the group mind. In B. Mullen & G. R. Goethals (Eds.), *Theories of group behavior* (pp. 185–208). New York: Springer-Verlag.

Wegner, D. M. (1989). *White bears and other unwanted thoughts.* New York: Penguin Books.

Weiner, B. (1972). *Theories of motivation: From mechanism to cognition.* Chicago: Markham.

Weiner, B. (Ed.). (1974). *Achievement motivation and attribution theory.* Morristown, NJ: General Learning Press.

Weiner, B., & Sierad, J. (1974). Misattribution for failure and the enhancement of achievement strivings. In B. Weiner (Ed.), *Achievement motivation and attribution theory*. Morristown, NJ: General Learning Press.

Weiss, R. S. (1973). *Loneliness: The experience of emotional and social isolation*. Cambridge, MA: MIT Press.

Weiss, R. S. (1982). Attachment in adult life. In C. M. Parkes & J. S. Hinde (Eds.), *The place of attachment in human behavior* (pp. 171–184). New York: Basic Books.

Weiss, R. S. (1986). Continuities and transformations in social relationships from childhood to adulthood. In W. W. Hartup & Z. Rubin (Eds.), *Relationships and development* (pp. 95–110). Hillsdale, NJ: Lawrence Erlbaum.

Welch, M. R., Tittle, C. R., & Petee, T. (1991). Religion and deviance among adult Catholics: A test of the "moral communities" hypothesis. *Journal for the Scientific Study of Religion, 30*, 159–172.

White, R. W. (1959). Motivation reconsidered: The concept of competence. *Psychological Review, 66*, 297–333.

White, R. W. (1966). *Lives in progress* (2d ed.). New York: Holt, Rinehart & Winston.

Wikström, O. (1975). *Guds ledning*. Uppsala: Acta universitatis upsaliensis, Psychologia religionum, 4.

Wilder, T. (1927). *The bridge of San Luis Rey*. New York: Pocket Books.

Wilson, J. (1978). *Religion in American society*. Englewood Cliffs, NJ: Prentice-Hall.

Wilson, T. D., Dunn, D. S., Kraft, D., & Lisle, D. J. (1989). Introspection, attitude change, and attitude-behavior consistency: The disruptive effects of explaining why we feel the way we do. In L. Berkowitz (Ed.), *Advances in experimental social psychology* (vol. 22, pp. 287–344). New York: Academic Press.

Wilson, T. D., Lisle, D. J., Kraft, D., & Wetzel, C. G. (1989). Preferences as expectation-driven inferences? Effects of affective expectations on affective experience. *Journal of Personality and Social Psychology, 56*, 519–530.

Wilson, W. P. (1974). Utilization of Christian beliefs in psychotherapy. *Journal of Psychology and Theology, 2*, 125–131.

Winnicott, D. W. (1971). Transitional objects and transitional phenomena. *Playing and reality* (pp. 1–30). London: Tavistock.

Wittgenstein, L. (1967). *Lectures and conversations on aesthetics, psychology and religious belief* (compiled from notes by Y. Smythies, R. Rhees, & J. Taylor). Berkeley: University of California Press.

Wittgenstein, L. (1971). *Tractatus logico-philosophicus*. London: Routledge & Kegan Paul.

Wobbermin, G. (1933). *The nature of religion*. New York: Crowell.

Wong, P.T.P., & Weiner, B. (1981). When people ask "why" questions, and the heuristics of attributional search. *Journal of Personality and Social Psychology, 40*, 650–663.

Wood, W. W. (1965). *Culture and personality aspects of the Pentecostal Holiness religion*. The Hague: Mouton.

Wood, W. (1982). Retrieval of attitude-relevant information from memory: Effects on susceptibility to persuasion and on intrinsic motivation. *Journal of Personality and Social Psychology, 42*, 798–810.

Worchel, S., & Andreoli, V. (1976). Escape to freedom: The relationship between attribution of causality and psychological reactance. In J. H. Harvey, W. Ickes,

& R. F. Kidd (Eds.), *New directions in attribution research* (vol. 1, pp. 249–269). Hillsdale, NJ: Lawrence Erlbaum.

Worthington, E. L., Jr. (1978). The effects of imagery content, choice of imagery content, and self-verbalization on the self-control of pain. *Cognitive Therapy and Research, 2,* 225–240.

Worthington, E. L., Jr. (1986). Religious counseling: A review of published empirical research. *Journal of Counseling and Development, 64,* 421–431.

Wortman, C. B. (1975). Some determinants of perceived control. *Journal of Personality and Social Psychology, 31,* 282–294.

Wortman, C. B. (1976). Causal attributions and perceived control. In J. H. Harvey, W. Ickes, & R. F. Kidd (Eds.), *New directions in attribution research* (vol. 1, pp. 23–52). Hillsdale, NJ: Lawrence Erlbaum.

Wulff, D. M. (1991a). *Psychology of religion: Classic and contemporary views.* New York: Wiley.

Wulff, D. M. (1991b). *Reflections on belief as an expression of personal faith.* Invited address to the 5th Symposium for European Psychologists of Religion, Louvain, Belgium.

Wulff, D. M. (1993). On the origins and goals of religious development. *The International Journal for the Psychology of Religion, 3,* 181–186.

Wuthnow, R., Christiano, K., & Kuzlowski, J. (1980). Religion and bereavement: A conceptual framework. *Journal for the Scientific Study of Religion, 19,* 408–422.

Wuthnow, R., & Glock, C. Y. (1974). The shifting focus of faith: A survey report, God in the gut. *Psychology Today, 8,* 131–136.

Wylie, R. C. (1974). *The self concept.* Lincoln: University of Nebraska Press.

Yankelovich, D., Skelly, F., & White, A. (1981). *The mushiness index: A refinement in public policy polling techniques.* New York: Yankelovich, Chalcey, Shulman.

Yates, J. W., Chalmer, B. J., St. James, P., Follansbee, M., & McKegney, F. P. (1981). Religion in patients with advanced cancer. *Medical and Pediatric Oncology, 9,* 121–128.

Yinger, J. M. (1970). *The scientific study of religion.* New York: Macmillan.

Zadeh, L. A., & Kacprzyk, J. (Eds.). (1992). *Fuzzy logic for the management of uncertainty.* New York: John Wiley & Sons.

Zaehner, R. C. (1957). *Mysticism sacred and profane.* Oxford: Clarendon Press.

Zajonc, R. B. (1968). Attitudinal effects of mere exposure. *Journal of Personality and Social Psychology, 9,* 1–27.

Zajonc, R. B. (1980). Feeling and thinking: Preferences need no inferences. *American Psychologist, 35,* 151–175.

Zuckerman, D. M., Kasl, S. V., & Ostfeld, A. M. (1984). Psychosocial predictors of mortality among the elderly poor. *American Journal of Epidemiology, 119,* 410–423.

Zukav, G. (1979). *The dancing Wu Li masters.* New York: William Morrow.

About the Book

Theory in the psychology of religion is in a state of rapid development, and the present volume demonstrates how various positions in this field may be translated into original foundational work that will in turn encourage exploration in many directions. A number of new contributions are collected with previously published pieces to illustrate the diversity of prominent theoreticians' thinking on topics pertinent to the psychology of religion. These essays span the psychoanalytic tradition and its derivatives: motivational, social, cognitive, and developmental frameworks plus the domain of coping and adjustment. Each section concludes with an extensive commentary.

This book is a valuable addition to courses in psychology and religious studies. It also will appeal to those professionals and lay audiences interested in how this field is evolving.

About the Editors and Contributors

William Sims Bainbridge is director of the Sociology Program at the National Science Foundation in Arlington, Virginia.

C. Daniel Batson is professor of psychology at the University of Kansas in Lawrence, Kansas.

Allen E. Bergin is professor and director of the Clinical Psychology Department at Brigham Young University in Provo, Utah.

David Elkind is professor in and chair of the Department of Child Study at Tufts University in Medford, Massachusetts.

Robert A. Embree is professor emeritus in the Department of Psychology at Westmar University in LeMars, Iowa.

Richard L. Gorsuch is professor of psychology at the Graduate School of Psychology at Fuller Theological Seminary in Pasadena, California.

Peter C. Hill is professor of psychology at Grove City College in Grove City, Pennsylvania.

Nils G. Holm is professor in the Department of Comparative Religion at Abo Academy in Turku, Finland.

Ralph W. Hood, Jr. is professor of psychology at the University of Tennessee at Chattanooga in Chattanooga, Tennessee.

Lee A. Kirkpatrick is assistant professor of psychology at the College of William and Mary in Williamsburg, Virginia.

Daniel N. McIntosh is assistant professor of psychology at the University of Denver in Denver, Colorado.

Elizabeth Weiss Ozorak is associate professor of psychology at Allegheny College in Meadville, Pennsylvania.

Kenneth I. Pargament is professor of psychology at Bowling Green State University in Bowling Green, Ohio.

Crystal L. Park is assistant professor of psychology at Miami University in Oxford, Ohio.

I. Reed Payne is professor of psychology at Brigham Young University in Provo, Utah.

Wayne Proudfoot is professor of religion at Columbia University in New York City.

K. Helmut Reich is research associate and assistant lecturer in the Department of Education at the University of Freibourg in Freibourg, Switzerland.

Phillip R. Shaver is professor of psychology and department chair at the University of California at Davis in Davis, California.

Bernard Spilka is professor of psychology at the University of Denver in Denver, Colorado.

Rodney Stark is professor of sociology and comparative religion at the University of Washington in Seattle, Washington.

INDEX